More Praise for *Venezuela Reframed*

'Until Angosto-Ferrández, no one had provided a probing analysis of Hugo Chavez's support for indigenous struggles. This book is required reading for understanding a key component of the Bolivarian revolution.'

Marc Becker, Truman State University

'An incisive analysis not just of Venezuelan indigenous movements but of Latin American radical politics in general. Truly essential reading!'

David Raby, author of *Democracy and Revolution: Latin America and Socialism Today*

'Angosto-Ferrández's outstanding analysis of indigenous collective action is a milestone in countering the disempowering anti-statism of the post-development era.'

Thomas Muhr, University of Nottingham

'Obligatory reading for students of indigenous societies and economies and for those of us suspicious of some of the more romantic approaches to the "Pink Tide" in Latin America.'

Barry Carr, La Trobe University

'This vital works offers a nuanced assessment of the often-contradictory relationship between the new indigenous movement and the Bolivarian political process.'

Miguel Tinker Salas, Pomona College

ABOUT THE AUTHOR

LUIS FERNANDO ANGOSTO-FERRÁNDEZ is a lecturer in anthropology and Latin American studies at the University of Sydney. He has extensive fieldwork experience in Latin America and Spain and has lived, worked and researched in Venezuela for nearly a decade. Recent academic publications include *The Politics of Identity in Latin American Censuses* (2015) and *Democracy, Revolution and Geopolitics in Latin America: Venezuela and the International Politics of Discontent* (2014). He has also been a contributor to various media outlets, such as Aporrea.org, Rebelion.org and Theconversation.com.

VENEZUELA REFRAMED

Bolivarianism, indigenous peoples and socialisms of the twenty-first century

LUIS FERNANDO ANGOSTO-FERRÁNDEZ

Zed Books
London

Venezuela Reframed: Bolivarianism, Indigenous Peoples and Socialisms of the Twenty-First Century was first published in 2015 by Zed Books Ltd, The Foundry, 17 Oval Way, London SE11 5RR, UK

www.zedbooks.co.uk

Copyright © Luis Fernando Angosto-Ferrández 2015

The right of Luis Fernando Angosto-Ferrández to be identified as the author of this work has been asserted by him in accordance with the Copyright, Designs and Patents Act, 1988.

Typeset in Bulmer by Swales and Willis Ltd, Exeter, Devon
Index: John Barker
Cover designed by Steve Marsden

All rights reserved. No part of this publication may be reproduced, stored in a retrieval system or transmitted in any form or by any means, electronic, mechanical, photocopying or otherwise, without the prior permission of Zed Books Ltd.

A catalogue record for this book is available from the British Library.

ISBN 978-1-78360-198-1 hb
ISBN 978-1-78360-197-4 pb
ISBN 978-1-78360-199-8 pdf
ISBN 978-1-78360-200-1 epub
ISBN 978-1-78360-201-8 mobi

Printed and bound by CPI Group (UK) Ltd, Croydon, CR0 4YY

To the Venezuelan people, and to Rosario and Manolo

Contents

ACKNOWLEDGEMENTS	ix
ABBREVIATIONS	xiii
PREFACE	xix
Introduction	1
1 Historical overview	26
2 Into the people	70
3 Balance of enfranchisement	104
4 Collective action through the electoral sphere	125
5 The state-supporting and state-sponsored indigenous movement	165
6 Contentious collective action in the margins of and outside the *chavista* bloc	187
7 Indigenous peoples, capitalism and the political economy of the socialisms of the twenty-first century in Latin America	208
8 Closing remarks	237

Appendix: Extraordinary Assembly	246
NOTES	254
BIBLIOGRAPHY	268
INDEX	281

Acknowledgements

I lived and worked in Venezuela for many good years, and my first acknowledgement is to all the people I lived and worked with during that period. This book, at least as it has come about, could not have been written without them. The ideas and arguments I present here are not only grounded on the research I have undertaken in the country, but also on that strange substance common to certain forms of knowledge and motivation that springs, always in whimsical outbursts, from lived experience – heard, seen, read, felt, imagined experience.

There is such a big list of people who, in one way or another, have helped shape this book. I am not going to name them all and I probably could not even if I wanted to, more for lack of space in my head than in my heart. I will nevertheless specially recall here, firstly, Maíta, Dalia and my family in Campearito, for it is there and among them that I completed the revisions of my original manuscript. To anyone who has gone through the pain of revisiting a previous creation in order to improve it this might sound totally mad, but the memory I have of those days brings me a smile every time it surfaces. It was a joy, and a laugh, to be thinking and writing in *la casa*, with dozens of people coming in and out every day in a frenzy of relations that defy any moderate notion of kinship one could ever come across. I then started to go through the proofs while in Spain, with my family there, and I want to specially recall them too in this acknowledgement, also with a smile and much joy. I dedicate this book to my grandparents, the eldest of this peculiar bunch of kin that I have. All crazy, except me, of course.

Here is also a salute to my *altísimos panas* Jesús Carneiro, Emilio Guzmán and Víctor Bejarano. And to Johan López, always ready to give a hand to back-packing characters in Caracas. And to my friend and colleague Javier Carrera, with whom among other things I share the experience of being *sin papeles* in Latin America. Javier, also among those other things, generously commented on one of the chapters of this book, so I share with him that one too, with much gratitude.

For their hospitality and the way they have nourished my ideas I should thank another thousand people or so, but let me name only a couple who come to mind right now: Antonia Carreño, Juan Caballero and Antonio Paredes. 'Here are the keys to the house', and off we go.

I also want to thank my colleagues at the University of Sydney, all of them, for what I have learnt over the past three years here in many respects. Institutions always have their own motion and constrains, but they are always inhabited by people, and one realizes that the latter can be stronger than the former. There is such a number of inspiring academic and administrative staff at the University of Sydney, and with such humane force. I am grateful to this community, and to the institution that makes my work possible.

I would also like to acknowledge as inspiring support the students I have worked with in Sydney, and in particular I am indebted to those who have come to seminars to discuss indigenous movements in Latin America, for the way in which they have contributed to refine my ideas over time.

I want to make a separate mention to my colleagues Michael Humphrey, Simon Tormey and Adam Morton, who commented on an early version of my Introduction to this book. It is such a privilege to have three colleagues take the time to share their views on one's work, and to provide generous orientation. Big thanks to them.

All the staff at Zed Books I thank for their extraordinary work in getting the book to this final stage, and to Kika Sroka-Miller in particular for her initial contact to discuss potential projects.

For this book I have used some material and ideas that I have previously published elsewhere, in journal articles. While empirical material has not been transformed in the journey from article to book, some of the ideas with which I interpret such material have been sharpened, and in some cases reoriented. These journal articles are all listed in the bibliography, except for one, entitled 'Indigenous peoples, social movements and the legacy of Hugo Chávez's governments', which is currently in press and will be published in a special issue of *Latin American Perspectives*.

There are many more people and things I should mention as positive influences on this book, but I will end these acknowledgements abruptly before I get too sentimental. Sincere gratitude to the people in Tuaken, a small place I have in mind and at heart even when thinking of big pictures. And, as in the dedication, here it is, in short: to the Venezuelan people, and to Rosario and Manolo.

Abbreviations

AD	Acción Democrática
ALBA	Alianza Bolivariana para los Pueblos de Nuestra América (Bolivarian Alliance of the Peoples of Our Americas)
AN	Asamblea Nacional (National Assembly [parliament])
ANC	Asamblea Nacional Constituyente (National Constituent Assembly [consitutional drafting body])
ASOCINSABAT	Asociación Civil Indígena Santa Barbará de Tapirin (Civil Indigenous Association of Santa Barbará de Tapirin)
ASOCOINBO	Asociacion Unica de Comerciantes Indigenas Bolivarianos (Extraordinary Association of Indigenous Bolivarian Traders)
AsoVAC	Asociación Venezolana para el Avance de la Ciencia (Venezuelan Association for the Advancement of Science)
CIN	Comisión Indigenista Nacional (National Commission for Indigenous Affairs)
CLEB	Consejo Legislativo del Estado Bolívar (Bolívar State Legislative Council)
CNE	Consejo Nacional Electoral (National Electoral Council)

COINKA	Comunidades Indígenas Kariña (Kariña Indigenous Communities)
CONAIE	Confederación de Nacionalidades Indígenas del Ecuador (Confederation of Indigenous Nationalities of Ecuador)
CONIVE	Consejo Nacional Indio de Venezuela (National Council of Venezuelan Indians)
COPEI	Comité de Organización Política Electoral Independiente (Political Electoral Independent Organization Committee)
CORPIA	Consejo Regional de Pueblos Indígenas de Apure (Regional Council of Indigenous Peoples of Apure)
CRBV	Constitución de la República Bolivariana de Venezuela (Constitution of the Bolivarian Republic of Venezuela [1999])
CVG	Corporación Venezolana de Guayana [state-owned development corporation for the development of Guayana region]
CVM	Corporación Venezolana de Minería (Venezuelan Mining Corporation)
DGAI	Dirección General de Asuntos Indígenas (Directorate General for Indigenous Affairs)
DICA	Directorate of Indigenous Cults and Affairs
FIEB	Federación Indígena del Estado Bolívar (Indigenous Federation of Bolívar State)
FUNDACIDI	Fundación para la Capacitación, Integración y Dignificación del Indígena (Foundation for the Training, Integration and Dignity of Indigenous People)

IAN	Instituto Agrario Nacional (National Agricultural Institute)
ILO	International Labour Organization
INE	Instituto Nacional de Estadística (National Statistics Institute)
INPI	Instituto Nacional de Pueblos Indígenas (National Institute of Indigenous Peoples)
IVIC	Instituto Venezolano de Investigaciones Científicas (Venezuelan Institute for Scientific Research)
LDGHTP	Ley de Demarcación y Garantía del Hábitat y Tierras de los Pueblos Indígenas (Law for the Demarcation and Guarantee of Indigenous Peoples' Habitat and Lands)
LOPCI	Ley Orgánica de Pueblos y Comunidades Indígenas (Basic Law of Indigenous Peoples and Communities)
LOPE	Ley Orgánica de Procesos Electorales (Basic Law of Electoral Processes)
LRA	Ley de Reforma Agraria [1961] (Law of Agricultural Reform)
MAS	Movimiento al Socialismo (Movement for Socialism)
MBR	Movimiento Bolivariano Revolucionario (Bolivarian Revolutionary Movement)
MEP	Movimiento Electoral del Pueblo – Partido Socialista de Venezuela (People's Electoral Movement)
MIBAM	Ministerio del Poder Popular para las Industrias Basicas y Minería (Ministry of Basic Industries and Mining)

MID	Movimiento Independiente Democrático (Independent Democratic Movement)
MINPI	Ministerio del Poder Popular para los Pueblos Indígenas (Ministry of Indigenous Peoples)
MOPIVE	Movimiento de los Pueblos Indígenas de Venezuela (Venezuelan Indigenous Peoples' Movement)
MUD	Mesa de al Unidad Democrática (Democratic Unity Roundtable)
MVR	Movimiento Quinta República (Fifth Republic Movement)
NGO	non-governmental organization
NGP	Nueva Geometría del Poder (New Geometry of Power)
OCAI	Oficina Central de Asuntos Indígenas (Central Bureau of Indigenous Affairs)
OCEI	Oficina Central de Estadística e Informática (Central Bureau of Statistics and Data Processing)
OCIGRANSA	Organización Comunidades Indígenas Gran Sabana (Organization of Indigenous Communities of Gran Sabana)
OIR	Organización Indígena Regional en Bolívar (Regional Indigenous Organization of Bolívar State)
OMAFI	Oficina Ministerial de Asuntos Fronterizos y para Indígenas (Ministerial Office for Border Zones and Indigenous Peoples)

ORPIA	Organización Regional de Pueblos Indígenas de Amazonas (Regional Organization of Indigenous Peoples of Amazonas)
ORPIZ	Organización Regional de los Pueblos Indígenas del Zulia (Regional Organization of the Indigenous Peoples of Zulia [state])
PARLINVE	Parlamento Indígena Venezolano (Venezuelan Indigenous Parliament)
PCV	Partido Comunista de Venezuela (Venezuelan Communist Party)
PDVSA	Petróleos de Venezuela S.A. [state-owned oil company]
PEMON 08	Proyecto Electoral y Movimiento de Origen Nacional del 2008
PODEMOS	Por la Democracia Social (For Social Democracy)
PPT	Patria Para Todos (Fatherland for All)
PSUV	Partido Socialista Unido de Venezuela (United Socialist Party of Venezuela)
ROC	Región Occidental (Western electoral region)
ROR	Región Oriental (Eastern electoral region)
RSUR	Región Sur (Southern electoral region)
SECONASEDE	Secretaría permanente del Consejo Nacional de Seguridad y Defensa (Permanent Secretary of the National Security and Defence Council)
TAWALA	non-profit NGO involved with 28 principal ethnic groups and 15 derivatives across Venezuela

TIPNIS	Territorio Indígena y Parque Nacional Isiboro–Secure (Isiboro–Sécure National Park and Indigenous Territory) [Bolivia]
TSJ	Tribunal Superior de Justicia (Supreme Court)
UBV	Universidad Bolivariana de Venezuela (Bolivarian University of Venezuela)
UCIW	Unión de Comunidades Indígenas Warao (Union of Indigenous Warao Communities)
UCV	Universidad Central de Venezuela (Central University of Venezuela)
UNERG	Universidad Nacional Experimental de los Llanos Centrales Romulo Gallegos (Rómulo Gallegos National Experimental University of the Central Plains)
UVE	Unión de Vencedores Electorales (Union of Election Winners)

Preface

A study of the politics of indigenous peoples is an unlikely place to find an apology of the state, but this example comes close to being one. Not candid, not devoid of concerns, but an apology nonetheless. The research condensed herein reveals the existence of a state whose political dynamics have both fostered and partially adapted to a variety of popular forces, interests and demands – including indigenous ones – and whose structures succeeded in massively improving Venezuelans' access to socioeconomic and political rights. The ultimate directionality of this state power is still undefined – it is driven by conflict. Needless to say, not everything about it is rosy – it suffers from and reproduces unresolved problems. But it is precisely now – at a time of economic difficulties, political adjustments, counterrevolutionary outbursts and imperialist threats – that a balanced discussion of the qualities and challenges of the Bolivarian state is most needed.

At this critical moment, a variety of critics queue eagerly to single out the alleged state-centric orientations of Bolivarianism as the ultimate cause of all – indeed of any – challenges that Venezuela faces. Among those critics, unsurprisingly, neoliberal pundits inside and outside the country seize the opportunity to try to gain ground for their political agendas. Their diagnoses and prognoses of the situation barely disguise a dogmatic belief in the need to reduce the state (and society) to a market-regulated model. But some sections of the Left, shouting 'we told you so' with a touch of self-righteousness, also consider the time ripe for a determined demolition of this 'bourgeois' state and a move towards a model that, here and now, would constitute a realistic solution to most socioeconomic problems.

In this scenario of crisis and widespread criticism, it might be tempting to let oneself go with the view that states are pernicious beasts by nature and that the very ideal of a transformative state is a recipe for failure, be it in Latin America or anywhere else. This temptation, however, might be shrouded in danger, and it certainly does not seem to appeal to the masses of Bolivarian supporters, among others. In Venezuela, and in Latin America more generally, resistance to that temptation is probably driven more by the stubborn wisdom of experience than by pusillanimous dictates of habit. Many have personally experienced the type of liberty that falls upon majorities as an unbearable yoke when the market and 'civil society' initiatives become the authoritative tutors of social and political life. None of the existing alternatives to left-leaning popular states have so far presented clear proposals to face up to the structural forces of really existing capitalism and the way in which it has created mass disenfranchisement in regions such as Latin America. Against that background, it might well be not only legitimate, but also sensible, to fear that, in our current global scenario, existing alternatives would sooner rather than later end up translating into some variant of the old formulas 'save yourself, if you can' or 'retreat to a small community where, perhaps, you will be able to realize your life ideals'. The debate is on, in any case, and a balanced discussion could be very valuable at this very point in time. Such a discussion requires solid foundations, and this book aims to contribute to their provision.

People in Venezuela are indeed giving their opinions about these and other questions – as they have done regularly, accompanying those opinions with their votes, since approval of the 1999 Constitution. And they are the only ones who can legitimately decide and continue shaping the political model they prefer for their country. This book, written in English, cannot contribute much to informing those decisions. But it will, I hope, enhance readers' understanding of current Venezuelan, Latin American and global politics, and stimulate new reflections about their own countries and the times we all currently live in. In many places, and not only in Latin America, people are posing questions that in one way or another relate to the role of the state in increasingly market-dominated societies. And in countries in which that role is abruptly changing, people seem particularly interested in discussing such questions – not necessarily on an abstract level, but certainly in ways that are politically transcendent.

Ask crisis-stricken people in Spain – just to name my own country – what they think about the rapid dismantling of social services and protections that many presumed to be almost natural constituent elements of their social contract. Ask them about what happens to the concepts of democracy and citizenship in our increasingly unequal class-based societies when even the fragile safety nets that the state safeguarded are removed – while capital holders, intertwined with political elites, are protected. It will not be difficult to find those crisis-stricken people, if you really want to talk to them: many of them are out on the streets, protesting and very willing to discuss the answers.

Some of those answers will appear simplistic to those who strive for a better, different, post-capitalist world. 'Is all this noise just about a return to the same old, business-as-usual, social democracy?', they may ask. 'Is it all about resuscitating the welfare state, at least until the next capitalist crisis strikes?', some may lament. Maybe. Yet many of those answers are already projecting other messages as well, voiced with indignation. They echo genuine concerns, restarting a far-reaching discussion about democracy, markets and collective social horizons. In that discussion markets do not come before people and, very often, appeals to (a certain understanding of) the state reappear as a handy means – not as an end in itself – with which to make that principle a reality.

The *Leviathan*-esque imagery that in one way or another remains associated with the state deserves yet another makeover. While never docile, it seems that the state is a human-friendly beast. Moreover, in this jungle of ours, it is about the last predator standing that, in certain conditions and with the support and guidance of multitudes, has been capable of fencing off our species from the wildest of carnivores around – one whose hand, once it became visible, revealed its merciless claws.

Introduction

This book studies the Bolivarian revolution from a largely unexplored but revealing angle: I will analyze how it has transformed, and been transformed by, relationships between the state and indigenous peoples, and how indigeneity in contemporary Venezuela is being defined by men and women making their own history. Over the past 16 years, the indigenous population has contributed to the shaping of its own and the country's future through a variety of forms of collective action. These tell us as much about the diverse composition and political priorities of the indigenous population as about the dynamics of contemporary Venezuelan politics and the Bolivarian state. This study will examine and characterize those forms of collective action and priorities, also discussing the extent to which constitutional rights for the indigenous population have come about. I will demonstrate that the current enfranchisement of this population, in political and socioeconomic terms, is unprecedented in Venezuelan history, despite lingering structural imbalances and significant tensions around issues such as autonomy and territoriality. Through the analysis of that enfranchisement (its causes, characteristics and limitations) I will also engage in ongoing debates about the present position of and prospects for indigenous and popular struggles, and the role of the state in Latin America.

Indigenous people constitute 2.8 per cent of the Venezuelan population, according to the 2011 national census. It is nevertheless important to note that the boundaries of this population's make-up are blurred, as for any population defined through social-identity criteria. This question, clearly expressed in national censuses, will be discussed further in the book, but I want to highlight this crucial question from the outset: despite generalized assumptions and simplifications associated with the label 'indigenous', this is a very diverse and quite fragmented collective in socio-political terms. The indigenous population is characterized by economic, cultural and other structural divisions, rather than merely being separated from other sections of the population by one or all of those divisions. This statement is not simply a theoretical premise with which to approach the study of a complex capitalist, post-colonial society; as this study will show, it addresses a reality that is revealed, among other things, by identifiable forms of indigenous collective action and the diverse political goals and priorities that they pursue. This should come as no surprise to those familiar with Latin American politics, but it is too often overlooked in generalized debates about indigenous struggles in Venezuela and other parts of the continent.

The study of current Latin American politics repeatedly shows that governments in the region operate with heterogeneous and rather fragmentary social support. Commenting specifically on studies of radical left-wing governments in Bolivia, Ecuador and Venezuela, Ellner (2014, p. 9) has highlighted a common ingredient: the non-elite groups that constitute the political base of these governments harbour a very complex, and not always harmonious, range of interests. These governments have indeed acknowledged this reality through their political actions. In their countries, the industrial working class – which remains central to some currents of Marxist thinking – is only part (and a relatively small one at that) of the forces from which governments have drawn political power and continuing electoral support. In theory and in practice, these governments have worked with the idea that marginalized sectors of society, including peasants, informal-economy workers and indigenous groups, occupy an important position, along with the 'working class', within their political movements. But here is another crucial caveat I want to add: this premise should not lead to a supposition that all those groups commonly identified as 'non-elite' and marginalized are objectively definable by homogeneous conditions within the country's class structure. That is certainly not the case with 'indigenous peoples' or 'the indigenous population', as I will demonstrate.

As a result of the concrete historical conditions of colonialism, state formation and capitalist expansion in the country, Venezuelan indigenous peoples and communities are engaged in very different ways in the economic and political structures of capitalism and nationality. There are nowadays, for instance, more or less territorialized peoples whose communities are sustained by semi-subsistence economies, but also other communities and individuals, in both rural and urban areas, absolutely deprived of independent means of production. These poles are only the tangible extremes within an established national social structure in which the indigenous population occupies very different positions. In this social formation, there are groups actively involved in or supporting the government and/or the construction of the so-called socialism of the twenty-first century, but there are also opposing organized groups. In short, the indigenous population is in practice segmented by heterogeneous material conditions, political demands and actions that complicate its treatment as a homogeneous, distinctively situated sector of society. And this heterogeneity, as pointed out above, is crystallized in particular forms of collective action that manifest those demands and priorities.

The current configuration of national politics in Venezuela has broadened social participation, and this has naturally brought out different priorities within the (heterogeneous) population. The constitutional rights granted to indigenous peoples in 1999 included differentiated political representation, which facilitated their political enfranchisement and their active incorporation into various aspects of national life. It also unavoidably implied exposure to a well-entrenched political arena – in the case of Venezuela, an extremely polarized one. Political and electoral enfranchisement have thus become an additional factor that contributes to the mobilization of (previously existing) socio-political differences within the indigenous population. Indigenous peoples and communities are rooted in history, and consequently they have been participating in a moment in time at which two political blocs (*chavismo* and *antichavismo*) compete to define the future. Contemporary indigenous struggles have not escaped this historical scenario. This question will be further explored and illustrated in Chapters 4 to 6, where I will examine different forms of indigenous collective action and the priorities they reveal. But let me pause to recall a single day in Venezuela, to complement these introductory reflections.

One day (or the social life of indigeneity)

On the evening of 2 December 2012 I was at the bus station in Ciudad Bolívar (in Bolívar state), passing the time before departing for Puerto Ayacucho (Amazonas state). Walking up and down, a couple of times I went past the encampment that a group of

Warao had set up in a corner of the station, right beside one of the embarking areas.[1] At that time of day they were winding down, some of the children already asleep. It was not an unusual sight. Bolívar's bus station had become home to groups of Warao and other *indígenas* who spent periods of time in the city, selling arts and crafts and begging. However, as on previous occasions, I could not help thinking of the contrast between the bus station as a place of transit and as a temporary residence – which is what it becomes to these Warao in their economic migrations to the city.

Off I went in my bus. Some twelve hours later, at a checkpoint before entering Puerto Ayacucho, a young national guardsman came aboard requesting identity documents. 'Only males', he clarified. In the very back row of seats, a youngster (in his late teens or early twenties) had no ID. The guard started asking why, and an awkward exchange ensued. The young man (whose Spanish was not fluent) and the group of people he was travelling with claimed that a *malandro* had stolen his ID.[2] As this was going on, one of my neighbours on the bus remarked indignantly: 'Can't he [the guard] see that the boy is Indian?' Giving a faint reprimand, the guard finally left and we resumed our journey. My neighbour started again: 'It is as if he did not see that he was Indian!' Another passenger added in agreement: 'Did the guard not see that he [the young man] is not like *racionales* [rational ones]?' And yet another, loudly: 'The National Guard bothers the Indians and does nothing to the *malandros*!'

As we entered the city, banners with electoral propaganda were everywhere. Regional elections were to be held within a couple of weeks, on 16 December. Some of the posters sought votes for Liborio Guarulla (incumbent governor of Amazonas state, and an indigenous Baniva): 'Liborio the Indian, Governor' (*El Indio*

Liborio gobernador); 'With the Indian there is progress and future' (*Con el Indio sí hay Progreso y Futuro*). The latter slogan was also printed on t-shirts that some of his followers sported around town.

We reached the station, and I got off the bus. A couple of hours later, I was walking through the so-called Plaza de los Indios, adjacent to Plaza Bolívar in the town centre. A small street market is held there in which indigenous arts, crafts, food and medicinal products are sold. On one of the stalls a banner caught my eye: it showed the photograph of an indigenous man, sporting a feather crown and holding the hand of Miss Amazonas – in turn exhibiting the sash that identified her as a beauty queen. Both had their eyes closed and a contrite expression, as if in spiritual communication. In the background was an image of Cerro Autana – a mountain that is a natural icon and symbol of Amazonas state. The banner announced: 'The Shaman of Amazonas: the Shaman who prayed Dayana Mendoza into becoming Miss Universe and Ivian Sarcos into Miss World'. Through the man behind the stall, one could contact the shaman for a spiritual service.

This series of events is anecdotal, but also relevant to the central discussion of this book. Is there a single 'indigenous question' that brings these episodes together? If so, is it based on the well-documented process of state-led capitalist development behind the dispossession and displacement of the Warao, who decades ago turned periodic or permanent migration to cities into a part of their subsistence lifestyle? How does that 'indigenous question' relate to the racialising codes and prejudices against indigenous people that linger on in sectors of Venezuelan society? And how are those prejudices in turn linked to the (patronizing) solidarity with the indigenous 'underdog' that spontaneously appeared on that bus en route to Puerto Ayacucho? Can one associate those racialising and solidarity codes with Liborio Guarulla's long and winding career in politics, which epitomizes the contradictions of contemporary Venezuelan politics?[3] Why would Guarulla highlight his indigenous identity as part of his election campaign tactics, when some people continue to make distinctions between 'Indians' and '*racionales*'? And how do those contrasting articulations of social categorization and indigenous identity merge with the commodification of culture that is condensed in the business of the shaman of Amazonas, who can pray you to worldwide success for a fee?

The answers to these and many other questions cannot be subsumed into a single 'indigenous question'. Despite some necessary reductionism among analysts and activists, it is simply misleading to presume that nowadays the material and cultural conditions of the indigenous population, and the demands that this population articulates, are homogeneous to the extent that they can all be analyzed as part of a single 'indigenous struggle' with unambiguous and common goals. The displaced Warao at the bus terminal and the shaman of Amazonas do not belong to the same social class. Liborio Guarulla and the ID-less young man on the bus do not occupy an equivalent position within Venezuelan 'indigenous cultures' that might explain their political alignments and electoral preferences. The Wayúu population living for decades (indeed generations) in areas of an urban centre such as Maracaibo (Zulia state) do not have the same economic priorities as the Pume in rural communities of Apure state. Pemon communities directly engaged in (and largely dependent on) mining activity in Bolívar state do not share the interests and priorities of Barí communities opposed to coal mining around Perijá (Zulia state). I do not present these cases and pose these questions as expressions of a post-modern, unintelligible world; I recall them at the very beginning of this book with Socratic purpose, in order to introduce some indispensable conceptual clarification to guide our discussion and as a necessary caveat against misleading analytical simplifications.

Indigenous struggles today are not constrained by homogeneous cultural or economic determinants, and neither are they teleologically pre-defined in their political direction. These struggles are in fact shaped by collective actions that reveal diverse political horizons – often in convergence with the bases and horizons of other social groups. Against this backdrop, we are better placed to undertake the study of contemporary indigenous struggles, whose contingent content is expressed in and defined by particular forms of collective action and the demands they advance. As I will show, a central part of these actions and demands has firmly located them as a constituent part of 'the people' that support *chavismo*.

The people

In Venezuela it had been a long time coming. The so-called Fourth Republic (1958–99) had faced small foci of revolutionary activism almost from its inception, but in particular from the 1980s onwards it harboured a gradually growing ferment of generalized discontent, civil disaffection and disenfranchisement among large sectors of society. When the economic crisis of the 1980s struck, the regime's imposition of the burden of that crisis upon the working classes through various neoliberal policies rapidly widened already notable social inequalities, and aggravated the perception of systemic failures. The so-called 'Black Friday' of 1983, marked by the collapse and devaluation of the currency during Herrera Campins' term of government, was only the first of a succession of dramatic February days in the nation's historical memory. The turmoil of the *El Caracazo* protests and crackdown in 1989 and the two coups of 1992 were milestones in a gradual process of the regime's demise, of which the extraordinary levels of extra-institutional protest throughout the 1990s became the most tangible expression. However, despite this background of struggle and the signs of the regime's coming end, the organized Left was incapable of building mass alternatives with the potential to govern. The engagement of large numbers of people (not just instances of organized activism or fragmented protest) in a commonly declared pursuit of a different future only occurred with the mobilization that led to Chávez's 1998 election victory. This mobilization was successfully based on a nationalist and populist strategy.[4] A nascent political bloc seized the country's presidency, and with access to state power it moved into an entirely new, catalyzing qualitative dimension. Its heterogeneous political base was soon realigned and further mobilized during the period of the 1999 Constituent Assembly. Disparate groups thus accelerated their gradual consolidation as constituent elements of that type of collective political subject known by social theory as 'a people' – a historically singular amalgamation of political forces. This collective subject, which also incorporated and reshaped a central share of indigenous collective action in the country, has been the support for *chavismo*.[5]

The emergence and development of the *chavista* movement can only be explained by simultaneously taking into consideration structural conditions, including class cleavages, and subjectively oriented collective behaviours. There is neither a rigid nor a direct relationship between the aggregation of collective actions that have shaped and reshaped this movement (and its countermovement) over the past 16 years and objectively measurable structural divisions in Venezuela. These divisions, economic and political, undoubtedly constitute the background against which the Bolivarian revolution emerged and has evolved, and as this goes on they have been partly modified in favour of the popular classes.[6] However, mobilization, activism and electoral behaviour in the country have clearly demonstrated that those divisions are only imperfectly reflected in the overarching collective political identities that have marked the field of struggle in the country: *chavismo* and its related, historically constituted opposite (*anti-chavismo*). These identities embrace political movements whose membership does not directly reflect the class (nor 'ethnic' or 'racial') structure of the country.

The late Hugo Chávez publicly recalled on several occasions the day, following the 2006 Venezuelan presidential elections, on which Fidel Castro told him that there were not 4,000,000 oligarchs in Venezuela. Castro was referring to the 4,200,000-plus votes for the opposition in that election, which Chávez had nevertheless won by a landslide (62.8 per cent of the vote and a 25-point lead over his rival Manuel Rosales). The 'oligarchy' was (is) one of the signifiers repeatedly used within the Bolivarian bloc to demarcate the political terrain in Venezuela – a signifier discursively associated with the dominant political bloc during the so-called Fourth Republic, and derivatively with the current opposition to *chavismo*. But of course, not everyone voting in 2006 for the opposition was a member of an 'oligarchy' – a term that, strictly speaking, would only refer to a very small percentage of the population in numerical terms. Behind Castro's comment was the idea that the *chavista* vote should be able to grow even more, capturing the 'middle' and 'popular'-class voters that in 2006 were among those 4,000,000-plus people supporting the opposition despite generally benefitting from the government's policies. Castro had a point. So do those *chavistas* who, in subsequent elections and before the relative growth of the opposition bloc, have noted that, in Venezuela, the 'middle class' (another signifier with which the *anti-chavista* opposition is broadly associated) does not account for over 44 per cent of the population – the percentage of voters that supported the opposition leader (Henrique Capriles) in the 2012 presidential elections. One can indeed make a class-based analysis of contemporary Venezuelan politics and government policy through different objective indicators expressing the historical contest between capital and labour, but it must be kept in mind that the electoral arena does not rigidly reflect the country's class structure. And the electoral arena has been, and remains, crucial for the Bolivarian revolution.

Despite the radical character of the process, it is (primarily and ultimately) elections that have made the pursuit of a transformative political process possible in Venezuela. For the Bolivarian movement, continuing successes in electoral competition have guaranteed access to a share of state power, and this power has *simultaneously* been used to facilitate socioeconomic inclusion and to foster popular mobilization, thus enhancing the possibilities of further transformation.[7]

The overall directionality of this state power, however, continues to be contested. It is not clear if the Bolivarian project will fade away as a post-neoliberal adjustment of capitalism or will take on some post-capitalist form. The latter is still a remote possibility, although over the past decade it has gained force. The transformative potential of the Bolivarian project, undefined as it is between its post-neoliberal and post-capitalist possibilities, is at present only plausible if *chavismo* continues to receive electoral majorities. Given the forces that dominate the opposition to it, a rapid return to an openly neoliberal path and greater dominance of capital in the country is otherwise a very likely probability.

In Venezuela politics is polarized between the *chavista* and opposition blocs, with diverse class divisions, ideological orientations and political horizons within them. The political contest between and within these two blocs has reached new heights at the time writing (2014–15), and its future definition is, as it has always been, crucially dependent on election results.[8] These were very tight in the last presidential round (April 2013), which Maduro secured by a narrow margin of 1.8 per cent. The study presented here therefore sits against a complex backdrop. It will explain aspects of Venezuelan politics that have already been defined, but it will also deal with prospects that are still uncertain. For good or bad, writing about the Bolivarian revolution continues to be a present-tense exercise.

Indigenous struggles in Latin America: positioning Venezuela

There is a vast body of literature addressing the impacts that indigenous mobilizations and the statutory shifts associated with the politics of recognition have had in Latin American countries over the past three decades (e.g. Assies et al. 2000; Becker 2013b; Laurent 2005; Postero 2009; Postero and Zamosc 2005; Sieder 2002; Van Cott 2000, 2005; Webber 2011; Yashar 2005). The phenomenon naturally affected and generated intense debates within countries politically shattered by (partly) indigenous mobilization but, significantly, it also attracted an extraordinary amount of international attention. In the 1990s, the decade of the forecast end of history and widespread neoliberal change at a global level, the indigenous protest phenomenon became a discordant note amid fundamental debates on the shape of post-Cold War democracy – a sort of anomaly. For many on the Left, it became a new symbol of resistance. But this symbol required translation and incorporation into new programmes of emancipation, and most often those translations ended up converging in a final condemnation of the state, from which it seemed necessary to separate emancipatory struggles. However, the arrival of the so-called post-neoliberal governments, with Venezuela, Bolivia and Ecuador as prime examples, brought new angles to those political emancipation programmes. Among other things, these governments have reintroduced the state back into left-wing and socialist-leaning programmes of transformation, with new opportunities and challenges. And indigenous collective action and demands are contributing to shape them, as this book will illustrate.

But let us continue recalling the historical background before embarking on an analysis of the present. At a statutory level, the so-called new Latin American constitutionalism was accompanied by the multicultural shift during the 1990s. Most countries in the region reformed their constitutions or sanctioned new ones with an explicit declaration of the multiethnic or pluricultural character of the nation, often recognizing indigenous peoples as a distinctive constituent element (Barié 2005; Roldán Ortega 2005). This shift brought countries in the region to comparable statutory positions, yet it did not stem from comparable processes of struggle. The shift was linked to top-down processes of systemic political relegitimization in the continent, but the systemic crises that preceded these processes had different national configurations and confronted diverse forms of social protest and mobilization. In countries such as Bolivia and Ecuador, multicultural reform and regime relegitimization became strongly (though not exclusively) associated with indigenous mobilizations (Becker 2011; Crabtree

2005; Petras and Veltmeyer 2005; see antecedents in Nash 1992). Yet in other countries this was not the case. In Venezuela, the collapse of the so-called Fourth Republic was underpinned by a long crisis and cycle of protests within which indigenous mobilization was not a prominent ingredient. In fact, there had not been a strongly positioned indigenous movement in the country, as I will demonstrate, but the 1999 Constituent Assembly nevertheless transformed the legal status of indigenous peoples. With the new constitution, to which indigenous organizations contributed according to their quite limited strength, Venezuela came to the vanguard of the Latin American countries that throughout the 1990s included differentiated rights for indigenous peoples in their constitutions (Barié 2005; Roldán Ortega 2005; Van Cott 2002).

In any event, the multicultural shift in constitutional reform was soon accompanied by growing scepticism and sharp criticism. At the continental level, statutory reform did not translate into any substantial socioeconomic transformation or political empowerment for the indigenous population. On the one hand, criticism of the multicultural euphoria became framed as criticism of ongoing neoliberal governance (Díaz-Polanco 2009; Hale 2002), which could take over and incorporate the celebration of cultural diversity as a new idiom within its leopard-like repertoire: (nearly) everything had to change so that (nearly) everything could remain the same. On the other hand, it was not only a problem within the state sphere. Beyond the state's normative rearrangements, the landscape of indigenous rights advocacy in the 'civil society' sphere was a long way from providing avenues of empowerment. In the 1990s, it was already giving clear signs of being strongly influenced, when not determined, by bureaucratic conflations of international normative arrangements and NGO programmes guided by deceptively depoliticized notions of the indigenous subject: the hyperreal Indian (Ramos 1994). This subject, which Alcida Ramos suggestively characterized as a projection of Western virtue, stoicism and heroic ideals, became the preferred subject for the new operating model with which indigenous rights and development could be pursued – in harmony with national and international 'civil society' agencies. To the puzzlement of advocates of the model, not all Indians were interested in pursuing what they considered their interests and rights in accordance with that hyperreal model. During the 1990s and 2000s, Indians continued to be engaged in overtly politicized forms of extra-institutional and institutional collective action, and in countries such as Bolivia and Ecuador they facilitated greater governmental reorientation – even new constituent processes in which 'plurinationalism' replaced 'multiculturalism' as the ideological framework for statutory incorporation of recognition. The state was being reconfigured, this time with an explicit anti-neoliberal orientation.

In a comparative study of indigenous protest in Latin America, Yashar argued that one of the central factors helping to explain its 'uneven emergence, timing, and location' was the politicization of indigenous identities that would have taken place 'where state policies challenge the material and political foundations necessary for local community autonomy' (Yashar 2005, p. 283). Along with what she called 'political associational space' and the existence of 'transcommunity networks', she suggested that this extension of state policies could help explain indigenous mobilization in Ecuador, Bolivia, Guatemala and Mexico throughout the 1990s. Maintaining that proposal as a working hypothesis depends both on how one defines 'autonomy' and on what type of state policy reaches indigenous communities. A significant share of indigenous protest throughout the past two decades has projected demands that can be associated with *more* state – as the apparatus that channels and guarantees social rights and can facilitate enfranchisement. In these cases, indigenous mobilization has not been a reaction *against* state reform, and in fact has been deployed *in support of* the state. I will argue that forms of state-supporting mobilization help to explain the increased degree of political participation among the indigenous population in Venezuela.

While some authors consider that local government is the sphere in which the impact of indigenous participation in state politics and the development of radical democracy can be best evaluated (e.g. Van Cott 2008), for the understanding of indigenous collective action in Venezuela it would be misleading to separate national politics from the local variety. In Venezuela, where indigenous collective action had been reactive, episodic and marginal in terms of national impact, from 1999 onwards it underwent important changes. There was a qualitative and quantitative increase in indigenous participation in national politics, including social movement activity. This phenomenon cannot be explained merely by the introduction of the statutory changes that, through the 1999 Constitution, guaranteed political rights and differentiated representation to the indigenous population. Electoral politics became a very important channel of indigenous collective action in the country, yet it is not the only one. This increased participation and mobilization has been inextricably connected with the political dynamics sparked by the Bolivarian process and its impact on state power, which has become a mobilizing force. This will be a central concern for this book: the way in which the dynamics of the Bolivarian state have transformed indigenous collective action. In Venezuela, this action is strongly intertwined with the polarized dynamics of national politics, and a significant part of that action strives for a consolidation of state structures associated with the socialism of the twenty-first century. Furthermore, we will see that even collective action that openly confronts some aspects of government policy presents demands and actions that cannot be presented as anti-state: the state's appeal remains strong.

What state?

Fernando Coronil got it right to an extent he could not fully foresee. In the crisis-struck 1990s, seeking to capture the dynamics that had led to a 'deification of the state' in Venezuela, he resorted to an evocative and polysemic title for his now classic monograph (1997): 'the magical state'. Appropriately, the book opens with the reflections of a chameleon-like literary man, José Ignacio Cabrujas. With Cabrujas' sneering but insightful genius in the background, Coronil could set out to reveal the social foundations and social effects of an oil-based state structure that, intertwining the realms of nature and capital, had transfigured into a magical entity. Over time, this entity and its chief players had simultaneously become mighty and incapable, comical and sombre, theatrical but always too real: hyperreal. Two decades later, one cannot help recalling Coronil's provocative call when embarking on a review of debates on contemporary Venezuela: 'the magical state'.

The Venezuelan state has done wonders, once again. The interpretation of its marvels is more contested than ever, yet also more than ever no one seems able to resist the spell. Everywhere, inside and outside Venezuela, people seek the precise terms with which this new state magic could be characterized, as if thereupon its forces could be tamed and controlled – whether to multiply them or to extinguish them, depending on people's politics. The opening line of Poulantzas' now rejuvenated treatise on the state (1978) could have been written by someone with this phenomenon in mind: 'Who can today escape the question of the state and power?' Looking at the evidence, the answer is unequivocal: no one.

Yet if that question is inescapable, the answers flee in all directions. The 'state' is certainly back but, unsurprisingly, it did not return alone: 'society' and its internal conflicts came along too. A myriad of analysts carry out the disenchanting task of characterizing the Bolivarian state, but no agreement ensues. Divergences stem partly from ideological reasons: the analyst's view of the transformative left-wing governments in today's Latin America. But ideological differences do not explain it all. Both sympathetic and hostile analysts present diverging characterizations of the Bolivarian state. The complexities generally associated with political analysis are in this case multiplied by the fact that the object of study, the contemporary Venezuelan state, is particularly elusive – not because it possesses essentially mysterious qualities, but because it is in a conflict-ridden creative transformation. This conflict is not only shaped internally, but also conditioned externally by the hostility of the United States, which ends up reinforcing political polarization within the country (Hellinger 2012, p. 155).

Because of its conflict-ridden transformative motion, this state is characterized by its contortionism. The political power the state deploys is being argued over and shaped by society and its antagonistic organizational dynamics – not only those of the *chavista* bloc, in itself heterogeneous. This makes the state twist and turn in awkward, unpredictable forms.[9] A wide variety of characterizations have been produced in the search for tools with which to accurately comprehend this form of political power in analytical terms. Within that range, some have paid attention to the state's inextricable connection with popular mobilization, to which this study of indigenous collective action will relate.

It has been called a 'state-in-revolution' (Muhr 2012) in a characterization that highlights the active role that the Bolivarian state has played in the organization of the popular classes. Rather than as a crystallized form, state power is also rightly presented by Muhr as a power undergoing reconfiguration, with reconfiguring forces stemming both from *within* the state and from *outside* it (2012, p. 20). It has also been called a 'state of revolutionary popular power' (Raby 2014), in an effort similarly aiming to pin down its defining political dynamics, including a mobilized population as one key characteristic element. Research has noted the existence of different relationships between social movements and state agents, discarding simplistic interpretations of the Bolivarian process as a top-down, government-controlled political participation process (e.g. Fernandes 2010; Hellinger 2012; Ciccariello-Maher 2013). I will critically engage these discussions, which address part of the crucial dynamics and characteristics of a 'magical state' that over the past 16 years has been performing magic of a different type – though some old tricks remain in the repertoire. This book will show that there is a mutually constituent link between state power and the current degree of indigenous mobilization, but will also place distinct emphasis on the fact that there is an original force in that relationship. This is an essential question for understanding this revolution.

Indigenous collective action has been participating in the shaping of the Bolivarian state and its democratic model through three main streams: electoral, the state-supporting and state-sponsored social movement, and extra-institutional mobilization (partly) against current government practice. These streams are not mutually exclusive in absolute terms (in fact, many actors move across the first two in particular); and all of them have been largely created as effective and sustained streams of action since 1998. It was the seizure of shares of state power by the Bolivarian bloc that facilitated and strengthened indigenous (and general popular) political participation and mobilization – and not the other way round. In this sense, the question that in politics equates to the dilemma of whether the chicken or the egg came first has a clear answer here. Before the *chavista* seizure of elements of state power, there were foci of organized but fragmented activism. Chávez's 1998 presidential victory was supported by an electorally mobilized but amorphous and uncoordinated social mass. What gradually consolidated afterwards was 'a people', a collective subject amalgamated around an overarching political identity but also sustained by strong currents of popular mobilization (not all of them harmonious). This mobilization has not resulted from the imposition of 'state power' upon 'society' in a top-down fashion; on the contrary, state power has been reoriented by invigorated popular organization, for which in turn the institutional apparatus of the state created favourable conditions. Particularly since 2006, government action and its supporters have explicitly searched for forms of strengthening 'popular power' as a democratic amalgamation of 'civil' and 'political' society.[10] I will present specific examples to illustrate this point in the realm of indigenous struggles, additionally showing that a trait of that amalgamation within the Bolivarian state is that it incorporates conflict and protest as dynamizing forces. The incorporation of conflict as a source of creativity turns upside down conventional wisdom about the absorption of social demands in institutional systems. This trait, however, characterizes the Bolivarian state, whose synergies with popular forces have brought both the latter and the former to positions that neither of them could occupy as separate entities.

Structure of the book

In addition to this Introduction, this book consists of eight chapters. The first two chapters complement each other in bringing to the fore key contrasts between indigenous organization and collective action before and after 1998. They show how the emergence of the *chavista* movement paved the way for a substantive transformation of that collective action, which gradually became *sustained and proactive* as opposed to its previous *episodic and reactive* character. The transition between these two distinct periods is mapped out in these chapters, particularly in Chapter 2.

Chapter 1 provides a diachronic contextualization of relations between the state and indigenous peoples in Venezuela throughout the twentieth century. It focuses on three defining aspects of those relations: (1) the impact of national censuses on defining the changing boundaries of indigenousness as a social identity; (2) state bureaucracies and government policy in the realm of indigenous affairs; and (3) indigenous organizations and forms of collective action during the twentieth century. The picture that emerges from examining these questions is one of erratic state bureaucracies and government policy, and fragmented and weak indigenous organization. Mobilization during this period erupted periodically, mainly as a reaction against immediate threats such as land invasions.

In Chapter 2 I will show how the emergence of the *chavista* movement and its seizure of shares of state power from 1998 onwards paved the way for a substantive transformation of that scenario.

Major indigenous organizations and activists gravitated towards *chavismo* as soon as it started to take off as a national-popular movement. Chávez's victory in the 1998 presidential elections and the subsequent constituent assembly period in 1999 focused and catalyzed indigenous activism, which started to take shape in new forms and largely incorporated itself into the *chavista* bloc. Out of this seminal process an indigenous movement gradually emerged. This movement did not exist beforehand: it was created by the dynamics of the Bolivarian revolution once the latter started to gain institutional power.

This chapter also discusses key ingredients in the constitution of the *chavista* collective identity, within which symbols and signifiers of indigeneity have played a very salient role. This is interpreted as part of the creative processes and logics through which mass-mobilizing movements generate collective identities.

Chapter 3 moves on to ask to what extent constitutional rights have materialized for the indigenous population, in respect of both their differentiated and their non-differentiated rights. It thus provides a basis for assessing the degree of political and socioeconomic enfranchisement of this population, which in many respects is remarkable and unprecedented in the country. In turn, that evaluation becomes a backdrop for subsequent chapters: it will be pivotal to understanding why different forms of indigenous collective action have developed in relation to the *chavista* bloc. As we shall see, these diverse forms reveal different interests and priorities among the indigenous population.

The following three chapters embark on detailed discussion of the three main streams of indigenous collective action that are to be found in contemporary Venezuela. Chapter 4 focuses on the electoral stream, whose overall importance cannot be overemphasized. Without access to the elements of state power that continuing election victories have guaranteed to the *chavista* bloc, the Bolivarian revolution would not be. If electoral dominance were weakened to the extent that it translated into the loss of significant amounts of institutional state power, the revolution would be fatally wounded. The process is dependent on state power, which simultaneously is a tool for the delivery of socioeconomic rights and an engine for popular mobilization.

In this chapter I draw attention to the fact that the electoral arena has itself been a strong focus of mobilization and convergence of indigenous and non-indigenous political forces. Indigenous actors have determinedly embarked on this avenue of political participation, which their new rights enhanced for them: the Bolivarian Constitution of 1999 guarantees differentiated indigenous representation in legislative organs. In this determined move, these actors have also fully incorporated themselves into the national-level political struggle, in support of either of the two political blocs that form it (*chavismo* and *anti-chavismo*). Against interpretations of this process as one of 'co-option' of indigenous activists and organizations, I will argue that it expresses the conscious choice of indigenous actors who see in their participation in institutional state politics a route for the advancement of their goals and, more broadly, for the creation and maintenance of broad popular blocs that can potentially present alternatives to neoliberal capitalism. The supporters of the *chavista* bloc within this electoral stream of collective action have strong connections with a state-supporting and state-sponsored indigenous movement that nevertheless constitutes a (partially) separate stream of collective action.

Chapter 5 focuses specifically on the analysis of that indigenous movement. This is a proactive movement in support of the state as a guarantor of enfranchisement, and its contentiousness is, rather, directed against unbridled capitalism and imperialism. This movement, actively incorporated in the *chavista* bloc, prioritizes socioeconomic enfranchisement and direct political participation in state politics before self-determination rights. Members of this movement have developed strong and continuing synergies with political parties, in particular with the PSUV, and with state agents. These synergies do not preclude occasional criticism of government or state organs, for the latter are recognized sources of creative tensions within the *chavista* movement. In this chapter I pay detailed attention to explaining how the creation of the Ministry of Indigenous Peoples in 2007 impacted on those synergies.

Chapter 6 addresses the analysis of a stream of indigenous collective action characterized both by its contentious nature – partly directed against government activities and/or state agents – and by its peripheral position in relation to the *chavista* bloc. I contend that the movement around the Yukpa of the Serranía de Perijá, whose dynamics I will examine, constitutes the epitome of the collective action undertaken in this stream. This stream is tangentially incorporated into the *chavista* bloc, where it has some active supporters. While often contentious in their approach to state agents, I will demonstrate that this movement is not fully 'anti-statist'. I will argue that the difficult relations between its activists and some government and state agents are significantly conditioned by the extreme polarization of politics in the country and by external interference in those politics – which in turn exacerbates polarization.

In Chapter 7 I analyze key factors in the national political economy that influence both government approaches to the shaping of indigenous rights and the forms of indigenous collective action that are deployed in the country. The fundamental importance of extractive industries to the national economy cannot be overlooked when analyzing the political arena. It must, of course, be taken into account when understanding government decision-making, but also when appreciating indigenous demands, as I will suggest.

In this chapter I will highlight the politics of some of the criticism levelled at countries such as Venezuela for their extractivist credentials, which I will place in a global context. I will also argue and illustrate that, beyond socioeconomic and political enfranchisement as a galvanizing goal, a very complex landscape of indigenous demands and social horizons emerges. This complexity complicates analysis of the Bolivarian process, as its direction remains unclear, but it also becomes an extra stimulus for discussion of global politics and the role of the socialisms of the twenty-first century within them.

Chapter 8 contains some concluding remarks.

ONE

Historical overview

Only by taking into consideration the history of colonization and the subsequent development of state structures in Latin America can one satisfactorily situate today's 'indigenous struggles' in the region. And that is as much a political history as a history of capitalism. The conceptual-juridical creation of 'indigenous' collective subjects and their subsequent social manifestations are inextricably linked to the history of colonization, accumulation and capitalist expansion in the continent. The colonial project out of which the 'Indian' subject emerged was also one of accumulation by dispossession and exploitation, and it was not fully extinguished with the nineteenth-century declarations of republican independence. Every metre that the so-called agricultural and capitalist frontiers have gained since has also been marked upon (or in the shadow of) that project, a project that was articulated through market-subservient states. At present, however, stopping and reorienting that project has led many indigenous actors, somewhat counter-intuitively, to embark on struggles in which the state, when directed by governments and political movements whose orientation protects the popular classes from increased degrees of capitalist exploitation, appears as a necessary ally. The reason for this political wager, even when these states do not fully meet the expectations of those who strive for contemporary forms of autonomous self-determination, is that these new states are facilitating forms of socioeconomic enfranchisement that were also part of the demands advanced by indigenous struggles in the continent. What seems to have been learnt along the long way of the twentieth century is that, in the absence of the statutory power of the state, what grows more naturally in this globalized world is not more freedom and self-determination, but more exploitation and dispossession.

Against that general historical background, this chapter will introduce a degree of diachronic analysis to position our discussion of the situation in Venezuela, setting out from the independence period onwards.[1] The scope of inquiry will be demarcated by three contextualizing issues: (1) the indigenous population in Venezuela according to national censuses; (2) state approaches to the administration of 'indigenous affairs' in the twentieth century; and (3) forms of indigenous political organization and collective action before the approval of the 1999 Bolivarian Constitution (*Constitución de la República Bolivariana de Venezuela* – CRBV). This contextualization is essential to understanding the trajectory of indigenous activism in the country, including its current synergies and creative tensions with the *chavista* movement.

Indigenous population and national censuses: historical overview[2]

Venezuelan national censuses have included distinctive quantifications of the indigenous population since they were first carried out as part of Guzmán Blanco's state modernization project in the 1870s. Despite significant fluctuations in relative proportions, national censuses always projected a minority status for the indigenous population, which in turn was presented as the only source of internal 'otherness' (no other social identity category was registered until 2011).

According to the most recent census (2011), 2.8 per cent of the national population is indigenous. It should nonetheless be noted that, in the past three decades, the relative weight within national counts of this population has increased by a factor of three: in the 1982 census, it constituted only 0.96 per cent of the total. This extraordinary increase is not principally determined by demographic factors. Although population censuses are generally associated with demographics and statistical information, they are politically loaded (and politics-sensitive) tools. In the particular case at hand, census numbers tell us more about the way in which the state defines and helps to shape indigeneity than about demographic changes among a clearly bounded sector of the Venezuelan population. Let us clarify some basic points about census-taking and social identities.

Census politics

National censuses generate crucial data for the design and orientation of government policy, but are also pivotal in the official representation of national imagined communities. Statistics bureaus represent themselves, and are generally regarded, as politically neutral administrative organs, and censuses are accordingly presented as scientific, apolitical enterprises – neutral apprehensions of social reality, as it were. However, the generation, interpretation, and use of statistical data, including census data, is inextricably shrouded in an 'arithmetic of politics'. First, the production of statistics is always inseparable from the political goals pursued by those who commission and/or produce them, as advocates of the so-called radical approach to statistical practice rightly remarked (Dorling and Simpson 1999; Irvine et al. 1979). Second, if we focus on population counts in particular, the measurement of social identities (e.g. 'indigenousness') is always shrouded in ideological preconceptions. When social identity categories are defined and articulated in censuses, they reveal particular 'conceptions of society and personhood' (Clark 1998, p. 185), conceptions that are contingent and subject to political contestation. Unsurprisingly, research converges in presenting censuses as political tools in nature (Angosto-Ferrández and Kradolfer 2012; Kertzer and Arel 2002, p. 18; Nobles 2000, p. x; Simpson and Dorling 1999; Skerry 2000, p. 7).

National population counts not only adapt and represent the social world, but also configure it through the conceptions of the world that they sanction. State populations are characteristically diverse in many respects, and including or not including social identity categories (such as 'ethnic' or 'racial' ones) as meaningful census classifications is necessarily the result of ideological decisions. Social class, gender, age, religion, sexuality, and regional and local identification, among many other structuring categories, diversify national populations. All these categories generate social identities that tell us about potential affinities and antagonisms in particular social structures, and often also become powerful indicators of unequal access to rights and resources. Yet not all these categories are considered equally significant for the representation of a national population – and certainly not all are made dependent on self-identification as the mechanism to determine ascription. The ways in which diversity is officially portrayed or ignored in censuses is thus always a telling testimony of prevalent governmental ideologies and aims.

The definition and conceptual articulations of a social identity category in census designs are always the result of ideological decisions. Social identities are contingent over time, and in social interaction they operate as situational and intersecting categories. There is no naturally objective way to understand them in numerical terms, and the criteria chosen to identify membership of such groups largely condition their numeric representation. For instance, it is not the same to identify the indigenous population by, say, place of residence, dress or primary language spoken (all of which are criteria that have actually been used in Latin American censuses), or to set self-identification as the mechanism of classification (thus making the category 'indigenous' dependent on people's subjective understandings of belonging to an 'indigenous' group in a specific social context).

Censuses help to make social identity categories a reality too, officially legitimating some of them. In this sense, they possess a degree of *creational power*. They officially 'nominate into existence' (Goldberg 1997) and can even 'make up people' (Ian Hacking, cited by Brubaker et al. 2004), institutionalizing signifiers of identity for sometimes loosely bounded groups. Regardless of the balance between recognition and creation of social identities in census-taking, the inclusion of such identities in national counts can significantly influence relations between the groups that are distinctively categorized (Cunin and Hoffman 2012, p. 158).

But the state's aim in census design is not influenced only by 'national' ideological traditions; especially at present, it is also crucially oriented by two distinct but complementary factors that currently influence national census design: (1) a socialization process led by supranational organizations; and (2) the bargaining power of actors that successfully place themselves in the sights of socialized states.

Supranational institutions 'socialize' states, as Martha Finnemore (1996) argued in her study of international society structures. Contrary to what realist and institutional neoliberalism theory contend, states do not always know what their interests are in a wide range of issues. Interests need to be defined before they can be pursued, and those interests are sometimes 'diffused to states by systemic norms from the outside' (Checkel 1998, p. 331). Finnemore argued that supranational networks in which states are embedded shape the latter's perceptions of the world and their role in that world; in that respect, 'states are socialized to want certain things by the international society in which they and the people in them live' (1996, p. 2). In the realm of census design, there is a long history of supranational coordination generating norms and ascendency over states since the International Institute of Statistics was created in 1885 (Nixon 1960), but it has certainly been strengthened over time. United Nations organs currently play an influential role in this respect, but it is shared with other, diverse supranational organizations (such as the World Bank and the Inter-American Development Bank). Today, the inclusion of 'race' and 'ethnic' categories in censuses is led by supranational interests, and not merely state-dependent and/or derived from 'bottom-up' demands. The advantageous shaping of these categories is open to organized groups that respond to that supranationally led state socialization. All this needs to be taken into account when reading census data on the ethnic or racial composition of a given country. Let us now discuss the history of national censuses in Venezuela, which well illustrates the key characteristics of censuses as political tools.

The indigenous population in Venezuelan censuses

Focusing on Latin American states, one of the ways in which population diversity has been recurrently (if contingently) portrayed since independence is through 'racial' and/or 'ethnic' categorization (Angosto-Ferrández and Kradolfer 2012). Since their introduction in Venezuela as part of modernizing statecraft in 1873, and until 2011, censuses classified the national population by a simple dichotomous division: a 'general' (non-indigenous) and an 'indigenous' population. The criteria through which indigeneity was defined fluctuated substantially over that period, but the 'indigenous' category remained as the only source of internal otherness against which the national population was shaped. Despite its central role in the shaping of the national image, the indigenous population has always held a statistical minority status according to censuses, as noted above: generally below 3 per cent of the total population and never as much as 5 per cent (see Table 1.1).

Despite the inclusion of new social identity categories in the 2011 census, the official dichotomous distinction between the indigenous population and the rest remains. In the most recent census, people could also identify themselves as 'black', 'Afro-descendent', '*moreno/a*', 'white' or 'other' – but only 'non-indigenous' people. Section Five of the questionnaire (which addressed the 'individual characteristics' of the population) had a filtering question that effectively articulated the 'indigenous'/'non-indigenous' dichotomization of the population. Question 4 of that section asked '*¿Pertenece a algún pueblo indígena o etnia?*' ('Do you belong to any indigenous people or ethnic group?'), with only yes or no as possible answers. However, the wording of the question was confusing due to the position of the adjective '*indígena*'.[3] Only those who responded 'no' were directed to Question 7 in order to self-identify in racial terms (i.e. in one of the categories mentioned above).[4]

The quantitative fluctuations of the indigenous population in Venezuela as reflected by censuses have been remarkable, as Table 1.1 shows. However, given the difference in conceptual definition, geographical scope and timing of the surveys (Allais 2004), the relative percentages are only to be used as an indication of official state data – not as accurate reflections of demographic change.

Indigenous censuses were conducted through specific and more systematized programmes from 1982 onwards. Since then, data on the indigenous population are considered to be more reliable and comprehensive, so I will focus on them in order to illustrate the way

TABLE 1.1 Indigenous population in Venezuelan national censuses

Year	National population	Indigenous population	Relative percentage[5]
1873	1,732,411	55,811	3.22
1881	2,005,139	70,154	3.49
1891	2,221,572	94,627	4.25
1920	2,479,525	48,855	1.97
1926	2,814,131	136,147	4.83
1936	3,364,347	103,492	3.07
1941	3,850,771	100,600	2.61
1950	5,034,838	98,682	1.92
1961	7,523,999	75,604	0.99
1971	10,721,522	—	—
1981/2[6]	14,516,735	140,040	0.96
1990/2[7]	18,105,265	315,815	1.71
2001	23,232,553	534,816	2.3
2011	28,946,101	725,141	2.7

Source: Angosto-Ferrández 2012b and Instituto National de Estadística (INE) (2011).

in which census-taking (and therefore census results) have been affected by ideological-technical and political conditioning.

As Table 1.1 shows, the percentage of indigenous population increased abruptly (by 125.5 per cent) between 1982 and 1992. The key to understanding this increase lies in conceptual and methodological changes articulated by the National Institute of Statistics (INE, after its Spanish name): the definition of indigeneity was radically transformed between those dates. In 1982, indigenousness was defined through objectivized criteria based on descent, language (spoken by the individual or by his/her mother or grandmother) and region of residence. 'Urban' indigenous people and those who did not speak an indigenous language therefore did not qualify. In the 1992 census, following the continental trend and, in this particular respect, the recommendation of International Labour Organization (ILO) Convention 169 of 1989 (which nevertheless had not been subscribed to by the Venezuelan government), self-identification was introduced – but with geographical restrictions. It was only applied in the eight federal states that, according to academic experts, were home to the 'traditional' indigenous population.[8] Even with this geographical limitation, the relative increase was extra-ordinary. It should be noted that 42 per cent of the total indigenous population was registered in urban areas.

In 2001, the census removed these geographical restrictions on the possibility of indigenous self-identification. Regardless of their place of residence, anyone could now identify themselves as indigenous, which partly explains yet another extraordinary relative increase (63.3 per cent) in this population. But this latter increase was also influenced by other identifiable political factors that contributed to a positive revalorization of indigenous identities: the approval of the 1999 Constitution – which granted recognition and differentiated rights to indigenous peoples – and the strong current of government-fostered revalorization of indigeneity that had become a central component of a new paradigm of national identity (Angosto-Ferrández 2012b, pp. 228–35). Of the 534,816 indigenous people enumerated in 2001, 62 per cent were registered in urban areas.

Between 2001 and 2011, the relative increase in the indigenous population was also quite remarkable – 41.8 per cent. Without methodological novelties of the type that facilitated increases in the two previous census rounds, this growth is even more directly associated with political factors derived from the process of indigenous enfranchisement that this study will discuss. This enfranchisement was expressed in broader access to both social services and institutionalized political participation, which adds to the continuing revalorization of indigeneity that has characterized Bolivarian governments over the past 14 years (Amodio 2007; Angosto-Ferrández 2008; Mosonyi 2009). In 2011, the urban indigenous population constituted two-thirds (66 per cent) of the total.

Beyond absolute or relative population figures, census sensitivity towards changing political contexts is even more strongly illustrated

TABLE 1.2 Indigenous peoples according to various state sources

Year	Source	Number of peoples
1974	DICA[9]	28
1982	National census	29
1992	National census	32
2001	National census	54
2005	LOPCI[10]	40
2011	Ministry of Indigenous Peoples	44
2011	National census	51

by the growing number of indigenous peoples registered in censuses and other state sources from 2001 onwards – evidently, demographics can never explain the appearance of indigenous people in census records. Let us look at the data.

In 1974, the number of indigenous peoples was determined by a group of academic experts according to prevalent anthropological criteria that identified indigeneity through a combination of objective criteria.[11] These criteria were essentially maintained for the 1982 census and thus the number of peoples barely changed.[12] However, defining criteria were fundamentally transformed by the (partial) introduction of self-identification in 1992, a factor that facilitated the registration of three new peoples. In 2001, in a political milieu of state-fostered reassessment of indigeneity and self-identification open to citizens in all federal states, preliminary results listed 54 indigenous peoples. Only 40 were subsequently sanctioned in 2005 by the National Assembly as 'existing and identified' indigenous peoples in Venezuela, when the Basic Law of Indigenous Peoples and Communities (LOPCI) was passed. That process of result-filtering (54 to 40) illustrated how notions of objectivized indigeneity still guide the work of census bureaus and some state organs, regardless of the self-identification criterion.

Before the 2011 census was conducted, the Ministry of Indigenous Peoples (MINPI), created in 2007, was circulating official documents making reference to 44 indigenous peoples.[13] According to preliminary results, the 2011 census registered 51 indigenous peoples. The decrease from 54 peoples in 2001 to 51 in 2011 might be associated with the fact that the 2011 census set national boundaries for indigeneity: it only addressed citizens who had been born in the country, whereas in previous censuses indigeneity had contained a factual transnational stipulation (Angosto-Ferrández 2012b, pp. 238–40).

National censuses certainly tell us about the blurred boundaries of social identities. But, in any event, the increased relative weight of the indigenous population and the increased number of indigenous peoples registered in the last two Venezuelan censuses are also strong indicators of a new social context in which: (a) indigenous identities have been positively revalorized; (b) differentiated indigenous rights have been legally recognized and developed; and (c) socioeconomic and political enfranchisement of the indigenous population has improved. These three points are central to our discussion and I will address them in detail in the following chapters. But it is also important to note what in practical terms has been at stake in censuses: potential access to collective title over territory and differentiated political representation.

Censuses have become the ultimate authoritative source to determine what are and are not indigenous 'lands and habitat'. As I will explain in Chapter 3, the process of indigenous territorial demarcation and titling has been slow and erratic and so far does not provide comprehensive information about which areas of the national territory are to be considered 'indigenous habitat'. In these circumstances, government agencies that need information about what those areas are end up resorting to the national censuses to obtain it. For instance, before MINPI was created in 2007, the state agency that coordinated 'indigenous affairs' (*Dirección General de Asuntos Indígenas* – DGAI) stipulated in its official regulations for the issue of fieldwork permits that the national censuses were the sources determining which territories were 'indigenous territories'. This translated into what I call elsewhere a 'bureaucratic tautology': census officials established that 'indigenous territories' were those in which 'indigenous communities' were located, but from the INE's perspective those communities were only to be found in regions that were previously labelled as regions of 'traditional occupation' due to a census tradition based on academically established criteria.

In an even better example, the Law of Demarcation and Guarantee of Indigenous Peoples' Habitat and Lands, passed in 2001, stipulated its scope of application in the following terms: 'This Law shall be applied in the regions identified as indigenous within national territory, *according to the last indigenous census* and other reference sources which identify them as such' (Article 13, my emphasis). The census was thus an initial filter for any indigenous people or community that wished to obtain collective title to the land. With the passage of the LOPCI in 2005, this circular trap was overcome: the territorial scope of application of this law is national (without restriction), and also contemplates the possibility of restituting lands to forcibly displaced indigenous peoples or communities (Article 24).

Censuses have also affected, and still affect, the possibilities of access to differentiated indigenous representation in deliberative state organs guaranteed by the 1999 Constitution. The constitution already stipulated in its Seventh Temporary Provision that 'For purposes of native representation on the State Legislative Council and on the Municipal Councils of Municipalities with a native population, the 1992 official census by the Central Statistics and Data Processing Office shall be used as a reference'. As we will see in Chapter 4 when discussing electoral politics, the 2009 Basic Law of Electoral Processes (LOPE, from its Spanish name) establishes that indigenous representatives will be elected in constituencies whose indigenous population is above certain quantitative quotas, which are based on census counts.

Let us now look at the type of state policy that accompanied these statistical data throughout the twentieth century.

State organs and orientation of indigenous affairs

Venezuela's policy on indigenous affairs throughout the twentieth century was so erratic that the absence of coherence appeared to be its main characteristic (Clarac 2002; Henley 1982; Villalón 1985). There was nevertheless something that remained strikingly constant in the midst of fragile bureaucratic structures and ineffective policy: the legally backed influence of religious orders, particularly Catholic, in the tutelage of the indigenous population. In 1915, the Venezuelan government passed a Law of Missions (*Ley de Misiones*) that underpinned and conditioned the state approach to the indigenous population for nearly a century. This law, subsequently clarified through several decrees and specific conventions with religious orders, granted extraordinary jurisdictional powers to the latter, as well as competences in the provision of services such as education and health. Religious orders substituted for the state. The law's original motivation was the securitization of border areas which had virtually no state presence, as well as the gradual incorporation of the indigenous population into the national economy. Yet it was maintained as a normative framework despite significant changes in the capacities of the state administration in subsequent decades. It was a telling testimony of the neocolonial legacies that shaped the Venezuelan public sector, and also proof of the lack of overt definition in the realm of policy-making on indigenous matters.

Within the Law of Missions framework, an initial convention between the government and the Capuchin order was signed in

1922 that gave rise to the Vicariate of Caroní in the south-east of the country.[14] Other conventions in the same vein, periodically renewed, were signed with different religious orders. The 1922 convention with the Capuchins, for instance, was renewed in 1956 and 1967. These renewals restricted some of the initial competences and powers granted to the order and augmented state supervision of its responsibilities, but the overall spirit of sovereignty delegation did not disappear.

Along with the function of border securitization and social tutelage, the missionary agents were instrumental for achieving state goals of economic development. The developmental function of the vicariates was explicit from the beginning and, among other things, the original law entrusted them with generating inventories of minerals, animals and plants of the areas they supervised for the Ministry of Home Affairs (Uzcátegui 2007). In addition, religious missions were expected to facilitate change and modernization in indigenous production methods. In a passage that illustrates the awareness with which the missionaries undertook their intertwined responsibilities, Mgr Mariano Gutiérrez (1915–95), who headed the Apostolic Vicariate of Caroní, explained the purpose of their work in the following terms: 'The task of the missionaries not only rooted *indígenas* in the land from which they learnt how to subsist with methodical work, new crops and more appropriate means. At the same time, patriotic consciousness [*conciencia de la nacionalidad patria*] was being created' (Gutiérrez 2006a, p. 20). Along with the nation-building task, what Mgr Gutiérrez was referring to when mentioning 'methodical work' and new production means was, without technically calling it so, new productive powers and relations more consonant with capitalist production methods. The task of the missionaries was therefore multifaceted, and against this one can easily understand, for instance, why president Rafael Caldera, of COPEI, in response to critics of missionary work during his first presidency (1969-74), did not hesitate to defend it, acknowledging their (non-religious) contributions to nationality: 'After all, Catholic missionaries are the cheapest, more effective and less problematic government employees; they just lack publicity' (Gutiérrez 2006b, p. 188).

The repeal of the Law of Missions became one of the slogans of indigenous activism when this began to develop in a more organized fashion in the late 1960s and early 1970s. The Second National Indian Congress in Venezuela (1972), one of the milestones in the hesitant process of organized indigenous activism in the country, demanded the repeal of the law as a central point of its final recommendations (Montiel 1992, p. 32).

The repeal of this law was also sought by a variety of left-wing and progressive nationalist actors committed to the country's modernization. Public intellectuals such as Miguel Acosta Saignes, founding figure of Venezuelan anthropology and pivotal in the creation of the *Comisión Indigenista Nacional* (National Commission for Indigenous Affairs) in 1947, summarized in the early 1980s the concerns of these groups: 'In administrative and political terms, the Law of Missions of 1915 is fundamentally anti-national. It concedes privileges of extraterritoriality that are inadmissible for the sovereignty of the Venezuelan state' (quoted in Villalón 1985, p. 75). Though Acosta Saignes did recognize that not all the dispositions of the original 1915 law were in force by the time he was writing, he understandably wondered 'why and for what should an anti-national instrument be maintained' seven decades after its approval (ibid., p. 76). As in the rest of Latin America, in Venezuela the recovery of sovereignty remained a constant goal of progressive actors, including indigenous ones, throughout the century.

This nationalist vein is a strong ideological driver among the continent's progressive forces, and acknowledging it is crucial to understanding the orientation of both contemporary Latin American left-wing governments and the emergence of the so-called new Latin American regionalism as an anti-imperialist, sovereignty-promoting project (Angosto-Ferrández 2014a and 2014b). The recovery of sovereignty and national independence, which were early pillars of Chávez's movement from its inception (Harnecker 2002; Raby 2006, pp. 145-6), have indeed been driving goals of legislative and executive action over the past 15 years in Venezuela, and a number of key decisions in the realm of indigenous peoples' rights have pointed in that direction. This nationalist vein, on the other hand, is politically double-edged in the realm of indigenous rights. In one of its variants, it has traditionally been used by Latin American elites as a platform from which to erode indigenous demands for land and autonomy, and this has not disappeared from the continent's national arenas.

In any event, Acosta Saignes's question, which was shared by key indigenous activists and their allies from the 1970s onwards, remained blowing in the wind for two more decades. Meaningful answers were only provided with the approval of the Bolivarian Constitution in 1999 and subsequent normative changes introduced by the National Assembly (AN), particularly the LOPCI: with this, the 1915 Law of Missions finally came to an end.

Education also became a central concern for indigenous activists and their allies from the 1970s onwards. The 1915 law had delegated educational responsibilities to religious orders, with few limitations or effective public controls despite subsequent normative efforts. In 1975, the Ministry of Education created a special branch for Borders and Indigenous areas, and the ministry would soon become the organ with major competences in indigenous affairs. The Basic Law of Public Administration of 1976, for instance, gave responsibilities to the Ministry of Education in the supervision of teaching materials used by any religious groups working with indigenous peoples, but it was not effectively implemented. In a report written in 1985, Venezuelan anthropologist María E. Villalón complained that '[despite the clarity of the law in this respect] evangelical missionaries in particular have been implementing tasks of alphabetization and evangelization among the Panare, Pemón, Sanema and Ye'kuana using materials and methods that are not supervised nor approved by the Ministry of Education' (1985, p. 63). These criticisms, widespread among activists, were particularly serious against the New Tribes Mission, which often operated in remote indigenous territories with virtually no state supervision.[15] Complaints against this organization for the style of its proselytising activities and its alleged connection with foreign economic and political interests had been continuous since the 1970s, but were never acted upon. It was in the midst of the Bolivarian process (in 2005) that the New Tribes Mission was formally expelled from the country, in what many considered another milestone in the recognition of a claim expressed for decades by indigenous organizations and activists.[16] This decision was certainly also in line with the government's concern at the time about the recovery of national sovereignty.

Let us now look at the state organs that, in parallel with the structure created by the 1915 Law of Missions, regulated policy on indigenous affairs before 1999.

State bureaucracies

As mentioned in my previous reference to Acosta Saignes, the Comisión Indigenista Nacional (CIN) was created in 1947, in the spirit of the Inter-American Indigenist Institute proposals. This occurred during the so-called *Trienio Adeco* (1945–8), a period of democratic transition with popular overtones dominated by Acción Democrática (AD). The *Trienio* would be interrupted by the coup against president Rómulo Gallegos in 1948, but its 1947 constitution had included an article summarizing *indigenista* orientations: the state would facilitate the incorporation of the Indian into national life 'taking into account the cultural characteristics and the economic conditions of the indigenous population' (Article 72).

The CIN initially reported to the Ministry of Home Affairs, as a consultative organ in charge of conducting research and providing information about the situation of indigenous peoples in the country. From then on, and without interruption, there have always been state agencies – with different names and competences and subsumed within the structure of various non-specialized ministries – that addressed indigenous affairs.

In 1952,[17] the *Junta de Gobierno* moved the CIN to the Directorate of Cults at the Ministry of Justice.[18] In 1968, the same ministry created the *Oficina Central de Asuntos Indígenas* (OCAI) (Central Bureau of Indigenous Affairs) as the new technical agency in charge of indigenist policy, with the CIN remaining as a consulting body (Villalón 1985, p. 102). In 1974, in a period of booming oil prices and renewal of national development projects, the Ministry of Justice set up so-called Regional Centres of Indigenist Action, and subordinate Nuclei of Indigenist Action (Montiel 1992, p. 44). A total of 21 such nuclei would emerge, accompanied by a regionalized bureaucracy

HISTORICAL OVERVIEW 45

around six Regional Centres (Heinen and Coppens 1986, p. 369). Civil associations were being promoted in indigenous communities during that period as a means to facilitate productive development and regularize land tenure, which as I will show in the next section remained an unachieved goal. These associations had a communal assembly as their directing organ and soon had pilot activities in areas such as the Perijá region (Zulia state), which for different reasons would become a continuing focus of indigenous social movement activity (see Chapter 6). By 1975, 22 such associations and 24 communal enterprises had been created, but they gradually faded away due to a combination of poor results and changes in the state bureaucracy that initially promoted them.

In 1977, the OCAI was converted into the *Oficina Ministerial de Asuntos Fronterizos y para Indígenas* (OMAFI) (Ministerial Office for Borders and Indigenous Peoples' Affairs) and transferred to the Ministry of Education. In 1979, the *Dirección de Asuntos Indígenas* (DAI) (Directorate for Indigenous Affairs) was created, also attached to the Ministry of Education. It would remain as the agency linked to indigenous affairs for more than two decades. Also in 1979, a presidential decree was passed providing the basis for a bilingual intercultural education system for indigenous communities. The programme gained some momentum in the early 1980s, but political fluctuations and financial restrictions soon weakened it; by the 1990s, it was seen by experts as a testimonial project.

The lack of renewal and weak performance of official indigenist policy was well reflected in other statutory areas. For instance, a 1951 decree (No. 250), issued to regulate access to indigenous territories, remained in force for over 50 years, despite dramatic changes in activity within these territories. In the early 2000s, the DAI still used this regulation to grant permits, for instance, to researchers.[19] Reflecting on this question after Tierney's *Darkness in El Dorado* (2000) sparked an international controversy, Venezuelan anthropologist Arvelo-Jiménez (2001, p. 37) succinctly described the situation:

> [permits for activities in indigenous territories are granted by] the DAI, but its legal base is an executive decree of 1950 [*sic*] that the expansion of the internal frontier has rendered obsolete and which is regarded as a joke by explorers, visitors, tourists, cinema directors, etc., who sidestep the bureaucracy of permit-granting by using political influence and contacts.

This was but another example illustrating the anachronistic character of legislation on indigenous affairs and the generally ineffective state bureaucracies.

Beyond legislation, the perception that many had about the reality behind the nominal existence of state organs addressing indigenous affairs was not positive. Venezuelan experts with direct experience in the indigenist field openly recognized (and denounced) that the agencies created to coordinate indigenous affairs since 1947 had always occupied a marginal niche within the public administration (Arvelo-Jiménez 1990, p. 5; Clarac 2002). In 1975, Mosonyi argued that the lack of impact of indigenist policy was 'due to the extremely scarce resources allocated to *indigenismo*, in addition to their insensitive distribution and, fundamentally, to a generalized disregard and apathy' (1975, p. 79). One can find crude descriptions of some of those agencies as 'the dumping ground for personnel in disfavour with other ministerial sections and insensitive to indigenous affairs' (Heinen and Coppens 1986, p. 370).

However, the lack of clear direction in indigenist policy and the marginality of the bureaucratic agencies that coordinated it had other, paradoxical effects. With the 1970s boom in oil prices and renewed national development projects, sub-agencies with self-appointed competences in indigenous affairs mushroomed within the state apparatus. In the mid-1980s in a developing region such as Bolívar state, despite the cooling effect of the national economic crisis, there were at least 20 government agencies dealing with indigenous affairs (Heinen and Coppens 1986, p. 365). Analysts associated this mosaic of agencies with the incipient state decentralization programmes started during the first administration of Carlos Andrés Pérez (1974-9), but in the case of Bolívar it was certainly also exacerbated by the bureaucratic expansion of the *Corporación Venezolana de Guayana* (CVG), the economic development body for the Guayana region, in which Bolívar state is located.

Overall, the incorporation of the population into national life formally remained the goal for these bureaucracies throughout the century. In addition to the goals behind the Law of Missions, the 1947 Constitution stipulated in the chapter on the national economy (Chapter VII) that 'The State is responsible for facilitating the incorporation of the Indian into the national life ... taking into consideration the cultural characteristics and the economic conditions of the indigenous population' (Article 72). The 1961 Constitution, which shaped the political project of the so-called Fourth Republic, stated in Article 77: 'The law will establish the regimen of exception required for the protection of indigenous communities and their progressive incorporation to national life'.

However, if one believes that 'incorporation' should have found expression in full citizenship and access to public social services, the project was clearly a failure. By 1992, the national census established that 65 per cent of indigenous communities were deprived of schools and nearly 87 per cent lacked even a pharmacy (OCEI 1993). In addition, the growing degree of urbanization of the indigenous population exposed it to the general degradation of the educational system that affected Venezuela in the 1990s (Heinen and Seijas 1998, p. 160). While this affected everyone in the popular classes, it of course had a harder impact on a population which, in addition, was structurally marginalized and fared worse than the non-indigenous population in terms of access to educational services. By the early 1990s, 8 per cent of the general population was in university education, but only 0.62 per cent of the indigenous population (ibid.). And throughout the 1990s the situation worsened even more. In parallel with a general deterioration of the education system, private higher education provision grew from 34.5 per cent in 1993 to 43.9 per cent in 1999 (Muhr and Verger 2006, p. 169) – another indication of the unavoidable level of exclusion of sections of society, including the indigenous population, from education.

In 1983, Venezuela subscribed to the ILO's 1957 Convention on Indigenous and Tribal Populations (No. 107), but clearly had not carried out meaningful reforms (Colchester and Watson 1995). During the 1990s, Venezuelan governments did not subscribe to the ILO's 1989 convention of the same title (No. 169), which placed more emphasis on the distinctive recognition of indigenous rights within state frameworks. This convention would be subscribed after Chávez became president. Moreover, Venezuelan government representatives in international fora were reluctant to support proposals for distinctive recognition such as the Inter-American Declaration of the Rights of Indigenous Peoples (Sevilla 1997).

Against this background, in the 1990s the courts became the avenue through which some indigenous struggles were channelled, with the support of national and international actors. In 1990, the Attorney General's Office (*Fiscalía*) inaugurated an Office for Indigenous Matters. The Supreme Tribunal of Justice issued decisions in favour of indigenous demands, with milestones including the nullification of Decree No. 1850 dealing with the Imataca Forest Reserve, nullifying the Law of the Political-Territorial Division of Amazonas State, and the demand of the Kariña community Jesús, María y José against the Municipal Council of Aguasay (Mansutti-Rodríguez 2000, p. 84).

Let us now look specifically and in more detail at a crucial aspect of state regulation of indigenous affairs: access to land and territory.

Land and territory

The study of colonial and republican land ownership regulations in Venezuela still lacks a comprehensive general history, but their general characteristics are accessibly, if fragmentally, outlined in a variety of works (e.g. Amodio 1999; Coppens 1971; Cunill Grau 1987; Martens 2011; Samudio 1996, 2005; Uzcátegui 1995; Vivas Ramírez 2001). I will give a general overview of such regulations, mainly focusing on those that appeared in the second half of the twentieth century directly addressing indigenous lands.

During the colonial period, *resguardos* had enabled the maintenance of communal property regimes for indigenous peoples and communities, and dismantling such regimes became the goal of the independent republic.[20] That dismantlement was spurred by the group of large landowners that came to occupy political power, imbued in and favoured by the ideology of liberalism and individual rights. The Constitution of 1811, which declared the aim of integrating 'Indians' into the new republican citizenry, had already approved the distribution of communal property in individual titles, and an 1820 Congressional Decree for Indigenous *Resguardos* was similarly intended to facilitate the transition towards individualization of land property. In 1821, the Congress of Cúcuta passed a law along similar lines. *Resguardos* and any form of collective property were targeted as an obstacle by the new governing classes, seen as harmful to economic development and inimical to the rights of a republican citizenry. A law of 2 April 1836, after the disintegration of *Gran Colombia*, legalized the division of indigenous lands and their distribution to indigenous families, according to the number of adults in each. However, the young and unstable republic failed to realize those ideals, despite subsequent specific laws (Coppens 1971, p. 10; Uzcátegui 1995).

In addition to political instability and the limited capacities of the state apparatus, legislation generated parallel and contradictory approaches to *resguardo* lands (Hill 1994, pp. 13-14). While some legislation explicitly aimed to disperse communal lands in individually- and family-owned properties, other legislation protected some indigenous (communal) land rights. Thus a law of 9 April 1832, as well as another passed by the Senate in February 1836, exempted both *resguardos* and *ejidos* (commons) in indigenous parishes from the general regime of sales of untilled land. Further legislation protecting indigenous land was in fact sanctioned in 1837, 1840, 1848, 1859 and 1865 (Hill 1994, p. 13). In the context of antagonistic legislation at work, economic power prevailed with little resistance. The liberalizing branch of legislation facilitated the gradual weakening or eradication of communally owned indigenous land in some parts of the country. In 1882, President Guzmán Blanco sanctioned the Law of Reduction, Civilization and Indigenous *Resguardos* (*Ley Sobre Reducción, Civilización y Resguardos Indígenas*), seeking finally to achieve on a larger scale what the dominant classes of the republic had unsuccessfully pursued on this liberalizing front since independence. But, yet again, the law fell short of finalizing the partition of the *resguardos* and the incorporation of the indigenous population in the liberal ideal of 'civil life' (Samudio 2005, p. 252).

Beyond unsuccessful statutory reform and regulation, economic factors protected indigenous communities from dispossession and the transformation of their property regimes (Coppens 1971). Pressure upon large (and mostly frontier) parts of the national territory where indigenous peoples found refuge was *relatively* small throughout the twentieth century – unlike in other parts of the continent, where the so-called agricultural and extractivist frontier was undergoing rapid and violent expansion. Crucially, the emergence of oil exploitation in the early twentieth century gradually but fundamentally transformed the political economy of the country. With an extractive economy largely dependent upon oil exports, the regions of oil exploitation and the coastal areas around which harbours, administration and urbanization developed absorbed economic pressure and its associated social effects. The importance of agriculture dramatically diminished, and with it the incentives for 'entrepreneurs' to proceed with the old accumulative business of land-grabbing and dispossession. Not that the indigenous population benefited much from the wealth created by oil, but those communities that stayed and remained in *de facto* control of territory led a life of relative autonomy.

The Law of Agricultural Reform (LRA) of 1961, early in the so-called Fourth Republic, became a key instrument in the regulation of indigenous lands during a period when pressure on larger areas of indigenous territory gradually increased. In spirit, the LRA transformed the project of completely doing away with communal property. It explicitly referred to the indigenous population in Article 2, and contemplated the recognition of communal property.

Advocates of indigenous rights criticized the *Instituto Agrario Nacional* (IAN) (National Agricultural Institute) in its practical implementation for not distinguishing *indígenas* from peasants, which in their view would lead to the 'peasantization' of indigenous communities (Arvelo-Jiménez 1982). Holders of IAN titles were the so-called 'indigenous enterprises' (*empresas indígenas*), legal entities with a pre-established organizational structure to which indigenous communities had to adapt – which required adjustments from the traditional systems of organization that did not always run smoothly. Even with these characteristics and the limited reach of actual titling of indigenous lands that was achieved under the LRA, large landowners and many establishment politicians considered the IAN a 'communist' enclave, and actively opposed the completion of its work (Colchester and Watson 1995, p. 14).

In territories such as (today's) Amazonas state, which combines the largest proportion of indigenous people in the country with very low population density and an abundance of natural resources, state responsibilities had been largely delegated to Salesian missionaries under the stipulations of the 1915 Law of Missions. For most of the twentieth century, this region was completely cut off from the rest of the country, and pressure on indigenous territories – even when they were not included for official titling purposes – was relatively low.[21] The situation changed during the first government of Rafael Caldera (1969–74). The so-called 'Conquest of the South' development project was launched, seeking to extend the 'internal' (capitalist) frontier to include the region. This of course brought a new set of problems, including invasion of indigenous lands, mining exploitation, and associated issues of illness and violence (Arvelo-Jiménez 1990, 2000; Coppens 1972). Although this happened relatively late in comparison with other countries in the Amazon region, it was clear that the ruthless momentum of this process would not be very different. As usual in these circumstances, the process implied that developers and administrators changed the equation of the land they wanted as 'vacant' lands – disregarding all forms of use that would not fit with the idea of 'cultivated land'. But it also implied the use of violence when 'developers' deemed it necessary to consolidate dispossession.

In addition to the impact of the 'Conquest of the South' project, the pressures on indigenous territories increased significantly from the 1980s onwards in states such as Bolívar. The financial situation in the country had entered a crisis, and the government redirected its development-oriented strategies. Large-scale mining had already started, supported by CVG, with negative impacts on indigenous territories, but small-scale mining was at that time stimulated as a priority. Mining concessions were granted with simplified procedures (Colchester and Watson 1995, p. 19), often with absolute disregard for indigenous land rights or demands. In the 1990s, there was a return to large-scale investments, often in joint ventures between Venezuelan and foreign companies.

Other developments with apparently non-economic motivations impacted on indigenous territories. A trend of conservationist policy spread from the late 1970s, which also affected the regulation of land ownership – and the potential access to land titling by indigenous communities. Decree No. 2552 of 1978 prohibited the commercial exploitation of the forests of then Amazonas Federal Territory, and in 1989 Decree No. 269 declared mining illegal. A number of national parks were also created in the region in the late 1970s (such as Yacapana, Duida-Marahuaca and Serranía de La Neblina) and the early 1990s (such as the Parima-Tapirapeco, and the Alto Orinoco-Casiquiare Biosphere Reserve). In Bolívar state, the creation of forest reserves in Imataca (1961), Paragua (1963) and Caura (1968), and the national park of Canaima (originally in 1962) brought 81 per cent of the territory into a special regime. All these statutory developments halted the possibility of granting property titles to indigenous communities in accordance with the IAN regulations. Furthermore, conservationist legislation established restrictions on the local indigenous populations relating to the use of resources in the territory (from wood to hunting and gathering) (Villalón 1985, pp. 20–1).

Against this background, in 1982, according to the indigenous census, 76 per cent of indigenous communities in the country were absolutely deprived of land titles. By then, the legal position was even more precarious precisely in the regions with large proportions of indigenous population (and 'undeveloped' land) such as Bolívar (89 per cent) or the then Federal Territory of Delta Amacuro (97 per cent) (Villalón 1985). By the early 1990s, 72 per cent of indigenous communities did not possess any form of land title (OCEI 1993, p. 31). By then, conflicts over indigenous lands were nevertheless widespread across the country (Martens 2011; Silva and Mansutti-Rodríguez 1996).

Let us now examine the types of organization developed by indigenous peoples and communities in Venezuela.

Indigenous organizations

The organization, definition and mobilization of indigenous demands in the national political arena has been a patchy, uneven process, which is one important reason that its historical reconstruction is difficult. First, the organizations that emerged in order to articulate indigenous demands did so out of a diverse social landscape, as outlined in the Introduction: indigenous peoples and communities are and have always been differently incorporated into the national society and capitalist system, which partly explains their current diverse socio-political positioning. They have, of course, gone through common structural processes, and particularly those linked to territorial dispossession and discriminatory prejudice constitute common experiences for indigenous peoples across the country. But the historical period in which that dispossession took place or became a more acute threat varies greatly too. In these circumstances, supraregional, pan-group indigenous mobilization over territorial issues always had additional difficulties.

Second, reconstructing the historical process of organization is conditioned by the fact that research on the topic is still limited and fragmented, and also because its indigenous protagonists have not produced many written accounts themselves. Against this backdrop, my goal in this section is to provide a general overview of the process of organization and to characterize the type of indigenous collective action that predominated before 1999 – when the Constituent Assembly and the approval of the CRBV marked a qualitative change in the process of indigenous participation in national politics.

With an insider's touch, Nemesio Montiel, a Wayúu activist and an anthropologist, provided unique insights into the early organizing process of indigenous peoples in his seminal work *Movimiento indígena en Venezuela* (1992). The focus of the book, however, is on Zulia state, his home region, and he only tangentially touches on extra-institutional collective action. While contentious activity had taken place since the 1970s in response to indigenous land invasions in various parts of the country, Montiel's overview mainly addresses the institutional process of the emergence and early development of indigenous organizations. But let us start with some antecedents.

In the 1940s, during a period of gradual democratization following Juan Vicente Gómez's dictatorship, there was in Zulia an incipient organizing process in experiences like the Indigenous Committee for Mutual Assistance (*Junta Indígena de Mutuo Auxilio*) and the Ziruma organization. It is no accident that these seminal processes were taking place in Zulia, the region that currently accounts for 61.2 per cent of the total indigenous population in the country (the Wayúu population alone constitutes 55.7 per cent of that population). The local Wayúu population was shaped by the process of urbanization from the early stages of oil and mining development in the country. Significantly, Ziruma appeared in response to threats of eviction against the indigenous population, mainly Wayúu (Guajiro), from developing quarters of Marcaibo, the capital of Zulia state. The drive of Ziruma members and the early actions of indigenous organization were influenced by peasants and workers organizing in the region, which stimulated 'some *mestizo* and acculturated leaders' to give sustance to their own demands in dealing with official agencies (Montiel 1992, p. 19). With the coup against the Rómulo Gallegos government and the end of the *Trienio Adeco* in 1948, an understandable weakening of those hybrid but left-oriented organizing processes ensued. Only after Pérez Jiménez's military dictatorship (1953–8) did the organizing process draw new breath, in the new democratizing environment. Many of the activists involved in that organizing process came from or joined the ranks of political parties such as *Acción Democrática*, COPEI (*Comité de Organización Política Electoral Independiente*) and

PCV (Venezuelan Communist Party) (Montiel 1992, p. 21). In 1965, the Committee for the Defence of the Guajiro (*Comité de Defensa del Guajiro*), a seminal organization in Zulia, was created, and among its aims was gaining autonomy from political parties. That seems to have been wishful thinking, as we will see.

In the 1960s, the latter organization's mobilizing slogan was: 'For a full incorporation of the Guajiro into national life' (Montiel 1992, p. 22) – very much along the lines of the goal expressed in Article 77 of the 1961 Constitution. A list of the organization's demands is indicative of what they meant by 'incorporation': health, access to water, agricultural development, communications, education and so on (ibid., pp. 22–3). This ideal of incorporation would later be interpreted by Montiel and others as an expression of ideological subordination leading to socio-cultural dissolution, but current indigenous mobilization in the country demonstrates that those types of demand have remained central for important sectors of the indigenous population.

The 'new indigenist' currents of the 1970s brought new tones to the organizing process, and the idea of political and cultural autonomy partly displaced that of incorporation as a driving goal for many activists. In 1970 a (First) Congress of Indians was celebrated in Caracas. This is regarded as a significant milestone, given its nationwide ambition and its aims to gain public presence 'and strive for their cause and ethnic reaffirmation' (Montiel 1992, p. 27). Tensions sparked at this stage between the emerging organizations and state bureaucracies, with the OCAI allegedly attempting to mediate and control the former.

A second national congress was held in April 1972, and regional federations also started to emerge: in 1972 for the (separate) states of Zulia, Anzoátegui and Bolívar, and for the Federal Territory of

Amazonas; and in 1973 for Apure state and the Federal Territory of Delta Amacuro. A national-level umbrella organization was created in 1973: *Confederación de Indígenas de Venezuela* (Confederation of Venezuelan Indigenous People). It claimed to represent 23 ethnic groups. None of these organizations was perceived to be really outside the orbit of the main political parties.

The Confederation's founding Declaration, which makes a passing positive reference to the 1971 Declaration of Barbados (from a symposium on Inter-Ethnic Conflict in South America), clearly positions this project within the current of the 'new indigenism' in the continent. There was an emphasis on direct Indian participation in socio-political processes, on the 'growing ability to decide about our own destiny' (Point 7 of the Charter Principles of Indigenous Federations, in Declarations of the Venezuelan Federations of Indians, 1980). It is important to record that the Declaration also noted the value of progressive nationalism, anti-capitalism and the constitution of political links with other sectors of society. The Confederation's organizational principles called for a 'nationalism which expresses itself in a search for our national identity with a determination to take charge of our own wealth and labour'; it also pointed to the negative consequences of the continuing colonial subjugations 'that are kept in force today by the existing capitalist structure' and underscored that 'the liberation of the Indian peoples is something they themselves should achieve, in ever-increasing solidarity with the peasants, labourers and others on the edges of the national society' (Point 3 of the Charter, ibid.). In short, it presented itself as part of a larger process of popular democracy-building.

Beyond declarations, the organizational process was intermittent, and of course never isolated from the general cycle of national politics. A group of professionals linked to the IAN and academics at the *Universidad Central de Venezuela* (UCV), *La Salle* and the *Instituto Venezolano de Investigaciones Científicas* (IVIC) (Venezuelan Institute of Scientific Research) also participated in these processes, in growing opposition to the 'official' indigenism of the OCAI. Nonetheless, the Ministry of Justice (to which the OCAI was attached by then) started to recognize these indigenous organizations (Montiel 1992, p. 41).

In the 1970s and 1980s, changes of government often led to reorientation of the official approach to indigenous activism, and the latter – which was never really autonomous – was affected by those reorientations. For instance, under Carlos A. Pérez's first government (1974-9), the agency for indigenous affairs questioned the political credentials of the emerging organizations, arguing that they had been created by the Social Christians of Caldera's government (1969-74) – although COPEI's sympathies for the federations was negated by some of the people involved (Montiel 1992, p. 42). Pérez's government encouraged the creation of indigenous civil associations, in parallel with the indigenous federations.

The profile and political manoeuvring of indigenous activists and leaders varied over time. Initially, their profile was closely tied to religious orders in whose missions they had received formal education, and was perceived by external commentators as lacking 'autonomy' (Heinen and Seijas 1998, p. 161). Bilingual leaders emerged, but were often alienated from their communities of origin, in turn resenting missions and *criollo* (Creole) society. When on occasion they became civil servants, it was common to find discrepancies between non-traditional leaders and the majority of the indigenous population.

In any event, various links between indigenous activists and the dominant political parties of the so-called Fourth Republic were widely recognized. Commentators summarized perceptions as follows:

> The Social Christians tend to assign the Indians a theoretically more important role, as with the formation of federations under Caldera and the sponsorship of congresses by Herrera Campins. AD implements a more populist policy in attending to needs of food, housing, education, and health, while striving to integrate organizations into the peasant federation that the party dominates. (Heinen and Coppens 1986, p. 368)

Furthermore, somewhat cynically, they considered that indigenous activism in Venezuela was rather integrated within institutional channels:

> Seeing their relatives streaming into the country as a consequence of persecution and extreme land grabbing in Venezuela's neighbouring states, the Indians are among the staunchest defenders of the democratic system. While complaining loudly, they are well aware that in Venezuela the government pays them a per diem to attend Indian congresses in Caracas to complain about conditions. (ibid., p. 380)

Even if this account might be unfair as a generalized portrayal of all activism, the Venezuelan process of indigenous organization was, in fact, rather exceptional within the continent: at least in urban and peri-urban areas, and always in relative terms, the immense wealth generated by oil had for a while made it possible for the state to provide some basic social services, things that for the indigenous population (and the poor in general) were unthinkable in neighbouring countries.

In the 1970s, another significant focus of activism around indigenous rights had emerged. The aforementioned denunciation of the New Tribes Mission and the struggle for their expulsion was one of its central demands, begun in 1974 by a group of Ye'kuana in an evangelized area of the Upper Orinoco. This gained support from different sectors of progressive urban activism (Arvelo-Jiménez 1990, p. 8; Luzardo 1988). The 1978 Carlos Azpurua documentary *Yo hablo a Caracas*, in which the Ye'kuana elder Barné Yavari made a claim for the conservation of tradition and against New Tribes influences, became an iconic film and was widely distributed around the country. Student groups and cultural associations such as the *Movimiento por la Identidad Nacional* (Movement for National Identity) joined in the campaign. As was generally the case with activism associated with indigenous demands at the time, this was presented by the establishment as proto-communist subversion. In a continent in which theologians of the liberation and left-wing activists were being systematically targeted and assassinated during military dictatorships of different forms, this type of finger-pointing was never taken lightly by activists.

Scattered but significant events were also taking place during the 1980s with the cooperation of or as a direct initiative of so-called allies of the indigenous struggles. Examples are the First Warao Congress (*I Congreso Warao*) in 1981, organized by Walter Coppens and Bernarda Escalante from *Fundación La Salle*, and the First Pemon Congress (*I Congreso Pemón*) in Kavanayén in 1983 (Mansutti-Rodríguez 2010). It is worthy of note that these processes entailed indirect links with state agencies – that is, the former were never totally independent of the latter. For instance,

Fundación La Salle was basically dependent on government financing. The First Piaroa Congress of Caño Grulla (*I Congreso Piaroa de Caño Grulla*) took place in 1984, before the renowned conflict between a Piaroa community (the Wóthuha) and the developer Hermann Zingg.

The allies supporting indigenous struggles followed different approaches, but a central current was consistent in considering the struggles as part of larger, popular-democratic transformation projects. Acosta Saignes had noted the importance of incorporating indigenous peoples in national production, linking the indigenous question to the national development project (1948). Within the Left, this line was interpreted as implying a greater project of political incorporation into a progressive nationalist project, and it was kept alive as a strategy by other left-leaning intellectuals. In the 1970s, Marroquín, arguing that 'Indian' should primarily be seen as a socioeconomic category (1977, p. 8), advocated that nevertheless *indígenas* should indeed be actively involved in state processes, in alliance with other popular sectors. Also around this time, from the ranks of the so-called 'indigenism of liberation', Andrés Serbín advocated tactical alliances between indigenous peoples and popular and class movements with common goals (1980, pp. 204–5), considering at the same time that these peoples, as historical subjects, could lead their own 'social development' from their own cultural platforms of existence. In the 1990s, authors such as Rodríguez (1991) and Sanoja (1991) articulated Marxist-leaning approaches from the academic field. Rodríguez, for instance, defined ethnic consciousness as a complementary dimension to class consciousness that is present in inter-ethnic relations (1991, p. 62). He openly criticized the new indigenism that created a 'total separation between the so-called *indígena* [*lo indígena propiamente dicho*] and the regional and national contexts in which the insertion of the indigenous takes place' (ibid., p. 54).

This political current remained strong as part of the overall process of indigenous organization, and to an important extent explains the process of incorporation of the latter into the *chavista* movement, as we will see throughout this book.

By the end of the 1990s, all these various experiences had resulted in the shaping of a group of leaders with extensive political experience in different spheres but, crucially, without organizational structures backing them.

CONIVE

In 1989, the *Consejo Nacional Indio de Venezuela* (National Council of Venezuelan Indians) was created. It deserves a separate commentary as the only significant national-level platform to be formed in the process of indigenous organization. In its founding declaration, CONIVE characterized itself as part of a 'movement' and increased suspicion of political parties and electoral processes as avenues for the advancement of their cause. In its origin, in which members of the *Federación de Indígenas del estado Bolívar* (FIEB) (Indigenous Federation of Bolívar State) played a very important role, that concern was central. Article 1 of the Declaration of the First National Council of Venezuelan Indians sanctioned as a principle 'autonomy from political parties, the State and national and transnational private interests'; Point 1.1.1 explicitly highlighted a conscious positioning in favour of 'distinguishing party politics from the politics of Indian movements'. Along those lines, Point 5.14 summarized the goals of CONIVE before becoming involved in elections, which under certain conditions it did not discard for other indigenous organizations:

> In principle we do not oppose Indian peoples creating their own electoral formulas; but we consider that to do so there must be lengthy and forward-looking preparatory work to organize and train an Indian membership tried and tested in struggle, with a programme that is different to that of the current political parties and capable of basic self-financing – and this is a task that has not been seriously addressed so far. (Juncosa, 1991, pp. 135–43)

In the early 1990s, with the growing disintegration of the political system and falling confidence in political parties, interest was resuscitated among indigenous activists to gain greater detachment from the latter. This had never become a reality in the past, as we have seen, despite continuous declarations to achieve it. Indigenous activists had had close contacts with and often been active in parties such as AD, COPEI, MAS (*Movimiento al Socialismo*), MEP (*Movimiento Electoral del Pueblo – Partido Socialista de Venezuela*) and the Liga Socialista (Montiel 1992, p. 53). Summarizing the situation prior to 1999, Van Cott commented that 'political parties, which have monopolized channels to political power and resources for half a century, permeate indigenous politics', continuing that 'factionalism derived from ethnic identity and political party affiliation impeded the consolidation of a national movement until 1999' (2003a, p. 53). As I argued in the Introduction, these differences are primarily to be expected from a very diversified population in socioeconomic terms, and to present them as principally stemming from 'ethnicity' or party-political activity is misleading. In addition, there was the counterbalancing force of other types of 'civil society' organizations with an apparently less political outlook but with strong links with political elites. For instance, in 1989, the *Fundación para la Ayuda de la Familia Campesina e Indígena* (FUNDAFACI) (Foundation for Assistance to Peasant and Indigenous Families) was created by Cecilia Matos, an intimate companion of president Carlos Andrés Pérez. That organization was described by Arvelo-Jiménez as soon gaining 'absolute political power' (2001, p. 33).

In any case, it is a fact that 'autonomy' from political parties has not come about over the past 15 years for CONIVE, either. Like most indigenous organizations, CONIVE has become deeply involved in party politics in an active move that I believe cannot be read merely as resulting from 'co-option'. Several studies of indigenous collective action have been unable to understand the relationships that over the past 16 years have arisen between indigenous organizations (including CONIVE), Bolivarian political parties and state organs. I will elaborate on the changes experienced by CONIVE in the next chapter, and more broadly on the involvement of indigenous organizations in electoral and party politics in Chapters 4 and 5. But, before closing this chapter, let us look at the realm of non-institutional indigenous collective action, which left clear imprints in these organizational processes and in the field of popular democratic struggle.

Contentious activity

Extra-institutional indigenous mobilization between the 1970s and 1990s, rather than a sustained challenge against power-holders that could be characterized as a 'social movement', was episodic and reactive, erupting in response to threats such as land invasion.[22] Illustrative examples of this episodic and reactive approach are the processes sparked by invasions of Ye'kuana territory in the Upper Ventuari in the late 1960s and early 1970s (Arvelo-Jiménez 2000, pp. 735–6; Clarac 2001, pp. 32–3; Coppens 1972), or by the occupation of Piaroa lands in the 1980s by the developer Hermann Zingg. In the case of the Yekuana of the Ventuari, it was land invasion that, as Arvelo-Jiménez put it, 'generated a political mobilization [of the Yekuana] in order to defend it'. This implied the emergence of a centralized and provisional leadership (Arvelo-Jiménez 2000, pp. 735–6), but it was not maintained over time as a unifying, mobilizing force.

There are parallels with the case of the Piaroa. In 1972 Zingg, waving the 'Conquest of the South' banner, seized Piaroa lands in Valle de Guanay, claiming some 8,000 hectares. There were constant physical threats and pressure on the local population for years, and Zingg's efforts to regularize his tenure of the occupied land were resisted by the IAN. The latter granted provisional collective title to the Piaroa of Caño Vera-Guanay in 1982, in an area that included all the 8,000 hectares claimed by Zingg (Hill 1994, p. 15); Zingg did not recognize the IAN resolution. A violent conflict began in 1984, including the capture and torture of local *indígenas* by Zingg's workers. The conflict escalated to national dimensions. A National Assembly sub-commission was launched to investigate the conflict, which gained substantial media coverage – often accusing the Piaroa and their supporters of things such as independentism, terrorist subversion influenced by Castro, Brezhnev and Gaddafi, or drug-trafficking (Arvelo-Jiménez 1990, p. 11; Hill 1994; Mansutti-Rodríguez 1986). The conflict did stimulate supra-community political organization among the Piaroa, but this never developed into a force with the capacity for sustained mobilization.

There were also horrible massacres, such as those by the Haximú against the Yanomami (1993) and the La Rubiera against the Jivi, which were not unrelated to land-grabs. Activists and scholars involved in the defence of indigenous rights generally recognize land invasions as an important trigger of mobilization.

The emergence of the *Organización Regional de Pueblos Indígenas de Amazonas* (ORPIA) (Regional Organization of Indigenous Peoples of Amazonas) was to some extent exceptional. It was triggered by changes introduced by the transformation of Amazonas from a federal territory into a state. Organizing to influence the drafting of the 1993 state constitution and the proposed politico-administrative territorial divisions, ORPIA – which had strong links with the human rights office of the Catholic Church in the region – achieved the symbolic declaration of the state as multiethnic and pluricultural, as well as rights still without parallel in the national constitution.

Indigenous collective action before 1999: a characterizing synthesis

When the dynamism of indigenous mobilization in countries such as Ecuador, Bolivia, Guatemala, Colombia and Mexico started to draw widespread attention in the 1990s, comparable mobilizing activism was relatively rare in Venezuela. Indigenous organizations with a regional base had existed in some regions from the 1970s and, although they gave rise to optimistic predictions about their potential at a national level, they were fragile and mostly short-lived. Those that lasted were weak and operated through institutional channels, rather than contentiously. They were also linked to party politics or, when they tried to maintain a more autonomous position, under continuous siege from political parties (see Figueroa 2005, pp. 34–49, for his account as the president of FIEB).

From the 1970s to the 1990s, indigenous organizations counted on non-indigenous allies from academia,[23] the progressive church, certain sectors of the public administration, and left-wing political activism, but lacked mobilizing capability despite some connections with other progressive forces.[24] The latter themselves remained fragmented during the 1980s and 1990s, until the Bolivarian movement channelled and dynamized their forces. And, particularly during the 1980s, they were aware of their weakness and disunion. Recalling the reflections that had taken place among those involved in supporting the Piaroa in the case of the Hato San Pablo at a meeting of the *Asociación Venezolana para el Avance de la Ciencia* (AsoVAC) (Venezuelan Association for the Advancement of Science), Arvelo-Jiménez wrote:

> We, the stigmatized [by the aggressive campaign of the independent media], could not have broken the media siege [*cerco mediático*] because we had never been a pressure group with a destabilizing project that brought us together, and it did not occur to us either to get together in adversity because there were no bridges of community among us. (1990, p. 13)

Although in those days other scholars talked of 'indigenous movements' when analyzing the situation of indigenous peoples in Venezuela (e.g. Mosonyi 1992; Silva and Mansutti-Rodríguez 1996), the term was used as being synonymous with 'indigenous organizations'. Mosonyi referred alternately to 'indigenous movements' and 'indigenous organizations' as synonymous, without any particular differentiation. Other analysts considered lack of success in indigenous claims to territory as resulting from 'the political and economic weakness of these [indigenous] movements' (Silva and Mansutti-Rodríguez 1996, p. 350); these authors were referring to indigenous organizations, which in turn were characterized as 'not sufficiently effective' (ibid., p. 351) and 'frequently divided [and lacking] human, material and financial resources' (ibid., p. 357).

So there was neither an indigenous movement as such nor strong indigenous organizations. This was the backdrop against which we come to the preamble of Chávez's victory in 1998.

TWO

Into the people

When studying the sphere of indigenous collective action, we find the basic sequence of events in the Bolivarian revolution: electoral victory, political revolution, (partial) economic transformation. This sequence has subsequently been reproduced, and reoriented, in the opposite direction: (partial) economic transformation, (reoriented) political revolution, election victories. These interconnected sequences, unfolding within a historically situated socio-cultural battleground, underline the cycle that has sustained the Bolivarian process thus far – albeit with contradictions, distortions and fluctuations in each of its constituent parts. Weaknesses in the sphere of economic transformation and ambiguities within the sphere of political revolution have impacted on the electoral arena, but successive Bolivarian election victories have so far provided the *chavista* bloc with new opportunities to make adjustments in the economic and political spheres.

In this chapter, I will focus on analyzing how the basic sequence of events in the Bolivarian revolution both shaped and was shaped by indigenous collective action. In particular, I aim to explain the political process that catalyzed the transition between a pre-1999 landscape of indigenous organization and mobilization (with fragmented, episodic and reactive collective action) and the current situation (with sustained and largely proactive collective action). Three main questions will be examined in this exercise: (1) the impacts of Chávez's 1998 election victory; (2) the catalytic effects of the 1999 *Asamblea Nacional Constituyente* (ANC) (National Constituent Assembly) on indigenous processes of organization; and (3) how and why indigeneity became a central source of symbols for the emergence and maintenance of the collective identity that helps to sustain the *chavista* bloc.

First election victory

Widespread discontent and rising levels of protest during the 1990s in Venezuela have been documented, and are generally considered as expressions of systemic crisis. Successive government attempts at political reform failed and, along with the weakening of the party system, illusions of the 'near perfect' Venezuelan democracy came to an end (Buxton 2001; Ellner and Tinker Salas 2007; Hellinger 2000; López Maya 2000). During this process, the Bolivarian movement, led by Hugo Chávez, gradually emerged as a stronger force embodying the proposal of profound socio-political renewal.[1] In 1997, this movement-in-the-making was central to the conformation of the *Polo Patriótico*, an electoral coalition that would eventually compete in the presidential election of 1998 (Raby 2006, pp. 156-7).[2] This initial process of galvanization of the Bolivarian movement incorporated into its political dynamics not only minority political parties, but also a variety of discontented and disenfranchised individual and collective actors, including indigenous organizations. The latter had never been prominent actors at regional or national level, nor had they ever constituted a sustained 'social movement'. These organizations and actors had been affected by internal differences – partly resulting from the diversity of positions that the indigenous population occupies within the country – and, despite their nominally declared goals of autonomy, they had always been directly involved in or exposed to party-political dynamics.

In the context of the realignment of forces that the regime's collapse was facilitating, and before the emergence of the Bolivarian movement, the majority of the experienced indigenous organizations and activists naturally gravitated towards the newly emerging platform. Commenting on the process surrounding the 1998 election, an analyst remarked that 'indigenous leaders vigorously incorporated themselves into *chavismo* when it did not yet appear as the winning force', adding that 'as the possibilities of victory for the presidential candidate began to be foreseen, the *indígenas* got ready to go to the National Constituent Assembly in a strengthened manner' (Mansutti-Rodríguez 2000, p. 84). Understanding this dynamizing force behind the 1998 presidential election and the subsequent ANC is crucial for the analysis of current indigenous struggles in the country. The involvement in the emerging Bolivarian movement and the constituent process that followed Chávez's election victory in 1998 were catalytic for indigenous organizations and activism.

The catalytic Constituent Assembly

Preparations

The 1999 constituent period was an effective catalyst for the activation and realignment of social forces in the Venezuelan political landscape. The relative bargaining strength of different groups was revealed, but so was the possibility of enhancing such strength through alliances in an assembly that had been given a strong mandate for change. This period brought to the surface the characteristics and limitations of indigenous organizations in the country, but in turn widened the channels for their effective incorporation into the broader popular movement which was building up by then. The call for the Constituent Assembly had received 82 per cent support in the April 1999 referendum, and in the July elections *Polo Patriótico* candidates won 119 of the 131 available seats.

The subsequent reconfiguration of indigenous peoples' rights in the new constitution was determined by a combination of factors that focused and catalyzed the capacities of previously fragmented and weak indigenous organizations and activists. CONIVE had been founded a decade before, but in practice remained a weak organization with very limited mobilizing capacities. It lacked fluid organic connections with regional organizations and had meagre resources and, more importantly, it had been weakened by continuous and unresolved internal differences. By 1997, the year before the presidential elections, CONIVE was characterized as being 'in a limbo-like state [*en un estado de inopia*]' (Mansutti-Rodríguez 2000, p. 82). Chávez's election victory and the ensuing constituent process stirred up the organization and obliged those who were in its orbit to (at least temporarily) suspend internal differences.

The ANC abruptly transformed CONIVE into an indispensable political interlocutor. The ANC needed an organization that could legitimately process and coordinate the election of indigenous representatives. CONIVE, though weak, was the only national organization sufficiently developed and with enough recognition and legitimacy to work with the National Electoral Council

(CNE) in that process. This institutionalization of CONIVE as an interlocutor with state organs suddenly empowered the organization; indeed, it created it as a powerful actor. The tactics and political alliances of CONIVE members during the ANC and their subsequent organic links with the parties that have led the Bolivarian bloc – first the MVR (*Movimiento V República*) and, since 2007, the PSUV (*Partido Socialista Unido de Venezuela*) – have firmly positioned CONIVE within that bloc and have transformed it into a pivotal organization in the selection of candidates for seats allocated for indigenous representation at national level (see Chapter 4).

However, this new privileged status for CONIVE did not come smoothly. Two fundamental challenges sprang up during the process of (re)organization stimulated by the ANC (Clarac 2001, pp. 363–5; Morales and Morales 2003, pp. 22–4): first, confrontations with the CNE and second, internal divisions within and between indigenous organizations and activists. The first issue revolved around legal and procedural questions affecting the actual degree of autonomy that should be granted to indigenous organizations in the election of their representatives. The second question – in part a natural expression of the divergent interests that segment a socially heterogeneous, identity-based collective – was heightened by what was at stake: for the first time in their history, indigenous actors were guaranteed direct participation and representation in state legislative organs.

As soon as his presidential term was inaugurated in February 1999, Chávez called for a referendum (eventually held in April) to decide on the convocation of a constituent assembly; more than 80 per cent of the valid votes backed the proposal. In this scenario, the members of CONIVE and the main indigenous organizations, which had in fact started to manoeuvre as soon as Chávez began his term, reacted without hesitation. In February and March, various indigenous organizations held workshops on constitutional reform and indigenous rights in Zulia and Amazonas – in the latter state, with the support of the Catholic Church (Van Cott 2003a, pp. 54–5). CONIVE, despite its fragile institutional position, promoted these types of event. Its leaders aimed to generate a consensus proposal for the Constituent Assembly and were in contact with actors linked to the *Polo Patriótico*. José Poyo, by then CONIVE's general coordinator, highlighted this cooperation as crucial to the consolidation of the organization's visibility and its links with government agencies and other organized groups (ibid., p. 55). CONIVE's change in status was well illustrated by the fact that the DAI directly provided it with technical support and even with physical space for its operations.

The DAI also supported the Extraordinary Congress of Venezuelan Indigenous Peoples held in Ciudad Bolívar on 21–25 March. This Congress had the re-emerging CONIVE at its core and gathered a total of 320 delegates from different regions. The Congress aimed to elect three indigenous representatives to the ANC, according to '[indigenous peoples'] customs and ancestral norms'. Behind this vague principle lay the idea that indigenous organizations and leaders would be responsible for the election, without the involvement of state organs. However, the Supreme Court ruled that the CNE had to mediate in the election process for all ANC candidates, and indigenous organizations were obliged to observe CNE's regulations. Noelí Pocaterra (Wayúu), Guillermo Guevara (Jivi) and José Luis González (Pemon) were elected at the Ciudad Bolívar meeting for the indigenous representation seats in the ANC, but the CNE declared that the election was illegitimate due to its timing (it had been held *before* the 25 April referendum that backed the call for the ANC), its limited representativeness (groups that considered themselves excluded complained to the CNE) and its lack of direct supervision by the CNE (Mansutti-Rodríguez 1999). The CNE's position prevailed, and in June a new election was called. In July, a new meeting was held in Los Caracas, with increased participation – over 600 delegates attended, including representatives of organizations that had not participated in the Ciudad Bolívar meeting.[3]

Despite these tensions, CONIVE came out of this process strengthened and with a new institutional position as the (only) legitimate organization of indigenous representation at national level. These empowering creative tensions experienced by CONIVE would in fact stretch into the Constituent Assembly period.

The constituent period

The drafting of the chapter of the Constitution dedicated to the rights of indigenous peoples (which would become Chapter VIII of Title III) generated intense debate between those for and against the recognition of differentiated rights (Combellas 2003, p. 200; Van Cott 2002, pp. 49–55).[4] This is unsurprising for a topic that, at both ideological and practical levels, has traditionally generated mistrust on both the left and right of the political spectrum: it impinges on notions of equality and, of course, it is underscored by questions of land and resources ownership and redistribution. But this topic was also resisted in the name of that conservative nationalist vein that has reactively framed indigenous territorial claims as being inimical to sovereignty. Against this background, there are two significant questions to consider in the case of Venezuela. First, the ANC was virtually an assembly of *chavismo*, so its debates and negotiations demonstrated the existence of a varied political spectrum within the movement. And second, the actors who, both inside and outside the assembly, publicly addressed the confrontation over indigenous rights avoided a head-on ideological debate – that is, they shifted it towards deceptively apolitical fields of discussion.

At the ANC, different positions on the ideology of multiculturalism, differentiated citizenship and ownership of resources were basically lost from sight by debates around three questions: (1) repayment of the so-called 'historical debt'; (2) the importance of gaining equal footing with South American neighbours in the recognition of indigenous peoples; and (3) the affirmation or negation of dangers for the country's territorial integrity – presented as a political principle beyond discussion.

The tone of the constitutional debate and the manoeuvres that accompanied it were well condensed in a speech by Aristóbulo Istúriz on the day on which Chapter VIII would finally be approved (Angosto-Ferrández 2010, p. 101):

> It is important that public opinion knows that the issue here is not a confrontation between those who defend the rights of indigenous peoples and those who are against the rights of indigenous peoples ... The issue is that this Assembly in its entirety has the moral, patriotic obligation of guaranteeing full rights to indigenous peoples without placing at risk ... the defence of the sovereignty, unity and integrity of the Venezuelan nation.[5]

Istúriz, who was second vice-president of the ANC, had also been appointed as coordinator of a Mixed Commission created specifically to unblock the discussion generated by the indigenous rights chapter.

When the ANC started its work, it had dedicated a specialized commission to indigenous rights. In early September, still in the assembly's early stages, that commission and CONIVE gathered more than 300 indigenous representatives from different parts of the country to come up with an agreed proposal. This CONIVE-drafted proposal, with some technical additions made by advisers, was adopted by the commission.

Detractors of particular indigenous peoples' differentiated rights had complained that they were linked to territorial recognition and the term 'people', given the dangers that this would allegedly pose for national sovereignty – a constant in the continent as soon as the so-called 'new constitutionalism' started to recognize separate indigenous rights. Indigenous members defended the need for this recognition, rejecting any risk of secession, emphatically proclaiming the compromise of indigenous peoples with Venezuelan nationality, and appealing to the historical debt that the state had contracted with aboriginal peoples – the debt that Hugo Chávez had symbolically undertaken to pay during the 1998 presidential campaign (see next section). They explicitly resorted to the legal character that ILO Convention 169 (1989) gave to indigenous peoples about their relationship to nation-states (Article 1.3), while developing a general tactic that presented the indigenous population as 'more Venezuelan than any Venezuelan'.

The supporters of indigenous deputies in the ANC articulated their position by emphasizing two of the foregoing points: the 'historical debt' and the need to match neighbouring countries in indigenous rights recognition. In an epitomizing remark, A. Briceño criticized the resistance that members of the Mixed Special Commission were showing towards the indigenous rights proposal, arguing that at this moment, after hundreds of years of insults against these *indígenas* of Latin America and the world, we [members] want to propose as a previous point that Chapter VIII be specifically voted on as a bloc, so that we decide in favour of the history we want to construct.

Yldefonso Finol, supporting Briceño's position in the advocacy of indigenous rights recognition, added: 'I agree, for it is a matter that has been sufficiently debated not only by this Assembly, but also by the entire continent, [a matter] that corresponds with the new Latin American constitutionalism'. Also from the ranks of the *Polo Patriótico*, Adán Chávez (brother of president Hugo Chávez), remarked on similar lines that 'the biggest historical mistake would be not to take advantage of this moment to give constitutional status to the centenary right of our indigenous brothers'. Venezuelan indigenous leaders also emphasized the experiences that had led to constitutional recognition in neighbouring countries, such as Bolivia, Brazil, Colombia, Ecuador and Paraguay, and other powerful figures within the government, such as Foreign Minister José Vicente Rangel, similarly defended the indigenous recognition proposal by recalling the examples of Bolivia and Ecuador among others (Van Cott 2003a, p. 61).

These statements represent the steady pressure that was leading to recognition: it was *formally* presented as a matter of symbolic value, historical justice and pertinence, displacing references to resource ownership and management or to the statutory justification of differentiated rights. Among the left-wing forces at the ANC, the predominant issue was the payment of a historical debt and levelling the playing field with other South American countries. The universalist arguments of the Left that distrust the politics of recognition as diversions of its original mission did not emerge.

This current links the growing demands for identity recognition to specific interests that can endanger proposals for substantive social change (Díaz Polanco 2005, pp. 50–1). Although this had advocates among prominent left-wing intellectuals throughout the 1990s, in statutory terms it is in retreat. There were some scattered appeals to the achievements of the ideology of *mestizaje* ('racial democracy') so strongly associated with the Venezuelan national imagery for decades (Wright 1990), but they did not explicitly connect with universalist visions of (undifferentiated) citizenship. Thus, for example, the ANC member Freddy Gutiérrez contended that distinctive indigenous recognition would be counterproductive because Venezuela represented 'perhaps the best *mestizaje* that has ever occurred in the world'.

At the other end of the political spectrum, the distrust of the political Right and the non-pluralist liberals towards collective rights did not gain any prominence. The neoliberal right had been left virtually outside directly controlled representation at the ANC. Outside the *Polo Patriótico*, only a weakened *Acción Democrática* party (with two members) and *Proyecto Venezuela* (with one) had entered the ANC as vestiges of the traditional parties. From outside the ANC, members of the opposition such as Henrique Capriles, the now (contested) opposition leader, criticized indigenous recognition, arguing that it created in the country 'a kind of division in three classes: *indígenas*, civilians and military. Why should they be differentiated? If we wanted to establish equality, let us then establish completely equal citizens'.[6] We will see later on how much Capriles's position changed (at least nominally) as soon as he wanted to run against Hugo Chávez in elections, and why that change took place.

Among the other members, two independents led the 'nationalist' criticism of separate indigenous recognition. One of them, Jorge

Olavarría, abstained when the chapter on indigenous rights was finally approved, as did Eliécer Otaiza, Gerardo Márquez and Florencio Porras.

Without open discussion of other questions of political principle, the clash of positions over indigenous rights was finally resolved through a negotiation of terminology: 'people' and 'territory'. ANC members who opposed indigenous recognition had focused on anticipating problems if recognition was confirmed and associated with the term 'territory'. This so-called nationalist argument, based on questioning the terms in which the recognition of indigenous peoples were proposed and on the defence of the pre-eminence of a national sovereignty principle (Combellas 2003, p. 200), was nucleated around the ANC's Security and Defence Commission that, with the Indigenous Peoples Commission, constituted the ad hoc Mixed Special Commission created following the controversy over the first drafts of the indigenous rights chapter.

The constitutional text finally brought to a referendum in December included a formal disposition through which the term 'territory' was replaced by 'habitat and lands', whose connotations were more neutral in international law. A paragraph was also added at the end of Chapter VIII stipulating that 'the term "people" shall not be interpreted in this Constitution in the sense that it is given in international law'. The chapter was approved at the ANC with the majority support of the members from the *Polo Patriótico*, a bloc that was absorbed by the dynamics of the constituent period and followed the lead of the massively popular figure of Chávez who, as already mentioned, had made the idea of paying the 'historical debt' to indigenous peoples one of the early slogans of his political project.

A Twelfth Temporary Provision was also included in the text, establishing a two-year time frame for the demarcation of indigenous habitat and lands, while another (Sixth) Temporary Provision established that 'the National Assembly, within two years, will legislate on all the matters related to this constitution. Priority will be given to the organic laws on indigenous peoples, education and frontiers'. Neither of these time frames was met,[7] which evinces that the demarcation and titling of indigenous territories was a process for which there was no real preparation (nor, probably, the political will) within the Constituent Assembly. Analyzing the current government's hesitant approach to land titling, the absence of ideological debate at the time of the ANC appears as political weakness – and as a symptom of the volitional inclinations of constituent periods. A constitutional framework was approved whose essential contents were viewed with distrust, though for different reasons, both by the government bloc and by the economic forces supporting the opposition. The euphoria of the creation of a constitution, the symbolic weight of a process dedicated to remodelling the identity of the republic, the interest in joining in the indigenous recognition of the new Latin American constitutionalism, and technical inexperience in issues of land demarcation, led to the approval of a chapter that has subsequently offered symptoms of atrophy. Within the government, current praxis does not contemplate the possibility of 'free determination' models of autonomy for indigenous peoples in the country. The opposition, which harbours the most orthodox neoliberal forces interested in eliminating collective territorial rights as well as sectors of non-pluralist liberals, was and continues to be an unlikely supporter of indigenous rights.

The Defence Commission basically brought together former members of the military, among which were declared sympathisers of the *Polo Patriótico*. This commission's arguments enabled neoliberal forces to disguise their interests in unrestricted purchase, sale and seizure of land. An openly neoliberal line was obviously disadvantageous for political actors at a constituent assembly dominated by political forces with an explicit mandate to seek an alternative to neoliberalism. Given this strategic disadvantage, in public even neoliberal lobbies and business organizations endorsed the 'nationalist' position. Thus, for instance, *Fedecámaras*, the largest business federation, had its views presented in the independent press with headlines such as 'The rights of ethnic groups fracture the Republic'. Pedro Carmona, vice-president of *Fedecámaras* and later known for becoming the figurehead in the 2002 coup against Chávez's government, was one of the prominent voices anticipating the alleged dangers of indigenous recognition for the nation and its economy.

This nationalist position, after all, had deep roots in Venezuela. It had been central for the military and state security bodies for decades. Hence, for instance, in the early 1970s, when the Ye'kuana of the Ventuari organized themselves to repel the land invasions that were by then flourishing again in Amazonas, members of the military in the Atures department (Amazonas state) disqualified those claims as originating in 'separatist groups' (Arvelo-Jiménez 1990). In that particular case, the military's reaction was allegedly spurred by the fact that some of them were direct beneficiaries of land-grabs, and the Ye'kuana mobilization worried them because it had stimulated reactions among other ethnic groups similarly affected by land dispossession in Ature. During the 1970s and 1980s, parts of the military responded with similar accusations every time that indigenous communities organized themselves against land seizures.[8]

The links between this particular nationalist position and extreme right-wing factions in the military and economic elites were also expressed in a range of independent media. In practice, these media outlets were doing the work of political parties not represented in the ANC. A clear example could be seen on 7 December 1999, just before the referendum on the constitutional text, in 'Vox Populi', a programme broadcast by Venevisión. The journalist Nelson Bocaranda, the programme's presenter, gathered a group of guests that represented the concerns of the political right and the conservative military.[9] Bocaranda opened the debate with no shortage of drama: 'Did the Constituent Assembly betray Venezuela in order to please Venezuelan Indians or indigenous people? Is the country going to disintegrate?' Among the guests invited to respond to such apocalyptic questions were military figures such as Fernando Ochoa Antich, but also the author of a book entitled *Conspiracy South of the Orinoco* (*Conspiración al Sur del Orinoco*) (Madi 1998).[10] This latter guest was not short of suitably dramatic warnings either: 'The alliance between theologians of liberation and the Marxists south of the Orinoco is leading to the creation of a dangerous power vacuum which forms the basis for the territorial dissolution of Venezuela'. For some reason, Fidel Castro and Gaddafi – who had been among the usual suspects in the criticism of indigenous rights activism in the 1980s – were spared direct responsibility on this occasion.

The transition to the people

The Constituent Assembly period facilitated the realignment of social forces and opened avenues for the participation of politically marginalized sectors of society. The case of indigenous actors is typical of this process. Indigenous activists and organizations began to participate institutionally in the shaping of national politics, and with that new forms of collective action developed. From then onwards, an important part of that collective action was channelled through state structures, including the electoral arena. The notion of independence from party politics that nominally guided indigenous organizations has in practice been transformed into synergic relationships with the political blocs that currently form the political field: the *chavista* bloc (especially, though not exclusively, through its main political party – initially MVR, and now PSUV) and the opposition bloc (whose less cohesive union impinges on its relations with the indigenous organizations that have gravitated towards it).

The careers of prominent indigenous activists make a good illustration of the way in which this process has taken the form of specific political action. Let us look at the illustrative cases of José Luis González (Pemon) and José Poyo (Kariña), both of whom played important roles at this time: González occupied one of the three ANC seats reserved for indigenous representation and Poyo was CONIVE's general coordinator.

On 2 August 1999, at the start of the constitutional process, both men were invited to a television programme entitled '*La Constituyente*' ('The Constituent Assembly'), broadcast by Globovisión (a channel that was to become a bastion of opposition mobilization in subsequent years). After the difficulties surrounding the election of indigenous members described in the previous section, proposals for a chapter on indigenous rights began to gain some public interest. González and Poyo were invited on the programme as indigenous representatives in order to comment on their proposals and political allegiances. The presenter asked González, 'Are you or are you not a member of the Polo Patriótico?' González did not hesitate in his response: 'I am not. I am a Pemon, and always work in defence of our indigenous rights'. Moreover, he also underscored that the MVR and the *Polo Patriótico* included people such as the former minister Atala Uriana Pocaterra (a Wayúu politician), who opposed some of the positions of elected indigenous members (e.g. the aforementioned González, N. Pocaterra and G. Guevara). When his turn came, Poyo explained that CONIVE was an 'autonomous' organization, though he recognized that it had established some working links with the *Polo Patriótico*.

Poyo and González were also questioned about the controversies generated by CONIVE's extraordinary assembly for the election of indigenous representatives to the ANC. Poyo pointed out that the indigenous activists who had protested against the legitimacy of the CONIVE-coordinated election were very close to political parties (such as AD) in Amazonas and Zulia states, and that they could therefore not be considered to be representatives of indigenous organizations.

Next, González and Poyo presented a summary of the demands that they had placed before the nation. Along with the possibility of establishing 'autonomous regions', economic development was clearly stated as a central concern. González remarked that mineral and forest resources had to benefit indigenous peoples so that they could stop being poor while actually being rich in resources; he explicitly linked this transition from poverty to well-being as dependent on territorial recognition.

These public declarations contain keys to understanding what has happened in Venezuela over the past 16 years at the forefront of indigenous activism. These two actors, with extensive experience by then in the realm of indigenous politics, underscored their political autonomy despite recognizing links with the *Polo Patriótico*. In subsequent years, both have become strongly identified with the PSUV and particularly with the *chavista* bloc, embodying the creative tensions between 'autonomy' and 'centralization' that characterize the internal politics of that bloc. Nominated by CONIVE and supported by the MVR/PSUV, both González and Poyo have subsequently occupied one of the National Assembly seats reserved for indigenous representation (the former in two different terms). Furthermore, they have competed against each other for that seat. While both have criticized some aspects of the government's approach to the implementation of indigenous rights, they have also vehemently defended the improvements that that approach has generated on various fronts. In political terms, they have remained firmly situated within the *chavista* bloc, remaining at a clear distance from the opposition bloc at critical moments (from the 2002 coup against Chávez to the 2004 pre-recall referendum period and the 2014 destabilizing *guarimbas*).

Let us now continue with the identification of the elements that characterized the incorporation of indigenous organizations into the *chavista* bloc.

Guaicaipurismo and the crystallization of *chavismo*

Any political system, regardless of its institutional arrangements and ideological affiliations, requires narratives to sustain its legitimacy and to facilitate a minimum degree of identification and cohesion among its members. The political sphere is always in need of meaningful (re)construction, regardless of, or rather in addition to, the material structures that sustain it; recall that the latter are not necessarily or automatically expressed in collective political identities. A 'nation', as a political system, is a complex entity whose original definition and subsequent development has always required the production of such legitimating and encompassing narratives, with the state's institutional apparatus becoming a central element in the generation of such narratives – more or less in harmony with the private enterprise, depending on the balance of power in the battle for hegemony. State-fostered symbols and narratives facilitate the shaping and reshaping of national identities, which are nevertheless always complemented 'from below'.

It follows from this premise that any attempt at a substantial systemic political transformation will be accompanied by the creation of new legitimating narratives of identification. In Venezuela, this process, visible in the project of republican refoundation that the 1999 Consitution encapsulated, runs in parallel to the formation and crystallization of the *chavista* movement. Indeed, republican refoundation had been one of the mobilizing slogans of the nascent *chavista* bloc for the 1998 election campaign, and that refoundation required a redrawing of the parameters that defined national identity, which was accelerated as soon as the bloc gained a share of institutional power. That redrawing has seen intensive use of the imagery of indigeneity and a re-evaluation of the indigenous contribution to nationality that had already been employed by Chávez in his successful 1998 presidential campaign. Chávez formalized his promise to help pay the nation's 'historical debt' to the indigenous population in a famous 'Act of Compromise with History' signed on 20 March 1998:

> Taking into full consideration that we are historically indebted to the half a million *indígenas* grouped in the 28 ethnic groups within the country, I make public, nationally and internationally, the commitment to pay back that sensitive debt from the Presidency of the Republic, in which I will arrive by the decision of the Venezuelan masses at the elections of 6 December 1998.

This declaration helped to give shape to the vaguely defined Bolivarian project and contributed to the formation of the new popular collective subject on which it depends. From early on, the emerging Bolivarian movement had been linked to the so-called 'tree of the three roots' (referring to the ideas and ideals embodied by Simón Bolívar, Simón Rodríguez and Ezequiel Zamora), with calls for national sovereignty and Latin American integration, and opposition to neoliberalism, but it was obviously not constrained by an identifiable theoretical corpus to guide its actions. Rather, it developed as a flexible matrix that, defined as an antagonist order in opposition to the status quo, facilitated the convergence of diverse demands (and political currents) within an alternative project to neoliberalism. As Laclau (2007) has consistently argued in his theoretical approach to explaining the logics of populist movements, this type of 'indefinition' is typical of these movements, which facilitate the convergence of fairly heterogeneous demands into a new collective identity by, among other things, producing (partially) empty signifiers.

The declaration of compromise towards indigenous peoples in 1998 constituted one of the public milestones adding a pluricultural ingredient to that Bolivarian matrix, and was accompanied by specific political alliances. As previously explained, Chávez and his collaborators had established direct contacts with prominent indigenous activists, especially with members of CONIVE as the most important platform of national indigenous representation (Silva 2007, p. 363; Van Cott 2003a).

The indigenous element within the *chavista* movement gradually became a prominent discursive current, to the extent that it well deserves a distinctive name. It is in response to this analytical requirement that I coined the term *guaicaipurismo* (after Guaicaipuro, the most celebrated native chief in the early struggle against Spanish colonialism and today an established icon of national lore). *Guaicaipurismo* is a crucial complement to Bolivarianism as a source of symbolic and narrative production that supports and expresses the collective political identity that takes form as *chavismo*. Let us see how this finds practical expression, after some historical context.

In general, notions of indigeneity pervade various aspects of the country's social imagery, from naming places to naming people. And the use of indigeneity as an ingredient of state-fostered national identity is not new (Barreto 1995; García Gavidia 2003; Heinen and Coppens 1986, p. 380). Venezuelan scholar Nelly García Gavidia (2003) demonstrated that appeals to images of heroic Indians had to some extent become a tool for political actors as early as the 1920s, but also that it was an appraisal that had fixed 'the Indian' as a symbol of the past, petrifying it and to a large extent removing it from the present as a living subject. In artistic spheres, at least since the 1940s milieu of democratic transition following Juan Vicente Gómez's autocratic rule (1908–35), a variety of localist and nationalist themes depicted blacks and *indígenas* as having progressive political intent – not merely as part of *costumbrista* (local custom) themes (Barreto 1995; Mayhall 2005). These trends changed after the coup against Rómulo Gallegos in 1948. The dictatorship of Marcos Pérez Jiménez ([1948]1953–8) cultivated a degree of official recognition for black and indigenous cultural expression, but relabelled them. The military government commissioned grand works that, balanced against modernist inclinations, celebrated nationalist narratives with the presence of indigenous and black protagonists. The *Nuevo Ideal Nacional* ('New National Ideal') that Pérez Jiménez proclaimed as a framework for the country's development accommodated those figures in association with the country's glorious traditions. The depiction of black and indigenous peoples in those works, as epitomized by the painter Pedro Centeno Vallenilla,[11] projected the idea that the peak of these populations was in the past, thus removing them from a project of future development informed by *blanqueamiento* ('whitening') goals.[12] With state control over its outlook and divulgation and limited grass-roots organization in search of identity recognition, art and folklore forms fell under a formula of 'permitted' cultural expressions useful to a national whitening project.

This did not disappear with the collapse of Pérez Jiménez's regime. Within the military, fortresses and camps throughout the country have also traditionally been given indigenous names (from Fuerte Tiuna, in the country's capital, to those in frontier areas) and gestures of identification with an indigenous past are widespread (as epitomized in the archaeological park at the military barracks in Maracay, one of the most important in the country). At present, these gestures remain strong. For instance, one can see military parades on Independence Day in which a loincloth-clad Indigenous Military Unit marches with silent weapons.[13]

In the field of education, school texts had also incorporated references to the heroic indigenous leaders that personified the resistance to Spanish colonization. In religion, the María Lionza cult, with a significant following in parts of the country, includes Guaicaipuro as one of its central pillars (with María Lionza herself and Negro Felipe being the other two). Nelly García Gavidia summarized the way in which the Indian had become an emblem of national identity, suggesting that it had created a singular dialectic: 'flesh-and-bone Indian' would be equivalent to the 'other', whereas 'heroic, past Indian' had become equivalent to 'us' (García Gavidia 2003, pp. 314–15).

With the arrival of *chavismo* as a radical populist movement, these trends were intensified and relabelled as part of what I have called *guaicaipurismo* – they became incorporated as central elements in the creation of the *chavista* collective identity. *Guaicaipurismo*, as a complement to *chavismo*, is the source of (partially) empty signifiers, which explains its effective flexibility: it facilitates and inspires the discursive praxis of government agents in the transformation process of national identity, and in a dialogical context *guaicaipurista* discourse becomes an active bottom-up expression of identification.

Since the approval of the 1999 Constitution, there has been a regular succession of events and executive decisions that clearly illustrate the prominence of indigeneity in a government-led re-evaluation of the national identity parameters. While some of those events are well known in isolation, bringing them together provides solid evidence for the understanding (and of the prominence) of this process. Let us see how *guaicaipurismo* has manifested itself and has been given meaning through the actions of state agents and *chavista* supporters in general.

Expressions of *guaicaipurismo*

A fundamental milestone was the erection of an altar for Guaicaipuro in the National Pantheon, the shrine of nation-builders, in December 2001.[14] Guaicaipuro is the most highly-praised native hero of the resistance against the Spanish *conquistadors*, invested with the heroic aura of those who prefer death rather than submission. He had long ago been incorporated into nation-building lore, but had not received state recognition of this significance prior to 1999.[15] In 2001, Guaicaipuro gained the status of a forger of the country's identity, and the inscription at his Pantheon's altar epitomizes central tenets of the broad *guaicaipurista* discursive framing:

TO GUAICAIPURO
As a representative symbol of the peoples and chiefs of the resistance
1560–68
In recognition of the first dwellers, as the most ancient, constant and
specific of
The country and the continent in all its historic development.
And for his undeniable contribution to the construction of our
nationality.
By the government of the President of the Bolivarian Republic of
Venezuela,
Hugo Chávez Frías, Caracas 8-12-2001

A year later, Presidential Decree No. 2028 (2002) replaced the annual 12 October celebrations of 'Day of Race' or 'Discovery of America Day' with the commemoration of 'Indigenous Resistance Day'. This rejection of the symbols of colonialism remains strong within *chavismo*, and the country's capital has remained a central objective of the symbolic indigenizing production of national identity. For instance, in 2005 the then metropolitan Mayor of Caracas, Juan Barreto, advocated from the ranks of the Bolivarian movement the suspension of the traditional festivities of 25 July in the city, as they commemorated the victory of Spanish over Guaicaipuro in 1568. In 2008, then Mayor Freddy Bernal proposed changing the name of the Paseo Colón to Indigenous Resistance Avenue. In March 2009, Mayor Jorge Rodríguez removed the Christopher Columbus statue from El Calvario, a decision that was publicly backed by

Chávez with the comment that, in addition to being horrible, 'it did not have anything to do with our national heritage'.[16] Rodríguez suggested that the replacement statue, for which an international competition would take place, should have an indigenous theme. On 12 October 2004, the Columbus statue in Plaza Venezuela had already been torn down by a group of protesters, emphasizing that its colonial symbology was unworthy of occupying such a central position in the city.

In March 2006, the crest of the national flag was redesigned, with a symbol of indigeneity (a bow and arrows) as one of the new features. Around the same time, the Ministry of Culture and Education adopted as its new institutional symbol 'The dog and the frog', a design taken from a Panare indigenous petroglyph. Significantly, the director of the National Library, Arístides Medina Rubio, remarked at the time that the new symbol was an expression of the 'new cultural establishment' [*institucionalidad cultural*]. This cultural establishment, it is clear, is largely characterized by a positive symbolic re-evaluation of indigeneity at state level which is far from complete.

As part of the failed constitutional reform initiative led by the presidency and the National Assembly in 2007,[17] Article 18 proposed recognizing the capital as both *Cuna de Simón Bolívar* ('Cradle of Simón Bolívar') and *Reina del Warairarepano* ('Queen of Warairarepano') – the latter term evoking the indigenous name of the mountain that the Spanish colonizers had renamed El Ávila. The measure was a good illustration of the central sources of discursive production among government agents and supporters in present-day Venezuela: Bolivarianism (a source of narrative and symbols associated with Bolívar, and more generally with independence leaders and republican patriots) and *guaicaipurismo* (linked to the pre-colonial indigenous population, and primarily to the leaders of resistance against the colonizers). The proposed constitutional reform came to nothing, but Warairarepano gradually gained official status as a placename.

With the strengthening of the Venezuelan currency, the strong bolívar, in 2008, national banknotes incorporated the figure of Guaicaipuro among the icons of nationality. Interviewed about the forthcoming changes in December 2007, the Director of the Central Bank, Armando León, underlined the historical novelty of adding both indigenous and Afro-descendent figures on the notes, along with the tradition of celebrating the patriots.[18]

The trend in *guaicaipurista* messaging is also visible in the selection of names for new state infrastructure projects, which are not anymore automatically named after independence heroes or republican patriots. The use of indigenous placenames (or names that evoke indigeneity) by state organs is not new, but it is increasingly noticeable. Thus, for instance, a new bridge that was planned over Lake Maracaibo pays tribute to the tribal chief Nigale, who was referred to in newspaper coverage of the announcement as 'a martyr of indigenous struggles'.[19]

In another significant instance of the *guaicaipurista* current cultivated by members of the *chavista* bloc, in Vargas state the Municipal Chambers and the Legislative Council started a process of renaming streets and districts with references among which indigenous placenames stood out. The regional anthem was to be changed too, and in the call for proposals from the regional Legislative Council A. Moscoso remarked that the proposed compositions would have to be based on symbols of regional identity that, along with others, included 'our indigenous people' and the 'Waraira Repano' (*Últimas Noticias* 2009). It should be noted that among the district names that members of the regional municipal councils wanted to change were 'Marlboro' and 'Week End'. After a CNE-supervised referendum in the *municipio*, the Parroquia (parish) Raúl Leoni had already been renamed as Urimare (recalling a female Indian figure of national lore).[20] The Municipal Council of Guaicaipuro (Miranda state) similarly announced around this time by decree the creation of a new flag and crest that included symbols evoking indigeneity.

Alongside this process, Chávez occasionally proudly identified himself as Indian, specifically claiming Cuiva and Yaruro ancestry.[21] This was in clear contrast with the intentions of those who described him as '*zambo*' (a pejorative term for people with indigenous and black ancestry), a contrast that emphasized the political dimension of Chávez's statements. This self-identification, far from passing unnoticed, had political significance: it reinforced Chávez's connection with indigenous actors in the country. As Noelí Pocaterra, one of the principal indigenous leaders in the country, put it at a UN forum: 'President Chávez has given indigenous peoples dignity. In addition to listening to their problems and responding with helpful executive decrees, he identified himself as an indigenous person'.[22]

The *guaicaipurista* current of course finds expression outside government circles. Indeed, many *chavista* supporters actively participate in the production of symbols that facilitate the maintenance of the *chavista* collective identity, and its *guaicaipurista* ingredient is evident in that 'bottom-up' participation. It is, for instance, noticeable all over the country in the denomination of communal councils, cooperatives and *chavista* cultural associations with terms that assert this form of identification.

Unsurprisingly, the *guaicaipurista* tendency is not always welcomed. Since it is recognized by both its supporters and its detractors as part of a symbolic confrontation that expresses the overall political contest in the country, it is often contested by government critics. Some of the latter publicly reject *guacaipurismo* in a logical reaction against symbols of identification that are strongly associated with *chavistas*. When the 12 October celebrations began to commemorate the 'Indigenous Resistance Day', some negative reactions were aired. 'It is ridiculous', declared the historian Guillermo Morón to *El Nacional* in 2003; 'They want to try and convert a universal historical date into a day of indigenous resistance that in fact was no such thing at that time'.[23] The declarations of a *varguense* before changing placenames in his state to indigenous replacements was another example of these reactions: 'This obsession with changing the name of everything, regardless of the costs that this implies, instead of occupying themselves with priorities such as security, the channelling of creeks and the generation of employment' (*El Nacional* 2008).

It could be said that colonial symbols have become the centre of a discursive war, as different opinions about them demonstrate. For instance, some local festivities throughout the country still commemorate the 'foundation' of a given city, underlining colonial legacies at the expense of pre-colonial history. Marcaibo (capital of Zulia state, with an opposition governor) maintains this type of celebration in its September festivities. In 2014, PSUV member Yldefonso Finol wrote an article entitled 'Genocide prize in Maracaibo' in which he complained about the fact and called for recognition of the region's indigenous past.[24]

It is worth noting that even the independent media in Spain, which have demonstrated notable rancour against the new left-wing governments in Latin America,[25] had something to say about these symbolic aspects of politics: in an editorial, *El País* hoped that

Mount Ávila, 'so Spanish and so Theresian [Saint Teresa of Ávila, a sixteenth-century Spanish nun] does not adopt in the baptismal fonts of the Bolivarian socialism of the twenty-first century some other denomination'.[26] For the author of the piece, it was even striking that the government supported the restoration of the vernacular indigenous (Pemon) name for the Angel's Falls, which are in Pemon territory.

The concern with symbols and sources of empty signifiers is not an apolitical matter. The political polarization of Venezuela has been reflected in the sphere of symbolic production nearly as much as in the ballot box, and the positioning that people take in relation to certain symbols becomes a clear indication of their sympathies. Taking into consideration the importance of collective identification processes in a polarized scenario is crucial. In the formation of the *chavista bloc*, the antagonistic frontier that facilitated its hegemonic emergence was strongly and systematically demarcated by symbols. Against this background, it is not surprising that when the opposition has tried to get more organized to compete against *chavismo* at the ballot box, as in the 2012 and 2013 presidential elections with Caprile's candidacy, they have tried to appropriate those symbols associated with their rivals, trying to capture votes in a period of border instability. In a highly illustrative example, Capriles began wearing clothes bearing the eight-star Venezuelan flag previously resisted by the opposition (which continued to use in its political events the older, seven-star flag that symbolically ignored Símon Bolívar's inclusion of the state of Guayana), and he appeared at public meetings wearing indigenous feather crowns.

Let us next see how this creative use of messaging has also influenced the conceptualization of the socialism of the twenty-first century and the field of indigenous collective action.

Indo-American socialisms

If the intensive use of the imagery of indigeneity that facilitates identification among members of the *chavista* bloc was evident before 2005, it became even more so after the call for the socialism of the twenty-first century. Following the government's lead, the appeal to socialism has often been presented as an Indo-American socialism. Chávez himself often promoted this formula as soon as, in 2005, he made explicit his intention of pursuing a socialist transformation of the country. The very night of his re-election as president in December 2006, when from the so-called 'balcony of the people' of Palacio Miraflores he addressed assembled followers, Chávez stated that the socialism of the twenty-first century, for which he had campaigned in the preceding months, should not be feared because it is 'an originary, indigenous socialism'.

More elaborately, at the inauguration [*juramentación*] of the Presidential Councils for Constitutional Reform and Communal Power in January 2007, President Chávez remarked:

> Our indigenous peoples, despite the bombardment of anti-values, despite capitalist abuses and the disintegration of many of their traditions, have been capable, just as they did in the resistance against European imperial aggression, of resisting the anti-values of capitalism and in a good part of their spaces they cohabit in an original, indigenous socialism. (Chávez 2007, p. 46)

Statements of this sort consolidate the discursive intertwining between the socialism of the twenty-first century and the indigeneity that Chávez and many members of his governments developed after 2005. And outside government, it is reinforced by the production of narratives that seek to link indigenous resistance with revolution and indigenous organization with socialism. The Ministry of

Education, through the *Fondo Editorial Ipasme*, has produced books with titles (in translation) such as 'Communal Indigenous America and the New Socialism: Twenty-one principles that orient socialism in Our America' (Linares 2011). The book 'The revolutionary thinking of Chief Guaicaipuro' (Beltrán Acosta 2003) presents a perfect example: the search for the establishment of a narrative that links the indigenous past of resistance with current liberation struggles. In fact, the idea that the Venezuelan people embrace the strength of Carib resistance is common with a variety of revolutionary activists is illustrated by Linares:

> We the peoples of South America's north and the Antilles have Carib spirit. We acquired ... their conscience as an indomitable people, their profoundly democratic notion of life [;] this stimulates us to oppose any attempt at colonization and to build societies where freedom, fraternity, cultural identity, dignity, collective self-esteem and resistance are promoted. (2011, p. 26)

Bolivarianism and *guaicaipurismo* converge

Since both Bolivarianism and *guaicaipurismo* have been seminal sources of identification in the construction of the *chavista* movement, it is not surprising that *chavista* supporters have developed creative discursive synergies between them. If what I have described above is largely a process of 'indigenization' of Bolivarianism and the socialism of the twenty-first century, the opposite process is equally evident. As it were, the figure of Guaicaipuro has also been bolivarianized.

On 7 August 2011, during the IV Bolivarian Congress Young Indo-America, MINPI minister Nicia Maldonado provided a perfect expression of how this phenomenon is produced. In her speech at one of the plenary sessions, she rhetorically asked: 'Why is this encounter Bolivarian?' [¿*Por qué Bolivariano el encuentro?*] She started to recall the struggles of Guaicaipuro and then moved on to link those struggles to the independence process: Miranda and Bolívar were then brought to the fore. Pointing out that she was speaking on the anniversary of Bolívar's victory at the Battle of Boyacá, Maldonado recalled that in the past some 'indigenous brothers' had reproached her for speaking so much about Bolívar, who was a *mantuano* (a white creole from the aristocracy) and a liberal, not an *indígena*. Maldonado then defended the importance of understanding what Bolívar's mission had been: [the achievement of] 'freedom, the independence of the motherland and the big motherland [*la Patria Grande*]'. Next she moved on to link these tasks and Chávez's impact on the geopolitical arena, pointing out that Bolívar 'rose against the Yankee Empire ...; he already rose against that Empire 200 years ago'. This type of argument, let it be said, is also cultivated from the 'bottom up'. In Bolívar state, where I lived, there were communal councils in indigenous communities with names such as 'United Indígenas for Bolivarian Ideals' (in Palmarito community).

This intertwining of Bolivarianism and *guaicaipurismo* was also very well expressed, for example, at an event commemorating the International Day of Indigenous Peoples (9 August, as established by the UN) in 2010.[27] Venezuelan indigenous representatives at the Latin American Parliament (*Parlatino*) exhibited that day the sword that *El Libertador* had presented to Mapoyo Indians for the latter's contribution during one of the campaigns in the wars of Independence.

The creative communion between these symbols of nationality is also well illustrated by the common phenomenon of indigenous choirs singing the national anthem in their vernaculars, which one can often see at cultural events at schools and various political activities, or at solemn commemorations. An example was the reading by indigenous activists of the Act of Independence during the commemoration of its anniversary that was celebrated in Ciudad Bolívar (home to the Congress of Angostura) in 2009, in the presence of President Chávez, members of the National Assembly and high-ranking military officials.[28] In the official parades that day, representatives of indigenous communities marched alongside participants of some government offices.

Conclusion

The emergence of *chavismo* as a national-popular bloc transformed and catalyzed indigenous organization and mobilization in Venezuela. Indeed, it gradually *created* an indigenous movement. Before 1999, indigenous organizations were weak and fragmented, and collective action episodic and reactive. The gravitation of indigenous activism towards the Bolviarian movement, and in particular its active incorporation into the *chavista* bloc during the National Constituent Assembly, catalyzed this activism and opened its transition to new forms of collective action. Central elements of this collective action, which has become sustained and proactive, have developed in synergies with state actors and other, non-indigenous groups within the *chavista* bloc. This collective action constitutes an indigenous movement that did not exist before the emergence of *chavismo*.

A creative demonstration of the process of transformation experienced by indigenous organizations in the country can be found in the sphere of identity formation. The *chavista* bloc made indigeneity one of the central sources for the creation of symbols and signifiers for its collective identity (which I have called *guaicaipurismo*). This identity is indispensable for the mass-mobilization of political movements, and is actively created and recreated in dialogical processes by leaders and supporters of these movements. In Venezuela, these re-creations have been very well illustrated by the strong investment from government and state agencies in reintroducing indigenous ingredients into the official narratives of nationality, while from sectors of indigenous activism there has been a creative association of indigenousness with revolution and, from 2005 onwards, with socialism.

THREE

Balance of enfranchisement

From the outset I stated that the current enfranchisement of the indigenous population, in socioeconomic and political terms, is unprecedented in Venezuelan history. We have already seen expressions of certain aspects of that political enfranchisement, particularly those stemming from the processes of indigenous organization and collective action that were stimulated by the emergence of the *chavista* movement, its seminal election victory in 1998 and the constituent period of 1999. The next three chapters (4, 5 and 6) are dedicated to analyzing the main avenues of indigenous collective action that can be identified in Venezuela today (as well as the goals pursued through them), which will bring us back to a discussion of political enfranchisement and how it is in practice expressed by different sectors of the indigenous population. We will see that, indeed, a central element of indigenous collective action has actively constituted itself as a supporting current theme of the *chavista* movement, but also that other elements of such action position themselves more tangentially in relation to that movement and actually deploy a contentious position with regard to some government policies and state organs. Here I will examine the different extent to which constitutional rights have come into being for the indigenous population, thus providing a basis for evaluating the character of its current degree of enfranchisement. This will help to explain why there are different forms of collective action and why they have developed synergic or antagonistic relations with the *chavista* movement, manifesting of diverse political priorities.

Let us start by taking an overview of indigenous rights legislation produced in the past 16 years, whose proliferation and reach is in itself an indication of how the political enfranchisement of the indigenous population has influenced the transformation of the country's normative frame.

Legislation

In 2009, when setting out to assess the first ten years of Bolivarian governments in relation to indigenous peoples, Esteban Mosonyi rightly remarked that the 1999 Constitution was an unavoidable starting point (Mosonyi 2009). It constituted a historical milestone that reframed relations between the state and indigenous peoples and recognized a wide range of differentiated indigenous rights. Advocates of those rights had to defeat strong resistance from outside and within the Bolivarian bloc that dominated the Constituent Assembly, but eventually succeeded in establishing indigenous rights as a symbol of progressive change in the country.

Six years have elapsed since Mosonyi's assessment, but an appraisal of indigenous peoples' struggles could not start otherwise: the Bolivarian Constitution, a landmark of the political process channelled by Chávez's victory at the 1998 presidential elections, transformed the legal status of indigenous peoples in the country. Venezuela came to the forefront of the Latin American countries that throughout the 1990s, adopting principles of liberal multiculturalism, included differentiated rights for indigenous peoples in their constitutions (Barié 2005; Bello 2005; Roldán Ortega 2005).

Subsequent institutional development of those rights has been prolific. In 2005, following approval of the Basic Law of Indigenous Peoples and Communities (LOPCI), some analysts even remarked that a 'maximum normative ceiling' had been achieved (Aguilar and Bustillos 2007, p. 30). However, setting limits to the possibilities for new legislative developments is pointless – it is always dependent on the balance of forces that dominate legislative and executive organs and on how they decide to express rights. And it is the case that since 2007 the 'normative ceiling' for indigenous rights had continued to reach new heights in Venezuela: two new major legislative projects were underway in 2013, specifically addressing indigenous education and special jurisdictions.[1] These new laws add up to a wide-ranging normative framework produced by a National Assembly with, let us remember it, a fluctuating but uninterrupted Bolivarian majority since 2000.

Milestones include:

- 2001: the signature of ILO Convention No. 169 and the Law of Demarcation and Guarantee of Indigenous Peoples' Habitat and Lands (LDGHTP)
- 2005: the LOPCI
- 2009: the Law of Indigenous Languages and the Law of Cultural Patrimony of Indigenous Peoples
- 2010: the Law of Indigenous Craftsmen and Craftswomen.

Presidential decrees that complemented and facilitated the consolidation of this standards framework are discussed below. Other significant decrees were no. 1393 (2001), which created the Presidential Commission for the Attention of Indigenous Peoples; no. 1795 (2002), on the Promotion and Application of Oral and

Written Usage of Indigenous Languages; no. 1796, which created the National Council of Indigenous Education, Culture and Languages; no. 2028 (2002), which transformed the 12 October national celebrations from 'Day of Race' (celebrating the colonial enterprise) into Indigenous Resistance Day.

However, as everyone knows, legislation alone is not enough to transform social structures, determine the implementation of public powers or guarantee the respect of private ones. Venezuela is no exception in this respect, and the solid normative framework for indigenous rights has not come to fruition in some key areas. The materialization of differentiated rights in particular is largely dependent on the demarcation and titling of indigenous territories. Only within the latter can special jurisdictions be formed, for instance, or the principles of 'free determination' gain substance. And the demarcation of territory has been a patchy and erratic process, as I will discuss next. This point is central to the current shaping of indigenous enfranchisement.

Indigenous rights and territory

By 1999, according to official data, Venezuela's indigenous population (315,815 people) constituted only 1.71 per cent of the national figure. The state had recognized 32 indigenous peoples through the 1992 national census, but that had not helped to change the minority and subaltern status of the indigenous population. Indigenous organizations in Venezuela had never been as strong and prominent in the political arena as some of their peers in the Andean region. When the constituent period arrived, they were in a weak position, and discussion of indigenous rights and territoriality quickly became a focus of important tensions. They were not only opposed by the weakened neoliberal forces that gained some representation in the Constituent Assembly, but also by a sector of Bolivarian supporters principally based around the military (Combellas 2003). As the key to accessing differentiated rights, the possibility of territorial recognition was eventually included. Indigenous land demarcation was in fact explicitly established as a government priority through the Twelfth Temporary Provision (which stipulated an unrealistic period of two years for completion of the process) of the 1999 Constitution. Decree 1392 (which created the National Commission for the Demarcation of Indigenous Habitat and Land) and the LDGHTP were issued in 2001. In 2005, the LOPCI finally introduced firmer regulations for demarcation and titling procedures. A new presidential decree (no. 7855) was passed in February 2011 and, after complaints from some indigenous organizations about its contents, partially reformed later on that year (*Gaceta Oficial de la República Bolivariana de Venezuela no. 39,665* of 3 May 2011) (see Bello 2011, pp. 39–44, for an overview of the objections and reform). This new decree placed the MINPI at the head of the National Commission of Demarcation, replacing the Ministry of Environment in that position. Some indigenous organizations complained about the lack of consultation prior to the drafting of the decree and objected that the new role given to indigenous representatives within the commission implied a weakening of their decision-making capacities – they were becoming '*voceros*' ('spokesmen').

Legal measures aside, territorial recognition is still minimal in relation to the terms contemplated by the 1999 Constitution. Ten years after its approval, there were only 36 titled indigenous communities, totalling 980,943 hectares (Angosto-Ferrández 2010, pp. 106–11). Since then, additional collective titles have been granted to other communities, and 2013 was particularly productive on this front. According to MINPI, 21 titles were granted throughout the year, demarcating property for 256 communities of six different indigenous peoples covering a total of 1,125,965 hectares (MINPI, *Memoria y Cuenta* 2013). The majority of these titles (14 of the 21) have benefited Cumanagoto and Kariña communities in Anzoátegui state, but the largest title in terms of area (597,983 hectares) was granted in Bolívar state to Pemon communities in the so-called Ikabarú sector, an important mining area. It should be clarified that this type of demarcation is not dependent on the termination of mining activities, in which some Pemon communities are in fact actively involved. It is most important to note that, in line with the government's overall approach to demarcation and enfranchisement (which I discuss below), these titles have been accompanied by financial support from the Government Federal Council for a variety of productive and essential projects; a total of Bs. 40,398,520 (US$ 6,396,220) was distributed for projects ranging from housing to transport and agriculture.

In April 2013, in an act publicizing new titles, Vice-President Jorge Arreaza stated that 74.6 per cent of land applications submitted since 2005 had been successfully processed, a total of 80 titles. President Maduro took the opportunity to back the approval of the remaining 28 applications being processed and framed this in explicit political terms: 'I can assure you that if they [the opposition] came into government again they would take the lands away from indigenous peoples'.[2] Maduro reminded his audience that Capriles, the opposition leader, had campaigned against the approval of indigenous rights during the 1999 constituent period. These remarks illustrate the importance that the Bolivarian bloc currently places in maintaining its position as the legitimate representative of indigenous interests, now that the opposition bloc has started to contest that previously unquestioned association as part of their electoral strategy.

Political manoeuvring aside, formal recognition of indigenous territories is still minimal. Analysts have associated this fact with state inefficiency and excessive bureaucracy, but there are two specific and interrelated political factors that more certainly influence the stagnation of the demarcation process: (1) government actions in the realm of indigenous rights prioritize political enfranchisement, social service provision and the development of production over territorial recognition; and (2) a large part of the indigenous population currently supports those actions.

The government position is clearly revealed by the emphasis on the creation of indigenous communal councils and communes as a way to integrate the indigenous communities into the state structure and national socioeconomic plans. The creation of MINPI in 2007 pursued those goals, as demonstrated by the ministry's declared objectives and its actual work, which has been in tune with the *Nueva Geometría del Poder* (NGP, New Geometry of Power) (Angosto-Ferrández 2010, pp. 119–25). Former minister Maldonado publicly favoured, from the very beginning of her appointment, communal councils and communes as the alternative to gain demarcation and recognition of indigenous territories (Aporrea 2007; García 2007, p. 32).

National development is a central element of the current stage of the Bolivarian project, as clearly outlined in the six-year economic and social development plans to which the MINPI is directly linked.[3] It necessarily implies an important degree of structural planning centralization, though it is combined with the current promotion of wider participation in political, cultural and economic aspects of social life (Ellner 2011). In line with the way in which leadership and organization has remained central to sustaining a politically plural movement such as *bolivarianismo* (Raby 2006, pp. 261–2), government development plans have shown a concern with organization at a national scale. Indigenous peoples' autonomies, as contemplated in the Constitution, constitute a challenge to that model. The national economy continues to revolve around the extraction and commercialization of natural resources by the state sector, which generates 97 per cent of foreign currency revenue (Sutherland 2013). A considerable part of those natural resources remain in territories with indigenous communities, for example minerals in Bolívar and Amazonas states, coal and oil in Zulia state, and oil around the Orinoco strip in general. The government has sidestepped these challenges by favouring a form of weak territorialization through communal councils and communes, which are not subject to legal titles of collective property in the way that indigenous territories would be. Even if, as we have seen, there has been a relatively significant increase in the number of community titles granted, the priorities of the MINPI (and the government) continue to be clearly reflected, among other things, in the way that this ministry distributes its budget: the 2014 MINPI operating budget allocated Bs. 1,350,500 to training related to the demarcation process, and Bs. 25,013,690 to the 'organization of the indigenous cities, communal councils and communes undergoing construction' (MINPI, *Memoria y Cuenta* 2013).

However, the spread of indigenous communal councils did not result from a mere 'top-down' process: they have been well received in many indigenous communities. Communal councils have been the avenue through which the government funded a variety of infrastructure, housing and production development projects. By the end of 2007, MINPI, then less than a year old, had facilitated the establishment of 1,159 indigenous communal councils (Angosto-Ferrández 2010, p. 123). Eight years later, many indigenous communities continue to apply for funds through communal council projects, and the ministry continues to make clear its aims to consolidate indigenous communities as 'collective and productive areas'. In 2013 alone, out of a total of 97 projects that MINPI funded in indigenous communal councils (to a total value of Bs. 25,870,979), 78 supported socio-productive projects (absorbing 45.6 per cent of the total budget). Remember that communal councils, in any case, define their own priorities when presenting funding requests, so that distribution of the budget also needs to be read as an expression of priorities in indigenous communities. In addition to this support of socio-productive projects through indigenous communal councils, MINPI channelled a further Bs. 6,508,311 to support productive projects in the so-called Units of Indigenous Socialist Production in Apure and Amazonas states (MINPI, *Memoria y Cuenta*, 2013). In order to understand the impact of this approach to stimulating production development and enfranchisement, it should be recalled that the design and implementation of these projects involves community participation, a process that is largely channelled in organizational terms by communal councils.

However, the ministry also underlines that the 'exploitation of strategic and mineral resources [needs] to be under the direction of the Socialist State so that it can be distributed with equity among communities'.[4] The aim of making those goals compatible explains why the government has so far favoured territorialization through communal councils and communes. Government priorities in this area are well illustrated by other sources of evidence. When collective land titles have actually been granted, they have been granted exclusively to *communities* (never to *peoples*). According to interested parties, when an application in the name of 'peoples' has been made and positively evaluated by the regional and national demarcation commissions, it has eventually been blocked by the executive (Mansutti 2006, p. 28). As a result, it is 'communities' – and not 'peoples' – that become the only plausible subjects of collective indigenous rights. This in turn implies that, in strict legal terms, differentiated rights can only be effectively enjoyed by the indigenous population inhabiting titled communities.

Towards a general balance of enfranchisement

While it is a fact that territorial recognition as set out by the 1999 Constitution remains underdeveloped and has been largely replaced by a form of weak territorialization rights, the indigenous population currently enjoys, like much of the previously disenfranchised population, a higher degree of other (non-differentiated) rights. Access to social services and options for productive development with state support have increased, which constitutes an avenue for enfranchisement through the materialization of socioeconomic rights. This question, generally overlooked by the opposition, is also disregarded by some advocates of indigenous rights who exclusively frame their criticism of government policy on the grounds of territory demarcation and notions of free determination. And this question is crucial to the discussion of the legacy of Chávez's governments in the realm of indigenous peoples' rights, as a large part of the indigenous population has shown sustained support for the ongoing socioeconomic and political enfranchisement as a priority over certain notions of free determination (such as territorial and political autonomy).

In the last national census (2011), the questionnaire for indigenous communities included questions addressing levels of access to social services in education, health, transport and communications. Some of these questions were unprecedented in census history and focused specifically on access to government *misiones* (special programmes), which were only launched in 2003 (Ellner 2006, p. 78; Maingón 2006). Others referred more generally to health, education and transport services,[5] which facilitate comparison of access to social services in indigenous communities over the past 20 years (similar questions about such access were posed in the 2001 and 1991/2 censuses).[6] There is scattered evidence that *misiones* and other government programmes have brought education, health, communications and transport services to some communities for the first time. To give but one example from my personal lengthy fieldwork experience in the Gran Sabana (Bolívar state), housing programmes and education programmes such as *Misión Ribas* (secondary school level) reached even relatively remote communities, and communications and telecommunications services have been substantially improved since the launch of the Simón Bolívar satellite in 2008 – one of its land support stations is in the Luepa military base, in the Gran Sabana.

However, it should be recalled that the indigenous community questionnaire in censuses is only applied in settlements that the National Institute of Statistics defines as 'indigenous communities' according to criteria based on objectivized notions of traditionality. This means that the questionnaire does not provide information about the indigenous population living in urban areas. And it must be noted that the latter constitutes a large majority: in 2001, it accounted for 66 per cent of the total indigenous population in the country (Allais 2004). For the urban indigenous population, as for the rest of the popular classes, access to social services depends on general government programmes. Although no disaggregated data yet exist for this urban indigenous population, it can be logically presumed that it has benefited from overall improvements in human development and the provision of social services in the country. Venezuela's improvement in the United Nations Human Development Index (which takes into account income, life expectancy and educational indicators) has been extraordinary even within the general positive trends in the region of the past decade: between 2000 and 2011, Venezuela's index rose from 0.56 to 0.735.[7] In addition, poverty levels dropped dramatically as a result of social investment during Chávez's governments. Up to 2011, income poverty fell from 42.8 per cent to 16.6 per cent; the reduction in extreme income poverty was even greater, from 20.1 per cent to 8.5 per cent. And it must be remembered that these categories measuring income poverty do not take into account other factors that foster social enfranchisement and rights, such as improved access to health services and education – both of which have improved in the country.

Other positive indicators relate, for instance, to improvements in levels of nutrition among the national population, an achievement that has received recognition from the UN Food and Agriculture Organization.[8] In the specific sphere of poverty in indigenous communities, MINPI has had, as one of its central goals, to deal with what it calls the indigenous population in 'extreme vulnerability', to which in 2013 alone, for instance, it dedicated Bs. 34,920,832.

Education

The comparison of 2001 and 2011 census data provides significant evidence of the improved access to education that has positively impacted on the indigenous population. The proportion of this population attending educational centres has increased by 7.76 per cent, with remarkable improvements in all age groups but particularly among the adult population. In the 25–54 age group, the proportion rose from 3.88 per cent in 2001 to 10.84 per cent in 2011; in the 55-or-over age group, it increased from 1.45 per cent to 3.09 per cent.

A very significant statistic is that among the indigenous population aged 25 or older the proportion currently registered in educational programmes is higher than the national average (9.3 per cent compared to 8.5 per cent). For a population with generally very low average income, access to education at that age is indicative of special public provision facilitating this type of enfranchisement.

Literacy among the indigenous population also improved during this period, with an average of 9.6 per cent – including a 15.2 per cent increase for those aged 55 or over. In this respect, the positive impact of *Misión Robinson*, one of the earliest government *misiones*, should be highlighted. It is a literacy programme based on the 'I can do it' (*Yo sí puedo*) method developed by the Cuban pedagogue Leonela Relys, and was launched in 2003, immediately involving thousands of volunteers throughout the country – including bilingual indigenous ones. The number of *indígenas* that benefited from this programme varies between different sources (from 45,807 to 81,662), as well as the number of indigenous languages into which the teaching materials were translated (from four to fourteen) (Villalón 2011, p. 28). Yet it is evident that, in spite of facing the challenges of interculturalism, it had a positive impact among a population particularly affected by the weakened structures of the public educational system during the so-called Fourth Republic.

An important gap nevertheless separates the national average in this respect from the average among the population in indigenous communities, with particularly serious differences in states such as Apure and Delta Amacuro: in these two states, more than half the population in indigenous communities was registered as illiterate (54.54 per cent and 57.57 per cent respectively).

The general policy orientation in education, which in addition to access and non-payment has involved a variety of participatory programmes, has had extraordinary effects in the enfranchisement of sectors of the population (Muhr 2010; Griffiths 2010). This has included the Bolivarian Schools projects (with the Simoncito programme for primary education, secondary school and the Robinsonian Technical Schools), and the national literacy programme, but in addition the indigenous population has benefited from specific programmes. For instance, in 2008 the Ministry of Higher Education started a programme directly addressing this population and guaranteeing university access to at least 14,082 people. This was supported by a resolution of the National University Council, passed in May that year, stipulating this special attention to the needs of the indigenous population as well as other disadvantaged sectors of society with traditionally low access to higher education. This type of programme has been implemented alongside others such as the *Cacique Nigale*. This stems from an agreement between the Indigenous Health Department of the Ministry of Health and the National Experimental University of the Central Plains 'Rómulo Gallegos' (UNERG), and incorporated 200 *indígenas* from all over the country into university-based medical studies (Tillet 2011). These indigenous university students, who received a scholarship in addition to free residence, food and transport, came from 28 different indigenous peoples in eight federal states. The programme was designed in response to the structural lack of specialized medical personnel willing to work in indigenous territories, and selected students committed to return to their communities of origin following the completion of their studies.

The Bolivarian University of Venezuela (UBV), created by presidential decree in 2003 and now supported by a nationwide structure, has also been facilitating free access to university education for a large number of indigenous students, and doing so in their regions of origin – which was unthinkable until very recently. The UBV developed a special Coordination of Indigenous Peoples within its administrative structure, and through its municipalization programme has opened and maintained 'university villages' in various indigenous communities, in line with the university's municipalization project (see Muhr and Verger 2006 for an analysis of this project). This process of widening access to education of course implies massive challenges, but Venezuela, like other countries in the region whose government policies regard education as a right, is willingly facing them as an unavoidable part of widening social rights and enfranchisement.

These advances in the consolidation of the right to education are slow in some aspects that were contemplated by legislation addressing indigenous rights. In particular, the implementation of 'intercultural education' is proving a challenge for various reasons, ranging from financial (tight budgets) and bureaucratic (lack of direct influence on the supervision of the curriculum for indigenous schools) to conceptual (Quispe and Moreno 2011). In accordance with legislative guidelines, a specialized Intercultural Bilingual Education Department was created within the Ministry of Education, and there has been an attempt to relaunch the intercultural education project outlined in conceptual terms in 1979. However, the indigenous schools that are consolidating intercultural programmes (such as some Pemon and Wayúu ones, in Bolívar and Zulia states respectively) remain the exception, though there are examples of ongoing work to improve these programmes at all educational levels. From 2012 onwards, for instance, there have been meetings between members of the Permanent Commission of the National Assembly and the management of the UBV in order to revise part of the curriculum in line with the requirements of specific indigenous communities.[9]

Health

Health is an area in which, just like the right to education, improvements at a national level have also benefited the indigenous population in undifferentiated terms. Programmes such as *Mision Barrio Adentro* in particular had an extraordinarily positive impact among the indigenous population in urban and rural areas, particularly in its early stages. It guaranteed access to health services for the poorest and most disenfranchised sectors of society. In 2005, after the initial stage with the *Consultorios Populares*, the programme enhanced its scope and capacities in the provision of health services and *Clinicas Populares* (People's Clinics) emerged along with *Centros Diagnósticos Integrales* (CDI) (Integrated Diagnostic Centres), *Salas de Rehabilitación Integral* (SRI) (Integrated Rehabilitation Rooms) and *Centros de Alta Tecnología* (CAT) (High Technology Centres).

For the indigenous population in particular, other significant improvements started to come about from 2005 onwards. That year, the first group of graduates from the *Escuela Latinoamericana de*

Medicina (ELAM) (Latin American Medical School) in Cuba arrived in Venezuela, to form the so-called *Batallón 51* of medical doctors specifically based in indigenous and frontier communities – areas traditionally lacking any access to public health services (Tillet 2011). By 2011, there were 783 medical doctors working in this programme.

Within the Ministry of Health, an Indigenous Health Department was created in 2006, with regional offices in each of the eight federal states with 'traditional' indigenous population, directly incorporating a variety of community actors and members of indigenous organizations into the communication and management processes connected with the ministry. This is another aspect to be noted in these processes of improved access to health services: they have actively involved indigenous actors. A significant example was the Indigenous Health Office created within the Ministry of Health as early as Chávez's first government; its latest incarnation has grown to employ more than 100 staff, including many indigenous people in the regional offices in areas with a 'traditional' indigenous population: indeed, between 2006 and 2010 the office was headed by a Wayúu medical doctor, Noly Fernández, a woman with experience in indigenous politics. J.A. Kelly, an anthropologist who worked in this office, wrote in his study of healthcare provision in Amazonas state that this type of appointment facilitated the accomplishment of tasks within a 'painfully bureaucratized and frustratingly low state apparatus' (Kelly 2011, p. 207). Such appointments not only represent the inclusion of indigenous actors in policy-making and public administration and the possibility of activating social networks that can overcome bureaucratic inefficiencies, but also illustrate the existence of synergies between grass-roots organizations, state bureaucracies and politicians at different levels – what constitutes part of a state-supporting and state-sponsored social movement.

A specialized *Servicio de Atención y Orientación al Indígena* (SAOI) (Service for Indigenous People) was also created within the National Health Public System, aiming to facilitate the provision of services to indigenous people who attend public hospital. Bilingual facilitators were incorporated into this scheme, which extends to 27 outlets in ten federal states. Since 2005, more than 200,000 indigenous patients have benefited from this programme, which experts in indigenous health have not hesitated to describe as an unprecedented example, at both the Venezuelan and continental level, of the adaptation of a health service to indigenous people (Tillet 2011, p. 147).

Media and information

The right to information, as Kathryn Lehman remarked in her study of indigenous media in Venezuela (2014), became both a general goal of Bolivarian governments and a challenging task in a context of majority privately owned and politically hostile media. And the expression of this right in specific policy has translated into the promotion of a variety of both public media and community-based initiatives that broadened the spectrum of information in the country – despite the continuing majority of media remaining under the control of private interests and clearly not supporting the government. It is, however, the case that certain demands of indigenous peoples and communities are not generally aired by the main public outlets, which increases the importance of community media and other forms of communication to present some less well represented opinions of indigenous actors, advance demands and, in general, denounce inefficiencies in policy implementation when they occur. In this respect, as Venezuelan anthropologist Daysi Barreto has noted, media such as the Internet have facilitated the circulation of information and demands in a way that, to some extent, balances the broad reach of television and mainstream media (Barreto 2011, p. 262). And to achieve that type of balance, government initiatives such as *Infocentros* have now become a means to facilitate the right to information in many indigenous communities.

Lehman (2014) has provided an overview of indigenous media initiatives such as the bilingual (Wayuunaiki/Spanish) newspaper *Wayuunaiki* established in 1999 in Maracaibo, which has grown to establish itself as a diversified outlet with international connections. Like other outlets of its kind, it is critical of certain government policies but has grown out of an acknowledgement of the substantial qualitative changes experienced in the realm of indigenous political participation in Venezuela. This type of media, while often receiving support from state agencies, does not operate as a silent 'client', but rather shows independence in its incorporation within *chavismo* or in its criticism of government policy.

Improved access to information and increased access to media production has also found expression in the realm of cinematic production. And it is worth noting that this is another realm through which indigenous interests are advanced, sometimes in support of government policy and in other cases upfront opposed to it. For instance, the *Muestra Internacional de Cine Indígena de Venezuela* (International Festival of Venezuelan Indigenous Cinema), which took place on 15–19 June 2014, was entitled '*Sabino Romero vive*' and was dedicated to the struggles of Yukpa activists including Romero, who led Yukpa groups in a campaign highly critical of the state structures created under Chávez's governments. (Romero had been shot dead in 2013; see more in Chapter 6.) The festival was jointly organized by the Wayaakua Indigenous Audiovisual Foundation and the *Centro Nacional Autónomo de Cinematografía* and the *Fundación Cinemateca Nacional de Venezuela* – with public funding.

Conclusion

This chapter does not provide an exhaustive list of types of enfranchisement. It leaves aside important social programmes such as the *Misión Guaicaipuro*, which specifically targeted the indigenous population, or the massive investment in housing that the government is currently undertaking through *Gran Misión Vivienda*, which operates in indigenous territories through MINPI activities.[10] However, this chapter illustrates that enfranchisement in socioeconomic terms is significant and continuing. We will see that this enfranchisement complements (in fact is considerably linked to) forms of political enfranchisement that include legally guaranteed minimum representation in legislative organs. A good number of indigenous activists have been actively involved in the social programmes that bring services to and materialize socioeconomic rights in their communities. As noted above, projects funded through communal councils, for instance, also involve the participation of members of the community and provide invaluable learning experiences in many respects – including, of course, those stemming from the difficulties that arise in participatory processes of making, implementing and monitoring policy. Moreover, indigenous activists and groups have also continuously participated in political activities and election campaigns in support of a government, which has facilitated the introduction of basic social and economic rights (see Chapters 4 and 5). Against this background, it is not surprising that a state-supporting and state-sponsored indigenous movement has emerged, or that electoral support for

Chávez and Bolivarian candidates has generally been outstanding in constituencies with a large proportion of indigenous population; in states such as Delta Amacuro and Bolívar, for instance, there has been overwhelming sustained support for Bolivarian candidates (in some cases with more than 70 per cent of valid votes).[11] It follows that a large part of the indigenous population supports the ongoing socioeconomic and political enfranchisement as a priority over notions of free determination. The type of enfranchisement currently taking place was in fact a historical demand of the indigenous population, and is also a protection against the forces of existing capitalism that, in the absence of state structures to guarantee some basic social and economic rights, might transform free determination into a principle devoid of substance – or even into a wide platform for the creation of new spheres of unbridled capitalist growth and expansion in indigenous territories. These factors explain why overall government policy, and the state structures that implement it, is shaped and firmly supported by a large part of the indigenous population, despite the fact that some demands have not been met – at least for the time being. There are elements of collective action that deploy contentious tactics against the government or some state agencies (not so much 'against the state') and project the prioritization of different means in the delivery of indigenous rights, as we will see in Chapter 6. However, it would be misleading, and plainly a negation of reality, to say that only the latter represent 'real' indigenous interests, as some government critics do. At this highly politicized point in history, indigenous actors are defining their interests through their continuing actions, and ignoring central parts of this is equivalent to ignoring central parts of contemporary indigenousness.

FOUR

Collective action through the electoral sphere

How would political scientists categorize an electoral system in which, within a period of six years, more than 7,000 different political parties had entered the contest? It would surely be a textbook case of atomization, whatever the causes with which that panoply was to be associated. In this chapter I will touch on a case akin to that hypothetical phenomenon and which has been going largely unnoticed. This case is now taking place in Venezuela. And, more specifically, it is happening in the realm of indigenous electoral participation – precisely where conventional wisdom would expect to find undiversified political expressions of a socio-culturally homogeneous and politically cohesive population. As we will see, the way in which the right to indigenous representation in legislative organs (which in Venezuela is a right enshrined by the 1999 Constitution) was formally regulated has unveiled some of the long-lasting effects of 'civil society' growth in the administration and mobilization of indigenous demands during the heyday of neoliberal reform in the country. But, while extraordinary, this phenomenon is only a part of the novel and complex developments stimulated by mass indigenous participation in the electoral process. In this chapter I will explain and discuss such developments and the way in which the electoral sphere has become a crucial channel of indigenous collective action in Venezuela.

We shall see that the electoral competition for indigenous representation has been fully incorporated into the national-level political struggle. Whereas not too long ago 'indigenous politics' was marginal in the Venezuelan electoral arena, it is now pivotal to it, and part and parcel of the contest between *chavismo* and *anti-chavismo* to define the future of the country. Legislation stipulates that indigenous communities and organizations can participate directly in elections and put forward (indigenous) candidates, but in practice their participation and activities are inseparable from the contest between the two political blocs that structure national politics. While these two blocs and the political parties within them clearly determine the competition for indigenous representation, I will contend that reading this situation as merely an institutional 'co-option' of indigenous activists and organizations is a misleading conceptualization that not only ignores the openly declared conscious decisions of activists and organizations, but also becomes an image of teleological conceptions of 'indigenous struggles' that ultimately disguises a negation of the 'indigenous subject' as a 'political subject'. In particular, the participation in elections of indigenous candidates supported by the PSUV and the so-called *Gran Polo Patriótico* (the electoral bloc that supported Chávez and now supports Maduro) is linked to a state-sponsored indigenous movement that has developed in synergy with the Bolivarian movement, as I will explain in the following chapter.

But before analyzing the pragmatic manoeuvring that political actors deploy within and outside the electoral framework in order to gain access to institutional state power, let me start by giving an overview of this framework.

Statutory framework

The differentiated rights that the 1999 Constitution granted to indigenous peoples included guaranteed minimum representation in the National Assembly and in 'the organs of the federal and local entities with indigenous population, in accordance with the law' (CRBV, Article 125). In order to make this right available immediately (i.e. before basic legislation was passed), the CRBV included a (Seventh) Temporary Provision with the principles that would govern the election of those indigenous representatives. Indigenous communities and organizations were thereby enabled to put forward 'indigenous' candidates in the contests in which indigenous representatives were to be elected. This facility effectively reduced the cost of and simplified participation, while also recognizing the role of indigenous organizations and communities as intermediary political bodies between the indigenous population and state organs. In principle, no political parties needed to be involved: any indigenous community (recognized as such by the INE) or indigenous organization formally established for more than three years could thenceforward participate in elections through a simplified procedure of registration with the CNE.

In practice, this enablement also delegated the filtering of indigenous identities to organizations and communities: the latter were made responsible for ensuring that the selected candidates met the requisites of a legally sanctioned 'indigenous' profile. Candidates had to fulfil at least one of the following requirements:

1. to have previously exercised a position of traditional authority in their respective communities
2. to have a recognized background of social struggle in favour of the recognition of their cultural identity

3. to have implemented actions for the benefit of indigenous peoples and communities
4. to belong to a legally constituted indigenous organization with at least three years' activity.

Requirements 2 and 3 clearly offer wide scope for subjective judgement and pragmatic manoeuvring, and their inclusion exemplifies the benevolent moral assumptions that pervade this realm of politics, often conceptualized as apolitical. This idealist approach has some practical implications (see also Appendix). In practical terms, the guardianship of indigeneity entrusted to organizations and communities is subject to political manoeuvring. For instance, the relationship between some candidates and the organizations that put them forward is not always pre-existing; that is, the relationship is actually established by the nomination, in a clear example of electoral pragmatism. There are many instances of candidates participating in different elections with the nomination of different organizations or communities (Angosto-Ferrández 2011, pp. 48–9). Legal requirements are fulfilled, but that does not necessarily imply or guarantee the existence or continuity of social activism in the nominating organizations outside the electoral period. It should also be noted that ethnic ascription is far from being a limitation either. This is first because most indigenous organizations have traditionally worked as multiethnic platforms of representation. But, second, it is because those organizations which in principle are mono-ethnic also demonstrate pragmatism when it comes to election time – that is, they are willing to put forward a candidate who does not belong to the ethnic group that the organization claims to represent (ibid.). But let us now continue with the statutory framework.

The LOPCI (2005), the predominant legislation developing constitutional indigenous rights, confirmed the minimum representation guaranteed to indigenous peoples and communities at national, regional (federal states), local and parochial level (Articles 64 and 66). In the National Assembly, three seats are guaranteed for indigenous representatives. Their occupants are directly elected in multiregional constituencies specially designed for this purpose:

- Western (including Mérida, Trujillo and Zulia states) (ROC, *Región Occidental*)
- Southern (including Amazonas and Apure states) (RSUR, *Región Sur*)
- Eastern (Anzoátegui, Bolívar, Delta Amacuro, Monagas and Sucre states) (ROR, *Región Oriental*).

As is always the case with the design of electoral constituencies anywhere, these constituencies have some practical implications in the shaping of electoral politics that will also be explored in the subsequent sections. For the time being, let me note two central issues. First, indigenous representatives are elected by all registered voters within the relevant constituency, under a system of a relative majority of valid votes; that is, the indigenous representative is 'indigenous' and (so far) always put forward by an indigenous organization or community, but she/he is elected by both indigenous and non-indigenous voters. Second, the distribution of the indigenous population throughout the country is quite uneven (see Table 4.1).

In federal legislative councils, minimum indigenous representation is guaranteed in eight states: Amazonas, Anzoátegui, Apure,

TABLE 4.1 Distribution of indigenous population in Venezuela

State	Indigenous population (%)	State's share of total national indigenous population (2011) (%)
Zulia	12.8	61.2
Amazonas	53.9	10.5
Bolívar	4.0	7.5
Delta Amacuro	25.3	5.7
Anzoátegui	2.4	4.7
Sucre	2.5	3.1
Monagas	2	2.5
Apure	2.6	1.6
Other states	0.1	3.2

Source: Instituto Nacional de Estadística (INE) – Resultados Poblacíon Indígena.

Bolívar, Delta Amacuro, Monagas, Sucre and Zulia. These federal states are those officially considered to be 'areas of traditional indigenous occupation', thus identified through technical (objectivized) criteria which continue to guide the INE and other state organs. This contradicts the use of self-identification as the criterion for counting the indigenous population in censuses: the 2001 and 2011 national censuses registered indigenous population in all 23 federal states. The implication of this officially backed conceptual differentiation between the two forms of indigeneity (i.e. that of the 'areas of traditional indigenous occupation' and the rest) is not insignificant, for it makes differentiated political representation rights only available to a (technically defined) more 'traditional' part of the indigenous population.

The 2009 Basic Law of Electoral Processes (LOPE) stipulated that 'in each state with an indigenous population of or above five hundred people a [indigenous] Legislator for the Legislative

Council will be elected, along with his respective substitute' (Article 151). While this confirmed the possibility for every state to grant a seat for indigenous representation in their respective legislative councils, for the time being (including the 2012 regional elections) the determination of which states have the right to differentiated representation has been conditioned by the aforementioned criteria of traditionality – that is, disregarding the actual number of people who in each state identified themselves in the 'indigenous' category in the national census.

Minimum representation is also guaranteed in municipal and parish councils (*Concejos Municipales* and *Juntas Parroquiales*) when the national census, ethno-historical sources or other data demonstrate the existence of an indigenous population in those administrative units. The LOPE established that an indigenous councillor shall be elected in *municipios* with 300 or more indigenous people (Article 152), and an indigenous representative in *parroquias* with 180 or more (Article 153). However, just as in the case of regional elections, to date there has been a systematic disregard of constituencies that, though outside the areas of 'traditional occupation', reach that number of indigenous population according to the national census.

Article 144 of the LOPE explicitly stipulates that the 'indigenous population and their constituencies will be determined by what the last national census of indigenous population indicates, with the variations officially estimated by the competent organs once it is approved by the National Assembly'. If this legal principle were to be applied automatically by the CNE by consulting the existing census data in accordance with the law, the number of constituencies (including federal states) with differentiated indigenous representation would increase substantially. To give but two examples, Lara and Nueva Esparta states, with 2,112 and 2,200 *indígenas* respectively according to the 2011 census, would elect indigenous representatives to their regional parliaments. However, this contradictory state practice (recognition through censuses and no recognition through electoral rights) has so far been resolved only by specific appeals to the courts. For instance, before the local elections of 2005, a Chaima association from Sucre state succeeded in presenting its case before the Electoral Division of the Supreme Court (*Tribunal Supremo de Justicia*, TSJ). The association requested that an indigenous representative should be elected for the Municipal Council of Ribero (Sucre state), since this municipal unit had more than the minimum of 250 *indígenas* registered according to the national census.[1] The TSJ ruled in favour of the request and ordered the CNE to call for the election of that representative.

The LOPE also opened the possibility for indigenous candidates to be nominated by actors other than indigenous organizations or communities. Article 174 states that 'indi-genous peoples and communities have the right to participation, political protagonism and representation, and for that reason they may put forward members of the National Assembly [*diputados*], legislators, councillors and members of parochial councils'; on the other hand, it is now also possible to be nominated through other avenues, as long as it is demonstrated to the CNE that the candidate has 'realized actions for the benefit of indigenous peoples or communities' (Article 186.3), or that he/she has a 'recognized plan for the struggles in favour of the recognition of the cultural identity [of the indigenous peoples]' (Article 186.2). The vagueness of this type of arrangement, another instance of that benevolent principle that pervades statutory conceptualizations in this realm of politics, opens the way for pragmatism. The way in which it is interpreted in practice remains to be seen, but for the time being organizations and communities continue to be the formal channels of nomination.

Let us now look at what actually happens in the electoral contest.

Having anything to do with the Indians

In the prologue to Montiel's already cited seminal book on indigenous political organization (1992), Venezuelan scholar and activist Esteban E. Mosonyi stated without a qualm: 'From the very beginning, the militants of the indigenous cause have positioned themselves from centre to radical left within the broad Venezuelan political spectrum, for it is well known that the Right "does not want to have anything to do with the Indians"' (Mosonyi 1992, p. 9). By then, Mosonyi had already been in the orbit of the 'indigenous cause' for over two decades – he was one of the signatories of the 1971 Declaration of Barbados. He knew well the politics surrounding that cause, and had experienced first-hand the demonizing tactics that economic and political elites deployed through the mass media in moments of conflict – when not violently and directly through their paid lackeys. Unsurprisingly, like most sympathisers of the 'indigenous cause', Mosonyi recognized that in right-wing politics there was not much room for negotiating alliances. This helps to explain why, later in the 1990s, most indigenous activists and organizations gravitated towards the *chavista* movement as soon as the latter started to take off: it was a movement emerging precisely as a reaction against those elites and political forces that, more or less disguised within governing political parties and state institutions, had until then managed the political system.

The constituent period certainly showed that within *chavismo* there were factions that did not support demands for indigenous rights either, especially those related to land; but indigenous activists also learnt that those opposing forces could be defeated through alliances with sympathetic ones within that very *chavista* bloc. In parallel, the Consitutent Assembly had confirmed that important sectors of the *anti-chavista* opposition, which harboured the most extreme right-wingers, continued to approach the indigenous rights debate in a way that fitted Mosonyi's characterization: they '[did] not want to have anything to do with the Indians'. While they did not obtain much direct representation in the ANC, they were very vocal and put great effort into mobilizing public opinion against elements that, like indigenous rights, they considered dangerous for their economic interests.

Such was the situation in the late 1990s, but an amazing political transformation has since taken place in the magical state. A decade after the Bolivarian bloc started to gain shares of state power, everyone wants to have something (anything) to do with the Indians – political right-wingers included. An illustrative conversion is that of Henrique Capriles, current governor of Miranda state and (disputed) leader of the opposition bloc.[2] In 1999, he was adamantly opposed to the inclusion of differentiated indigenous rights in the Constitution;[3] in 2012, wearing an indigenous feather crown, he passionately proclaimed, at a climactic moment in a mass election rally in Puerto Ayacucho: 'I will demarcate all indigenous lands' (Angosto-Ferrández 2014b, p. 138).

The analysis of electoral pragmatism help to explain the logic behind Capriles' conversion, and more generally why everyone now wants to have something (anything) to do with the Indians – or rather, with *their* Indians.

Electoral expressions of the national struggle

In Venezuela, voters have been polarized in the face of two options: *chavista* or opposition candidates. Suffice it to recall that, in the last presidential election (April 2013), the candidates of those two blocs received 99.87 per cent of valid votes.[4] Electoral contests for legislative organs had remained relatively less exposed to this polarized scenario until 2008, but primarily because the *anti-chavista* opposition, unlike the *chavista* bloc, proved incapable of sustaining united electoral fronts for very long. The heterogeneous political composition of this opposition has been only glued together – and precariously at that – as a 'bloc against': lacking defined leadership and a common political project, their only galvanizing force has so far been their *anti-chavismo*. Key opposition actors have oscillated between competing electorally with *chavismo* and pursuing extra-institutional adventures to oust the government. For example, an important part of its leadership backed or directly participated in the 2002 coup against Chávez,[5] and then in the oil industry lock-out of 2002-3 which sought to precipitate a government collapse by economic strangulation. Temporarily returning to the electoral contest, the opposition regrouped around the so-called Democratic Coordinator (*Coordinadora Democrática*)[6] for the recall referendum of 2004.[7] A heavy defeat at the ballot box (over 59 per cent of voters backed Chávez) led to another disbandment of their forces and support base. Part of the latter was alienated by an errant leadership that, in what would become one of their central weaknesses in years to come, did not want to accept the results despite their transparency and legitimacy – backed by not only national but also international observers, including those appointed at the request of *Coordinadora Democrática* itself (Raby

2006, pp. 174-5). This disbandment translated into the opposition fiasco in that year's regional elections, where *chavismo* secured 22 out of 23 governorships as well as the vast majority of mayoral appointments.

In the National Assembly elections of 2005, opposition parties withdrew their candidacies only a few days before the vote, in an orchestrated attempt to delegitimize both the legislative body and the government. Unsurprisingly, this decision backfired in political terms: for five years they were left with no direct influence whatsoever in an organ which is not only the most important in legislative terms,[8] but also pivotal in the nomination of senior positions in other public bodies – a statutory role of the assembly. In the 2006 presidential elections, and despite renewed opposition efforts to find a united electoral front, Chávez obtained an extraordinarily clear victory even by his already high standards: 62.84 per cent of the valid votes supported his project, by then already under the banner of socialism of the twenty-first century. In addition to a favourable economic situation in which high oil prices facilitated the recovery from the devastating effects of the 2002-3 oil industry lock-out, the *chavista* bloc benefited from a weakened opposition that had previously opted out of the institutional contest.

It was actually a failed government initiative that resuscitated the electorally moribund opposition at that time. The government's defeat in the 2007 referendum on constitutional reform brought electoral unity back as a central, motivating goal for the opposition. Though a narrow victory, it constituted their first success in a national-level vote since 1998.[9] With that momentum, the opposition regrouped for the 2008 regional elections (after the so-called Agreements of 23 January) and subsequently for the 2010 AN elections, by then forming a coalition around the *Mesa de la*

Unidad Democrática (MUD). This organized return to the electoral contest translated into further polarization of the vote, as well as in a narrowing of the gap between the two blocs in election results.

The electoral contest became tougher. Legislative bodies, and particularly the AN, were indispensable for the government to maintain the production of legislation in line with the socialist transformation of the country, especially after the defeat at the constitutional reform referendum. Conversely, the opposition had experienced the weakening effects of not being involved in institutional state power, which meant a lack of control not only over legislation, but also over nominations for key positions in public bodies. The competition for the indigenous representation seats became fully drawn into this scenario, and indigenous activists participated directly in the shaping of this point in the country's history.

The unity of the opposition, however, has again proved to be fragile, and this might be reflected in forthcoming elections for deliberative bodies. The coalition held for the 2012 and 2013 presidential elections, but its defeat in the latter in particular led to new leadership and renewed organizational crisis. The MUD had collapsed as an effective electoral platform before the December 2012 regional elections – *chavismo* won 20 of the 23 governorships. But after the defeat in the 2013 presidential elections – the second in six months for MUD leader Henrique Capriles – this platform proved incapable of maintaining organic coordination and of reining in its most extreme factors. The latter openly supported destabilization through the so-called '*La Salida*' but, in general, opposition leaders maintained an ambivalent position over that plan and the subsequent *guarimbas* that ended up marking them as open to anti-democratic methods to oust the government.[10] As of 2015, the MUD is in a new and apparently irresolvable crisis. It is difficult to predict the extent to which this united platform might be rebuilt for the next AN elections, due in 2015.[11] The competition for indigenous representation, in any case, will undoubtedly reflect the balance of the struggle between *chavismo* and *anti-chavismo*.

Indigenous electoral participation within the national struggle

The strong and growing intertwining of the electoral indigenous collective action arena and the national struggle between the *chavista* and the opposition blocs is clearly expressed in election results. A simple comparative exercise demonstrates it.

As already noted, holders of the indigenous representation seats are elected by all registered voters within the relevant constituency, under a system of relative majority of valid votes. Consequently the electoral register is exactly the same in the election for those seats (i.e. indigenous representation) and for conventional seats elected through the list-system.[12] Comparing the results of the winners of each of those seats (indigenous and conventional) in a given constituency can therefore tell us about potential correlations. And we find that this correlation has increased extraordinarily, in line with the overall polarization of the electoral arena outlined in the

TABLE 4.2 Regional elections 2004–12: difference between winners of indigenous and non-indigenous seats

Year	Average difference (%)
2004	33
2008	18.1
2012	4.88

Source: Author's own calculations from the data of Consejo Nacional Electoral (CNE).

previous section.[13] Let us start by looking at what has happened at the regional elections.

In 2004, the difference between the winners of the list-vote and the winning indigenous candidates ranged between 14 per cent and 49.5 per cent (with an average of +/− 33 per cent); this was obviously too wide a range to speak of a strong correlation between one and the other. However, it is important to note that, except in Zulia state, elected indigenous candidates were those promoted by the same bloc that won in the list-vote (the *chavistas*). The *chavista* bloc counted on the participation of indigenous actors from the early stages of its formation, years before the opposition started political work on that front. Obviously, this had electoral consequences. In 2004, the opposition bloc won the list-vote in Zulia (with *Un Nuevo Tiempo Contigo*) but, since it was not well enough organized to compete for the indigenous representation, the elected indigenous candidate in that region was the one put forward by CONIVE and backed by the *chavista* bloc. At that stage, indigenous electoral politics still remained relatively marginal within the national struggle, and it is therefore unsurprising that, amid the low turnouts that characterized those elections, some indigenous candidates were elected by less than 10 per cent of registered voters.

In 2008, however, the difference between the list-vote and the winning indigenous candidate decreased abruptly, ranging between 9 per cent and 28.6 per cent (with an average of +/− 18.1 per cent). The difference had been reduced by half. Moreover, if we add to the existing differences the fact that (as Table 4.3 shows) the percentage of invalid votes was substantially higher for indigenous representation seats, we find another indication that the link between party vote and indigenous candidates vote was even more closely related. That is, those who voted for the Bolivarian bloc lists also voted for the indigenous candidate or generated an invalid vote. The transfer of votes to indigenous candidates not backed by one's bloc was minimal and there were signs that the opposition bloc, by then better organized as an electoral front (see previous section and recall the Agreements of 23 January 2008), began to compete effectively for indigenous representation seats. Thus in Zulia, where the candidate backed by Unidos por Venezuela (opposition) won the list-vote, the indigenous candidate put forward by CONIVE and backed by the PSUV was also defeated.

In 2012, the difference narrowed even more dramatically, with an average now of 4.88 per cent. Only in one state (Bolívar) did the difference between the list-vote (or the votes for the elected governor) and the winning indigenous candidate exceed 10 per cent. In states such as Delta Amacuro and Zulia, the difference was below 1 per cent (0.75 per cent and 0.28 per cent respectively), whereas in others such as Amazonas and Apure it was just above 2 per cent (2.03 per cent and 2.40 per cent respectively).

Yet if regional elections let us know about the growing intertwining between the competition for indigenous representation and the national struggle, National Assembly elections provide even stronger evidence (see Table 4.3).

TABLE 4.3 National Assembly elections 2005–10: difference between winners of indigenous and non-indigenous seats

Year	Average difference (%)
2005	21.47
2010	7.1

Source: Author's own calculations from the data of Consejo Nacional Electoral (CNE).

As explained above, the 2005 elections were marked by the orchestrated withdrawal of the opposition parties. In addition to the naturally higher levels of abstention that this generated, we find that within the *chavista* bloc there were signs of increasing discipline in the vote. In half of the states in which an indigenous seat was elected, the difference between this vote and the vote for the conventional seats was less than 10 per cent.

Yet much more revealing is the situation in 2010, when the high stakes at this extremely polarized juncture caused the two blocs to increase their efforts to secure the election of indigenous candidates linked to their blocs. Differences in all states dropped below 10 per cent except in Anzoátegui and Bolívar. For the first time, the opposition bloc defeated *chavistas* in the election of an indigenous candidate to the AN, winning in the Western constituency.

Organizations and communities in elections: the emergence of a fragmented political landscape

A total of 171 indigenous collective actors participated in the elections held in Venezuela between 2004 and 2010.[14] These actors are indigenous organizations and communities, which, as explained in the overview of electoral regulations, the country's laws enable to participate in elections directly (i.e. without the need to constitute themselves as political parties and without any formal involvement of existing parties). If we compare the relative size of the indigenous population (according to 2001 census data)[15] with the relative size of the non-indigenous population, those 171 collective actors in the electoral arena would be the equivalent of there having been 7,371 collective actors (political parties) competing to represent the non-indigenous population. This extraordinary atomization, however, has not received much attention, either inside or outside Venezuela. This is not entirely surprising for a country in which, until recently, 'indigenous politics' had not featured as a prominent constituent part of the national political scene and consequently not many analysts took it seriously. But the fact is that, even among national and foreign experts in indigenous politics, there has not been much said about this electoral phenomenon. This is evidence of how abrupt and transformative the incorporation of indigenous peoples into Venezuelan politics has been – it quickly rendered the tools of traditional analysis obsolete and incapable of explaining the new realities.

This multi-organizationism that came about with political enfranchisement also revealed the (largely unknown) existence of a myriad of 'civil society' organizations working in the sphere of indigenous rights and development – with very limited achievements, it must be said, if one looks at the cumulative impact. And that social landscape had not only been disregarded or ignored by commentators; it came as a surprise for many indigenous activists, too. Here is a telling episode.

In September 2011, I gave some classes at the Indigenous University of Tauca (UIT) in Bolívar state, a unique project of intercultural education in the country.[16] One day we were discussing indigenous participation in elections, and the students' reaction on the issue of multi-organizationism illustrates very well how striking (and unknown) it still is for a majority of people – activists directly involved in indigenous struggles included.

I asked how many indigenous organizations they knew of, and how many they thought had participated in elections since 2004. Among the students were Eñepa, Jiwi, Pemon, Piaroa, Pume, Sanema, Yekuana, Yukpa and Warao. 'Eight', 'ten', they responded, naming some of the organizations with a better established background. 'Many more', I said, telling them that, in addition to those more established organizations, a variety of smaller ones, along with some communities, had also formally entered the electoral contest. I invited them to think of big numbers and asked them for a guess. 'Twelve', 'fifteen', they guessed; 'many more', I replied again. Their wildest guess was twenty.

I then showed them the full list of organizations and communities that had participated in elections over the previous six years (2004 to 2010). Going through the names on the list and counting the numbers they added up to, one of the students exclaimed: 'If there were so many, we [*indígenas*] would be fine!' Incidentally, that young man knows all about indigenous land struggles and their complexities in parts of the country. He is the son of the late Sabino Romero, Yukpa leader and icon of indigenous land struggles who was assassinated on 3 March 2013 – two days before Chávez's death.

Elections to the National Assembly and Latin American Parliament: candidates' relations with the polarized national blocs

Tables 4.4 and 4.5 contain details of the candidates who occupied the leading positions in the AN elections of 2005 and 2010, and whose election results reveal their dependence on (and their participation in) the policies espoused by the national blocs that polarize the national struggle.

From a different perspective, these tables also provide valuable information about the incorporation of indigenous electoral politics into the national arena. Given the timing of parliamentary elections

TABLE 4.4 National Assembly elections 2005

Candidate	Nominating organization/ community	Constituency	Valid votes (%)
José Poyo	CONIVE	ROR	70
José Luis González	FIEB	ROR	7
Gladys Palmares	CI TAWALA	ROR	3
Noelí Pocaterra	CONIVE	ROC	98
Luz Brujes	ASOCOINBO	ROC	1
Nicia Maldonado	FUNDACIDI	RSUR	50
Carlos Pérez	CCPIA, CORPIA, Fundea	RSUR	25
Guillermo Guevara	CONIVE, ORPIA	RSUR	23

TABLE 4.5 National Assembly elections 2010

Candidate	Nominating organization/ community	Constituency	Valid votes (%)
José Luis González	CONIVE	ROR	47.10
Tulio Gudiño	TAWALA, OIR, Cerro e Mono	ROR	37.88
Wilson Espinoza	Evolución	ROR	3.36
José Rafael Chacón	AMANITA	ROR	2.76
Magda Marcano	ASOCINSABAT	ROR	2.66
José Poyo	COINKA	ROR	2.51
Arcadio Montiel	MiaZulia, TAWALA, PARLINVE et al.	ROC	50.18
Noelí Pocaterra	CONIVE, ASOCOINBA	ROC	47.52
Argelio Pérez	FUNDACIDI, CONIVE	RSUR	57.28
José Bigott	TAWALA, PARLINVE	RSUR	23.33

in 2005 (with the aforementioned orchestrated withdrawal of the opposition parties), the percentage of votes obtained by winning candidates in the ROC (Western) and ROR (Eastern) constituencies is unsurprising. The situation in RSUR (Southern), however, was exceptional and deserves explanation. Nicia Maldonado, the head of CONIVE, decided to break ranks in order to participate in the election in the RSUR constituency. Among others, she ran against the CONIVE-backed candidate (Guillermo Guevara, a former member of the Constituent Assembly). Maldonado was formally nominated by the *Fundación para la Capacitación, Integración y Dignificación del Indígena* (FUNDACIDI), an organization of very limited institutional presence; but she counted on the support of the MVR (*Movimiento V República*) of the *chavista* bloc. That enabled her to win the seat, but, significantly, only thanks to the votes obtained in Apure state; in Amazonas, her region of origin, Maldonado lost to Guillermo Guevara.

This revealed lingering divisions within CONIVE, but also the emergence of a new type of indigenous leader whose programme was shaped by the Bolivarian process and who was fully committed to the incorporation of indigenous struggles into the popular struggle at a national level. Maldonado was appointed to be the first Minister of Indigenous Peoples when MINPI was created by Chávez's government in 2007. This alienated part of the traditional leadership, and particularly that of organizations in Amazonas; as we shall see, this contributed to Maldonado's defeat in the 2012 election for the governorship of Amazonas.

In 2010 there was a very different situation at the national level. As explained in the previous section, polarization increased after the opposition organized to compete electorally. With two electoral blocs consolidated around the government (the *Polo Patriótico*) and the opposition (the MUD), and with the added strategic interest in winning (on the side of the former) or blocking (for the latter) qualified majorities in the National Assembly (crucial for organic legislation and appointments in other public bodies), the interest in securing the support of indigenous representation seats increased substantially. The MUD's backing of Arcadio Montiel in the Western constituency (ROC) enabled him to become the first candidate outside the Bolivarian orbit to be elected to one of the indigenous representation seats at the AN. In the ROR constituency, there was for the first time a relatively close contest for the indigenous seat. In RSUR, the Bolivarian bloc won after bringing together the efforts of FUNDACIDI and CONIVE.

It is worth commenting separately on the cases of José Luis González and José Poyo. During the constituent period, these prominent indigenous leaders presented themselves as peripheral to the nascent *chavista* bloc, although subsequently they have both been firmly positioned in its orbit. González, who was an indigenous member of the National Constituent Assembly, subsequently arrived in the National Assembly in 2000 with the support of CONIVE and MVR. In the 2005 AN elections, however, he lost the backing of CONIVE as the candidate for the ROR constituency in favour of José Poyo. González nevertheless opted to run (against Poyo), and he was put forward as a candidate by the FIEB (*Federación Indígena del Estado Bolívar*). Without the support of CONIVE/MVR, González's results fell dramatically (7 per cent of the vote, against Poyo's 70 per cent).

In 2010 the situation turned upside-down. González regained the support of CONIVE and the PSUV and obtained a seat in the Eastern constituency (ROR). José Poyo, now without the backing of CONIVE/PSUV, decided to run with the support of *Comunidades*

Indígenas Kariña (COINKA), a small and relatively dormant regional organization – and obtained only 2.5 per cent of the vote.

The latter nomination generated an exchange of accusations between Poyo and members of CONIVE. The former did not recognize CONIVE's Cumaná Assembly, at which González was elected as the organization's candidate for the election. A public controversy ensued, with CONIVE Executive Secretary Raúl Tempo criticizing José Poyo for dividing the organization and serving anti-revolutionary interests, and the latter criticizing Tempo very much along the same lines.[17] Poyo argued that he would compete against González because 'this is an Indian's business and not a political party's business', suggesting that CONIVE's assembly had been controlled by delegates alienated from grassroots activism, and furthermore that CONIVE did not represent *chavismo* in indigenous communities.[18] However, he continued to position himself within the Bolivarian bloc: 'I am a revolutionary and I have always supported the Bolivarian Government and Comandante Chávez with my work in the National Assembly and the American Indigenous Parliament'. He remarked that he supported 'the Bolviarian process that president Chávez leads and which gives inclusion to the indigenous peoples that for years were marginalized and excluded from all the processes generated in our country and were never taken into account by any other government'.[19] While Poyo has criticized the bureaucracy that delays things such as territorial recognition, he is among those who consider that indigenous struggles need to be fought from within the National Assembly.

Six candidates contested the indigenous seat at the Latin American Parliament (Parlatino) in 2010, each of them backed by a different indigenous organization.

TABLE 4.6 Elections to the Latin American Parliament 2010

Candidate	Organization	Valid votes (%)
Dalia Herminia Yánez	CONIVE	44.18
Bartolomé Pérez	PARLINVE	26.12
Émber Iguarán	TAWALA	15.63

The results were telling of the way in which the *chavista* bloc, unlike the *anti-chavistas*, operates with greater discipline at election time, as a result of its greater organic cohesion. In these elections, despite its increased efforts to create pragmatic links with indigenous organizations and activists, the MUD was unable to mobilize support around a single candidate. The opposition base, lacking clear direction as a result of the lack of leadership and organic cohesion at a national level, divided their vote between Bartolomé Pérez (for PARLINVE) and Émber Iguarán (for TAWALA).

Main organizations and their connections with the polarized blocs

Election results demonstrate that, despite the large number of indigenous communities and organizations that took part, only a few have developed any institutional capacity to play a meaningful role. That capacity is dependent on the synergies they have created with the political blocs that constitute the national struggle. Only three organizations have had a significant presence at national level, participating at least once in all three special AN constituencies and also in the 2010 election to the Parlatino (also of national scope): CONIVE, PARLINVE and TAWALA. Two other organizations have participated in at least one of the special AN constituencies and also in the PL 2010 elections: MOPIVE and Evolución.

In this distribution we can find yet more indications of the way in which the indigenous electoral contest becomes part of the national struggle. In 2005 CONIVE, which is firmly positioned within the *chavista* bloc, was the only organization that put forward candidates in the three special AN constituencies. In 2010, however, both CONIVE and TAWALA took part in all three constituencies – the latter establishing links with (part of) the opposition bloc. In addition, both the Movement of Venezuelan Indigenous Peoples (*Movimiento de los Pueblos Indígenas de Venezuela*, MOPIVE) and the Venezuelan Indigenous Parliament (*Parlamento Indígena Venezolano*, PARLINVE) nominated candidates in two constituencies. The fact that the parties gathered around the MUD had, for the first time, tried to find consensus candidates for the indigenous representation seats is essential to understanding this expansion in the geographical reach of these organizations.

Given the method of election and the polarized competition, the number of organizations or communities that have succeeded in elections is very low. Focusing on the national and regional

TABLE 4.7 Principal organizations in the electoral arena

	National Assembly			Parlatino	Regions[20]
	ROR	ROC	RSUR		
CONIVE	X	X	X	X	7
Evolución	X			X	5
MOPIVE	X	X		X	1
PARLINVE	X	X	X	X	1
TAWALA	X	X	X	X	8

TABLE 4.8 Indigenous organizations that obtained seats in regional and national elections

Organization	Regional 2004	AN 2005	Regional 2008	AN 2010	Parlatino 2010
ACPB	1*				
COIBA			1		
CONIVE	4*	2	2*	1*	1
FIEB	1		1		
FUNDACID			1		
FUNDACIDI		1		1*	
Mia Zulia			1*		
ORPIA	1*				
SOCICOIN/ KA			1		
TAWALA				1*	
UCIW			1		

* Obtained most votes for the winning candidate when backed by several organizations and communities.

spheres, CONIVE – which, despite its internal tensions, has been firmly incorporated in the *chavista* bloc since its inception – is the only organization that has had at least one of its candidates elected in all elections (see Table 4.8).

Different perspectives on the electoral contest

As previously noted, the Venezuelan indigenous population is small in relative terms, and two-thirds live in urban or rural areas – as opposed to those who live in 'traditional' indigenous communities as defined by the INE. The distribution of this population is also quite uneven, and only in a few political-administrative units and electoral constituencies does it reach high proportions. Amazonas state, where over half the population is indigenous (53.9 per cent), is the exception. In Delta Amacuro state, the indigenous presence is also relatively important – around a quarter of the total population (25.3 per cent) – and in Zulia state it is around one-eighth (12.8 per cent). In these states some municipal units have such a high concentration of indigenous population that this significantly influences the type of political alliance that can be made in the entity (cf. Lauer 2005), but these are isolated cases in the national context. With its very small and fragmented sociological base and the lack of organizational resources, indigenous political actors who are more reluctant to get deeply involved with the national-level political blocs are fully aware of their limited options in the current electoral system. In fact, their participation in elections is planned according to those limitations. These indigenous actors face three options:

1. participate in elections as part of an indigenous organization (which implies, as will be shown, alliances with political parties)
2. participate through a political party created by themselves (which also implies alliances with conventional parties)
3. remain outside the electoral contest.

During the 2008 regional elections campaign, I interviewed spokesmen for a variety of indigenous organizations and their responses reflect these three positions:

- Italo Pizarro, ex-president of the FIEB (the principal and oldest indigenous organization in Bolívar state); FIEB took part by nominating candidates in alliance with the PSUV/*chavista* bloc

- Juvencio Gómez, ex-president of the FIEB, former member of the Bolívar state legislative council (CLEB) and then also leader and co-founder of PEMON 08 (*Proyecto Electoral y Movimiento de Origen Nacional del 2008*), an ephemeral political party that included indigeneity as part of its identity; he opted for direct participation
- Arturo Rodríguez, then president of Kuyujani (an organization that represents the Ye'kuana and Sanema peoples); chose not to take part in electoral processes and avoided direct links with political parties.

Italo Pizarro offered the following explanation when asked about the FIEB's participation in elections, and specifically about their nomination of Yaritza Aray (a Kariña, a PSUV militant, and backed by an FIEB assembly after being announced by the PSUV as its indigenous candidate).

> Yaritza Aray had [first] been nominated as a PSUV candidate, under the guidelines of 'the key' of Chávez and all that kind of thing. When our colleague [*compañera*] Yaritza was chosen [by the FIEB's assembly], the decision was influenced by the [PSUV]. It is said that the PSUV is a new political movement, but it has the same behaviour as other previous political party movements, but with another colour and with another name. Despite the fact that there had been a certain antipathy on the part of some indigenous people [before the FIEB's eventual selection of Yaritza Aray], it was taken into account that, as the Constitution provides, indigenous organizations can nominate candidates, and this channel was used, respecting the guidelines that we have as an indigenous organization. However, the PSUV's influence makes itself felt, as Yaritza Aray is also currently the substitute [*suplente*] deputy to Juvencio Gómez, who is also from our organization. We

are concerned that we will see [Yaritza] be closely linked to the [PSUV]. In these circumstances, the indigenous representative is drawn towards the government. That is why he/she does not represent *indígenas* 100 per cent ... As we see it, he/she is the candidate of the PSUV or the government of the day [*gobierno de turno*]. And some – almost the majority of those who have been nominated [this way] at a municipal and regional level – have ended up better off at a particular level than they have benefited indigenous communities.

Here, Pizarro's position was pragmatic but also clearly critical of political processes that, in his view, are effectively co-optation. Others within the FIEB share some of Pizarro's concerns, but do not separate the organization's work from engagement with the current national struggle: they publicly defend the strategic alliance with the Bolivarian bloc.

Indeed, the current president of the FIEB, José Gregorio Cascante, has been openly supportive of the relationship with the PSUV and the *chavista* bloc, actively participating in maintaining it. This involvement, openly declared, explicitly promotes involvement in terms of support for the PSUV and the government: '[the leadership of the FIEB] will continue supporting the revolutionary process led by president Hugo Chávez and all his policies to give protagonistic participation to the *indígenas* who live in Bolívar state', Cascante revealingly declared in May 2011, when announcing the FIEB's involvement in PSUV indigenous political teams created in Bolívar, Amazonas and Delta Amacuro states.[21] In this respect, the organization is currently committed to providing electoral support to the *chavista* bloc, even in contests in which indigenous representatives are not required to stand as candidates – such as in presidential elections. To give a recent example of symbolic value, during the 2012 presidential campaign Cascante accompanied Chávez on the rostrum at the latter's mass meeting in San Félix (Bolívar state). This alignment, however, does not preclude occasional criticism of the government, which is considered part and parcel of the functioning of the *chavista* bloc.

Let us now look at other options taken by indigenous actors. Juvencio Gómez was president of the FIEB until 2004, when he won the indigenous representation seat in the CLEB – supported by the MVR. In 2008 he removed himself from active participation in the *chavista* bloc and helped to found PEMON 08, with the support of which he ran for the nominal seat in District 3 (South) of Bolívar state. Asked about the FIEB's political alliance with the PSUV at that election, he said:

> The indigenous representative is elected by the whole state, not only by the *indígenas*, and these are complications that we have to deal with. If the indigenous representative was only elected by indigenous electors, we would have our own space, but that is not the case. [That is why] alliances are sought with an organization that has wider popularity, such as the PSUV, in order to guarantee votes. That is what the FIEB did in order to have its candidate elected, because the official party then fits it into what they call the '*chuleta*' [card] that the PSUV distributes among its voters, and the indigenous candidate appears to be supported. That is going to guarantee the votes. In these circumstances, we looked to Andrés Velásquez, who is also popular, and that is why PEMON08 nominated him as a candidate, in order to obtain in that way votes for our indigenous candidate, Ricardo Delgado. Other [indigenous] candidates have also been shopping around; for instance, Tulio Gudiño has also approached Andrés Velásquez, and has accompanied him, in order to obtain [votes through

that alliance]. But the indigenous candidate who wants to go [independently] has very little prospect, even if he or she is good. Because ... *chuletas* are used and people, without knowing the candidate, say 'this is the candidate recommended by the PSUV, I am going to vote for him or her', without knowing him or her, without knowing who he or she is. These are the advantages and disadvantages that we have to face.

Asked what had motivated him to found PEMON08, Gómez said:

[Our experience in politics] made us reflect and look for avenues not to stay stuck within our achievements in constitutional terms. There are several forms of public power in Venezuela and, for the time being, what we have achieved constitutionally is participation in Legislative Power ...: that is what is written in the law, in the Constitution ... But then, what happens with the Moral Power, with the Judicial Power, with the Executive Power? As Venezuelan citizens we are not only beneficiaries of the rights of indigenous peoples, but also of citizens' rights, of economic and political rights, etc., which are in the Constitution. Thus, making a new evaluation, reflecting and assessing our participation and looking at the aspiration of indigenous peoples in their participation in different levels of the Legislative Power, we reached the conclusion that it was not enough. It is not enough that we only have one representative in the CLEB, out of the existing 13 seats there. It is the same in *municipios*, with only one councillor out of five or six on the council. Our representation in the Legislative Power cannot provide responses to the needs and demands of the communities when they relate to other powers. We have therefore decided to broaden our participation, trying to reach different levels and other powers, further increasing the number of representativews ... Creating a party, we ... can have our candidates opting for other political spaces. We created PEMON08 and with it we'll be able to register our candidates for the governorship, seats on the legislative council, and we will also do it, when the time comes, in the elections for councillors [and] when National Assembly elections arrive.

PEMON08 was the embodiment of ideas that some indigenous activists had harboured for years in a country in whose political arena they find new channels for achieving a share of institutional state power. Despite the challenges they recognize, this is yet another indication of the empowerment that currently pervades a segment of the population previously peripheral to such power. For instance, at least since 2004, activists from Bolívar state such as Ricardo Delgado (an indigenous Pemon, and former mayor of Gran Sabana *municipio*) had openly advocated that indigenous leaders should try to gain representation on the regional legislative council beyond the seat of differentiated representation that the law guarantees for them (see Appendix). The strategy set out by these activists is based on the fact that, by establishing alliances with non-indigenous actors and targeting certain constituencies, the bargaining strength of the indigenous peoples could become sufficient to influence the appointment of important positions within regional government.[22] The aim here is to gain a share of institutional power too, which, with different goals, remains a driving objective for most political actors, including indigenous ones, in the magical state.

PEMON08's results were very uneven. In Districts 1 and 2 the party came last; but in District 3, where Gómez's native community is located and where there is a significant indigenous population, he came second – a remarkable result for a party created ad hoc. With the exception of the *Unión de Vencedores Electorales* (UVE), an electoral platform linked to the PSUV and which has functioned as a link in the so-called '*morochas*',[23] PEMON08 received the most votes in the district. It must be noted, however, that the indigenous population does not automatically respond to the stimuli of 'descriptive representation'.[24] In 2008, for instance, in Gran Sabana – the *municipio* with a greater number of Pemon indigenous communities and voters – the *criollo* (non-indigenous) Manuel de Jesús Valles (with support from the PSUV, PPT and the Tupamaros) was elected, despite the fact that there was also an indigenous candidate: Cherry Rodríguez (supporting PEMON08 and various parties of the opposition bloc). Valles had already defeated Ricardo Delgado (also Pemon) in 2004.

Though this type of commentary is only indicative, close to the elections I asked the chief and several inhabitants of two indigenous communities in the constituency about their electoral preferences. How they assessed the work of the previous mayor, the Pemon Ricardo Delgado, was based on his actions and omissions in relation to the provision of public services and material support, not his ethnicity. For the indigenous voters in the *municipio*, 'substantive representation' seemed to be more important (that is, representation related to policy and legislation that prioritizes the interests expressed by that group, irrespective of the ethnicity of the representative).

Let us now look at the third option for indigenous collective actors: to remain outside the electoral contest. I asked Arturo Rodríguez if Kuyujani, the organization he coordinated at the time, would take part in the forthcoming election supporting any candidate. He stated:

> We are independent, though we work with governments. Until now, Kuyujani has not involved itself with political parties, because we want to keep our organization independent, as an NGO. Why? Because if Kuyujani did as the Federation [FIEB] does, it would

not be Kuyujani anymore; it would be a political organization. That is why we do not want our organization to fall into that space ...; we want to keep Kuyujani independent, 'indígena'. At regional elections, or for municipal councils or mayoral elections, we participate, most of our leaders participate, but only [by voting]. But we are not directly involved in political parties.

While this position is exceptional in the current landscape of indigenous organizations in the country (remember the exceptional number of such organizations that have taken part in elections), it should be taken into account as part of the range of tactics with which the indigenous population currently engages in national politics. A point worth noting in order to understand indigenous politics in contemporary Venezuela is that, even when the decision is made not to participate actively in the election cycle, the members of these organizations, as Rodríguez's comments made clear, do not consider the sphere irrelevant: voting in Venezuela – unlike in other parts of the world in which citizens have lost all confidence in its effectiveness given the lack of stimulating options – maintains its appeal as a form of active political participation in the orientation of public affairs.

Let us now look at other aspects of the pragmatics of election contests in which there is evidence of the new position that indigenous peoples, and indigeneity as a flexible identity, occupy in Venezuela.

Guaicaipurismo, empty signifiers and the election contest

Guaicaipurismo, which has been a central symbolic source in the discursive constitution of the *chavista* movement (see Chapter 2), has also come to occupy an important position in electoral tactics. The state-led reassessment of the 'indigenous' category, alongside greater political participation and redistributive policies specifically aimed at the indigenous population, have increased the visibility of indigenous identities in the public sphere. Significantly, this situation has found expression in processes of re-ethnification, culminating in the administrative recognition of peoples considered to be 'extinct': the sphere of national censuses provides strong evidence of this phenomenon. However, this positive reassessment of indigenous identities does not imply that in social interaction all actors use them with equal significance or finality. At election time in particular, one can find illustrative differences. 'Indian' and '*indígena*' have become 'floating signifiers' in this scenario. The polarization in the electoral arena and the existence of guaranteed indigenous representation and unsatisfied indigenous demands have stimulated a contest around these labels. Both political blocs claim to represent indigenous interests and develop discursive tactics to do so.

Let us see how this was expressed. First, here is Nicolás Maduro in the 2013 presidential election campaign during a visit to Amazonas state: 'I am a son of the people, I feel like an Indian of this people. In my blood there is Indian blood, my skin is Indian skin, my heart is the heart of Guaicaipuro and my dreams are the dreams of Chávez, the great cacique of the people'.[25] Maduro also made reference to Capriles' opposition to indigenous rights during the constituent period: '*Caprichito* called for people to vote against this constitution [CRBV] because he said that *indígenas* do not have rights to the land'.[26] He continued: 'I can assure you that if [the opposition] came to government again, they would come to take the land away from indigenous peoples'. In isolation, this is what some analysts disdainfully consider to be 'rhetoric'. In relation to other discursive phenomena identifiable in the electoral arena, however, it is a salient part of the current political competition in Venezuela. Let us see.

Remember the late Hugo Chávez in the 2012 presidential campaign: 'I am half-Indian; for I do really have Indian blood, and black blood, I am a mixture of the Indians of the savannah and the blacks who came from Africa to mix with us in this land'. And now let us relate both statements to this further comment by Chávez in thew same campaign: 'The cynicism of the little bourgeois knows no limits; now he wants to be an Indian'.

The 'little bourgeois' to whom Chávez was referring was the opposition leader, Henrique Capriles, who in that same campaign, addressing the people of Amazonas state as a presidential candidate and wearing an indigenous feather crown, had promised: 'I will demarcate all indigenous lands'.[27] Why would Chávez pay attention to that 'rhetoric', and why would he say that 'not even I, a half-Indian, dare to wear that sacred crown of the indigenous chiefs'?[28] Basically, because Capriles was giving a sign that 'indigeneity' had reached a point where it could be lost as a central signifier of his political movement.

These isolated quotes can thus be seen as expressions of the political logic that underlines the electoral contest. Both Hugo Chávez and Henrique Capriles competed for the legitimate possession of the 'indigenous crown' and the signifiers that can help to maintain or incorporate indigenous demands into the 'chain of equivalences' of their political movements. When Maduro succeeded Chávez at the head of the *chavista* bloc, he did not forget to 'Indianize' his identity as part of his electoral profile and to help maintain what has been one of the key elements of the overall identity of the *chavista* bloc. While some people disdain this type of tactic as futile rhetoric, politicians in Venezuela (and voters, I would add) certainly take them seriously.

Conclusion

The electoral arena has played a crucial and clear role in the revolutionary cycle: originally (1998), it stimulated the constitution of a 'people' as a new collective subject, gave it access to state power, and thus made political revolution possible. Subsequently, it has been the key to maintaining shares of state power and to the design and implementation of political and economic policy. Beyond this basic but indispensable value of elections per se, the electoral arena in general in Venezuela has been a strong focus of mobilization and convergence of political forces – including indigenous ones. It should be underlined that 19 different elections have taken place in the country since Hugo Chávez came to power in December 1998. From 2004 onwards, there has been on average at least one national vote every year, some of them preceded by primary elections in which supporters of the political blocs select their candidates. Indigenous candidates and many organizations have been actively involved in these elections, even when the polls were not electing indigenous representatives. This participation has been a source of continuing mobilization of support bases – particularly for the *chavista* bloc, which from the very beginning invested heavily in the maintenance of electoral fronts as both a guarantee of success and a mechanism for activating support.

Constitutional rights immediately identified the electoral arena as an avenue through which effective participation in national politics – one of the seminal demands of indigenous activism throughout the twentieth century – could occur. And indigenous actors have indeed made use of it. This form of mass political participation required rapid changes for indigenous activism in general, which in its institutional form was previously dependent on episodic and reactive mobilization and on fragile and divided organizations. The study of this new avenue of political participation has also demanded change in the way scholars and analysts discuss 'indigenous rights' and its politics. This latter adjustment has been slow and hesitant; most of the discussions among analysts in the areas of anthropology, sociology and political science completely overlooked this phenomenon, as if this new avenue of political participation, which has so strongly influenced political dynamics within the country's indigenous population, did not exist – or as if, now that indigenous actors do take part directly in electoral politics, they do not fit the heroic model of the 'hyperreal Indian' (Ramos 1994), always engaged in apparently apolitical and cultural demands and always a natural enemy of the state. From those perspectives, the electoral arena seems to be a secondary, unnatural, non-indigenous route for indigenous collective action. When (if at all) looking at the mass of indigenous activists and voters that do participate in electoral politics, those who join in the cult of the hyperreal Indian seem to hold the master key to explaining the phenomenon: co-option. With this token, in addition to presenting institutional state politics as a field of lobotomy that necessarily brainwashes those who approach it, we find a negation of politics – and, more particularly, a negation of the Indian as a political subject.

Yet Indians have once again demonstrated that, rather than being hyperreal, they have flesh, bones and brains. That amounts to being a political subject, and to making political bets as such. In this new demonstration of that fact, and in the Venezuelan context, many indigenous actors have decided to work actively and continuously on a political process in which they see advancement for their struggle. This explains why many indigenous activists and organizations have gravitated towards the *chavista* movement and their current involvement in its internal dynamics, which include internal conflicts as well as confrontation with a historically constituted opposition – represented by the *anti-chavista* bloc. As we have seen in this chapter, this finds expression in the electoral arena, in which there is not only a polarized contest between two blocs, but also differences and tensions within them – including tensions within indigenous ranks.

What new political rights brought to the surface was the sheer size of a silent and previously latent phenomenon. By enabling indigenous organizations and communities to register as electoral actors, we have been able to witness, on the one hand, a range of priorities and a strong desire to take part in elections – in other words, to obtain institutional power in order to pursue one's political goals. On the other hand, we saw the spectre of a fragmented political base, as well as the ghostly effects of the type of civic participation promoted in the heyday of neoliberalism and 'civil society' activism: dozens of organizations, about most of which no one knew or knows anything at all, were functioning in Venezuela – with similarly ghostly, but quite unnoticeable, results. Their origin, activities and sources of funding would be an interesting topic for research in itself, although one of titanic proportions – even in these days of digitalization, for most of these organizations one cannot find a single trace on databases, in published scholarly research, or in national and regional newspapers in the country. In any event, they become proof of the fact that, given the opportunity, the indigenous population will express politically something that characterizes it socially: diversity of conditions and interests.

One solution that is sometimes suggested in order to grant 'autonomy' to the indigenous population in the electoral arena is to make the election of their representatives directly dependent on a special electoral register made up only of the indigenous population in the respective constituency. In Venezuela, this has occasionally been proposed, not only by indigenous organizations but also by political parties such as PODEMOS and PPT. When the LOPE was being debated, for instance, members of the latter party proposed the creation of an Indigenous Electoral Register for the indigenous population in elections for their own representatives.[29] Even leaving aside other important considerations often debated in other parts of the world – Would such a legislator only legislate on matters that only affect the indigenous population? What are these? What happens to the non-indigenous population affected by those decisions? – that type of decision would not remove difficulties and pragmatism in the electoral arena. On the one hand, there would be the problem of setting boundaries for who was and who was not 'indigenous' which, as censuses show, is a far from straightforward matter. Dealing with these political difficulties would be transferred to new institutionalized ('indigenous') spheres of power, and this is a responsibility that some indigenous actors are indeed willing to take on. But of course the imbalances of power between stronger and weaker organizations and leadership figures, for instance, would not disappear, nor would the quite different interests of indigenous peoples and communities that partly stem from their inclusion in the structures of nationality and capitalism that I outlined in the Introduction. Needless to say, the interest of non-indigenous parties and the ever-present economic powers in influencing those indigenous spheres in various ways will remain a constant.

To sum up, the picture is complex, but it has not paralyzed indigenous actors. Whatever their shortcomings, and despite clearly different agendas, many of them have had a hand in trying to make the most of this scenario in which access to shares of state power to define social conditions is pivotal for their goals. That is precisely what political subjects do.

FIVE

The state-supporting and state-sponsored indigenous movement

In Venezuela there is a state-supporting and state-sponsored indigenous movement. Behind these labels there is a form of collective action that has been primarily channelled by and in support of the Bolivarian state. There are strong synergies between this stream of collective action and that activated in the electoral arena by the *chavista* bloc, within which both are actively incorporated. This state-supporting movement, which has been pivotal in the articulation of the so-called New Geometry of Power, prioritizes direct political participation in state politics and the consolidation of access to socioeconomic rights ahead of self-determination rights.

As a general form of collective action, it exemplifies the possibilities for synergic cooperation between social movements and state organs when there are shared goals; as a particular form of indigenous collective action, it evinces the existence of a variety of goals among the indigenous population. This movement, which is closely intertwined with branches of the state's executive power, has clashed with some indigenous activists and organizations that prioritize other political goals and pursue them through other forms of collective action. The way in which government policies have facilitated socioeconomic and political enfranchisement partly explains why, despite these differences, the state-sponsored and state-supporting movement has received mass support from the indigenous population: it facilitates the delivery of central indigenous demands. The participatory mechanisms involved in the government policies that delivered socioeconomic enfranchisement facilitated the mobilization of supporters of this movement, and in turn this mobilization partly overlaps with the stream of collective action that, as part of the *chavista* bloc, is deployed through the electoral arena.

Before moving to the specific analysis of the actions underlining this form of collective action, let me clarify the grounds on which the concepts of 'state-sponsored' and 'state-supporting' social movements operate. Given widespread preconceptions about what constitutes a 'social movement' and what such collective action pursues, this initial discussion may be very timely. Among those preconceptions is the idea that social movements spring and recruit from 'civil society', and also that they deploy their political activity contentiously and outside institutionalized state structures – and normally against them. As demonstrated in Venezuela, this is far from being necessarily the case.

Participants or clients

There is a curious convergence of criticism from the Right and some sectors of the Left in identifying indigenous supporters of the government as co-opted, passive or manipulated actors who, rather than consciously participating in a political process in which they see positive transformations, have been tamed or 'bought out for a bag of food', as one can hear from some radical right-wingers and some advocates of certain conceptions of indigenous self-determination alike. Authors who otherwise recognize positive changes in relations between the state and indigenous peoples criticize 'neo-paternalist' practices when referring to government social programmes (e.g.

Mosonyi 2009, p. 169). I argue that this positioning overrides and ignores the fact that indigenous actors are consciously involved in the implementation of government programmes, and also that it is crucial to note that, in addition to welfare projects, a variety of programmes have been funding productive and infrastructural projects too – in response to demands advanced by the indigenous population for decades.

Criticism that policy design and implementation generates clientelist relations among indigenous people does not explain the issue. Focusing on governmental programmes with broad popular support in other policy areas, researchers have noted that such support is not merely a product of client–patron relations. In the field of government-promoted community and public media, for instance, it has been shown that the actual interactions that develop between producers and government representatives are complex, with adjustments taking place on both sides (Schiller 2011). Similarly, it has been argued that indigenous communities in Venezuela use community media as a platform to renegotiate their position vis-à-vis other actors in society, including state agents (Lehman 2014). Commenting on popular participation dynamics among *barrio* (shantytown) women in Caracas, research has identified some vertical attitudes in state officials, but as only a part of broader dynamics in an ongoing political process in which women increase their negotiating power (Fernandes 2013). These studies certainly argue against simplistic depictions of top-down flows in government programmes. In this study, I demonstrate that it is simply wrong to portray the indigenous population that supports and has been actively involved in government programmes as subordinated 'clients'. Different dynamics in the relations between government and non-government actors arise, of course, and indeed some clientelistic networks develop, but it is about time that indigenous participation in those programmes start to be also seen in terms of involvement in political life and of the agency of actors shaping their own enfranchisement – which is what, indeed, many participants say themselves, in public and in private.

Indigenous movements in Venezuela: some clarifications

I have already pointed out why indigenous collective action before 1999 can be best characterized in two types: one channelled through (weak) indigenous organizations which were always to some degree involved, as the subordinate party, with political parties; and the other channelled through episodic and reactive mobilizations in the face of specific threats such as land invasion. Both types relied on a variety of networks of support and occasionally undertook contentious action, but analyzing them as 'social movements' could be misleading – if we want to use the concept with precision to describe a particular type of collective action, and not just any type of such action.

At present, similar conceptual (and political) challenges arise through attempts to understand indigenous collective action. Recent work on the Venezuelan case is being built upon the 'social movement' concept in ways that require clarification. For instance, this would be the case in analyses of the emergence of new educational institutions for indigenous peoples. These institutions have facilitated the formation of indigenous professionals and technicians, broadening participation and strengthening the democratic arena (Mato 2010). Precisely because these are positive changes, it is important to understand how they have come to be, and this is where questions about the use of the term 'social movement' arise. Some analyses end up assimilating any type of collective action, including that which takes place through regular institutional channels and even lobbying, to social movement action. This results in puzzling ambiguities.

Tertiary and technical education for indigenous peoples in Venezuela, for instance, depends on legislation that already favours it and has been advanced mainly through institutional channels relying on the work of experts, different forms of lobbying and occasional issue-related campaigns. This does not exclude the active participation of indigenous activists, of course, but many of them are actually working within state structures such as the national and regional legislative assemblies and ministries such as MINPI.

From another perspective, advocates of the so-called 'political opportunities structure' (POS) approach have resorted to the 'social movement' concept in ways that raise important questions. Used to explain the transition from 'indigenous movements' to electoral politics, the POS approach 'emphasizes the constraints on and incentives for collective action that the state and political system present to social movement mobilization' (Van Cott 2005, p. 40). Van Cott identified variables that encouraged indigenous social movements (or a part of them) to enter the electoral arena in Latin American countries, such as factions within ruling elites, wider access to institutional politics for new actors, the degree of the state's use of repression, and the influence of international actors and structures (such as supranational organizations). With these theoretical points of reference, comparative works attempted to explain the appearance of 'indigenous parties' in Venezuela (Martí i Puig 2006; Van Cott 2002, 2003b), presenting CONIVE as one such party. Yet this is inaccurate and misleading in two crucial ways, as became apparent in the discussion of electoral politics I have already undertaken: first because CONIVE, despite its participation in elections, remains a 'civil society' organization; and second because most members of CONIVE, and certainly its leadership, are in fact members of the PSUV. By overlooking these facts, studies of indigenous collective action have not understood the relationships that over the past 16 years have arisen between indigenous organizations (including CONIVE), Bolivarian political parties and state organs. The electoral participation of indigenous candidates supported by the PSUV and the *Gran Polo Patriótico* is related to the state-sponsored and state-supporting indigenous movement that has developed in synergy with the *chavista* movement. But let us tackle yet another theoretical-ideological issue that has complicated an adequate understanding (and the recognition) of this type of collective action. This relates to the widespread understanding of 'political society' and 'civil society' as ontologically separate entities; and, furthermore, it relates to a pre-established moral judgement passed on the inherent virtues contained in these supposedly separate entities.

Social movements, state and society

'Civil society' – as opposed to the state as the 'political society' – is mostly considered to be the sphere from which social movements emerge, recruit and operate. Yet the very definition of 'civil society' is inextricably linked to ideological preconceptions that affect the demarcation of its boundaries and opinions about its role and potential. One widespread notion of civil society presents it as constituted by secondary associations that come between primary ones (family and friendship) and the state. But even within this apparently basic definition there is substantial divergence. Some perspectives contend that this realm of association cannot (or ought not to) encompass 'the market' and economic agents such as corporations, while others hold that corporations and markets are essential to the constitution of a civil society (Edelman 2005, pp. 30–1). Both of those apparently opposed views are nevertheless pervaded by the assumption that civil society constitutes 'an arena of (at least potential) freedom outside the state, a space for autonomy, voluntary association and plurality or even conflict', a distinction that, not coincidentally, gained new momentum following the collapse of the Berlin Wall (Wood 1990, p. 63). That assumption is grounded on a dichotomous distinction between 'civil society' and 'state' that identifies the latter with coercion and the former with freedom and/or voluntary action.

Other approaches to the understanding of civil society present its intermediary capacities as a means to authoritarian ends. This view, popularized by certain interpretations of Foucault's work, also projects the idea that the distinction between political and civil society is artificial and impossible: the state's governmental might would shape the population through a myriad of ways, among them through civil society organizations. Against this background, it is not surprising that social movements (associated with 'civil society') and states (identified with the 'political society') are considered antagonistic.

It is, of course, the case that other theorists associate the state with the capacity 'to organize, recuperate, even produce social forces' (Hardt 1995, p. 31). Parts of this approach are closer to alternative notions of civil society such as those articulated by Gramsci. Gramsci refocused the analysis of class power as widely pervading socio-cultural practices – as opposed to presenting it as concentrated on a single visible point. His understanding of civil society was not supported by the clear-cut dichotomy discussed above, although the recognition of a 'civil' and a 'political' society is identifiable in some of his writing. Gramsci's distinction was underlined by the belief that 'civil society' could re-absorb the power that in capitalist societies is coercively situated in the state, responding to class interests; if that were to be achieved, the power previously appropriated by the state would be made part of a democratizing, emancipatory civil society hegemony (Cox 1999; Hardt 1995, pp. 30–1).

A substantial part of indigenous collective action in contemporary Venezuela demonstrates that there can be state-sponsored and state-supporting movements, in this case one that takes part in a process of socialist-leaning state reconstruction within a democratic electoral framework. There are other forms of collective action which diverge from that movement but, as I have been arguing from the beginning of this book, this is the expression of diverging interests within the indigenous population – and not, as is sometimes suggested, the fact that the political activity of the state-supporting movement is 'un-indigenous', not fitting the hyperreal model of the indigenous subject. We will come back to this discussion later. Let us now continue with the analysis of the state-supporting and state-sponsored indigenous movement, for which it is crucial to examine the origin and work of MINPI.

The creation of MINPI

After Chávez's landslide victory in the 2006 presidential elections, the government underwent an important ministerial reorganization in response to a new political strategy aiming to consolidate political revolution and socioeconomic change. The socialism of the twenty-first century had already become the explicit goal of Chávez's government, and had been widely supported at the ballot box. The 'five engines of the revolution' were launched to implement this project and Chávez decided to promote the creation of a united party to become the backbone of the Bolivarian movement. Ministries, which now incorporated 'Ministry of Popular Power' (*Ministerio del Poder Popular*) in their names, included for the first time in the country's history one specifically dedicated to indigenous peoples: MINPI, created in 2007.

The creation of this ministry marked a turning point in relations between the state and indigenous peoples. State bureaucracies had previously languished in a pool of unfocused efforts and resources, often without effective capacity for the implementation of policy. In parallel, given the absence of other channels of mass collective indigenous representation and mobilization, indigenous organizations, while weak, had played a legitimating role in the mediation between government, political parties and indigenous peoples. As occasional spokesmen for state policies through their links with political parties, some regional organizations had *de facto* attained a status that, while marginal, brought them closer to the state sphere. In practice, this had of course always hampered their goal to be independent civil society organizations, but in turn it gave them a degree of political relevance that they were never able to achieve through their actual mobilizing capacities or organizational strength.

MINPI emerged as an impetuous state agency to cover the function of state/indigenous peoples' mediation. It is linked to the executive power, both central to the constitutional system sanctioned in the CRBV and a political pillar for a *chavista* movement that grew out of a very fragmented and initially disorganized social base (Fuentes 2013, pp. 52-3). The government thus created its own organ for the expression and implementation of policy for indigenous peoples, and it was a powerful and clearly oriented one.

In administrative terms, MINPI occupied an all-embracing central position among the state agencies that, under different names and attached to different ministries, had addressed indigenous affairs in Venezuela since 1947. Moreover, the ministry's regionalized structure introduced executive branches of government in precisely the areas where indigenous organizations had previously been (or attempted to be) the proponents of indigenous representation.[1] The creation of MINPI thus reduced the (ineffective) role of the indigenous organizations as necessary political intermediaries. Prior to 1999, they had never been prominent political actors, and after that date those that gained momentum did so by consolidating their synergies with other political actors, and particularly with the nascent *chavista* bloc.

The emergence of this body required important bureaucratic changes that occasionally highlighted conflicts between different fronts of indigenous political activism. MINPI appeared after the LOPCI (2005) had sanctioned the creation of a new state agency to handle indigenous affairs (LOPCI Article 142): the *Instituto Nacional de Pueblos Indígenas* (INPI) (National Institute of Indigenous Peoples). The INPI was designed to be a decentralized, autonomous entity for the execution of indigenous policy, and the law established that it would be ascribed to 'the ministry with competence in indigenous matters, on which it will be dependent in budgetary terms' (Article 143). Before the creation of MINPI in 2007, the INPI was an agency of the Ministry of Education.

In political terms, MINPI operates with a practical focus on three interrelated fronts, all of them in relation to the new government strategy: (1) the promotion of the New Geometry of Power in indigenous communities; (2) the facilitation of redistributive policy and productive development for indigenous communities; and (3) the political mobilization of indigenous supporters of the government and the socialism of the twenty-first century project.

MINPI and the New Geometry of Power (NGP)

MINPI prioritizes the creation of indigenous communal councils and communes at the expense of the ideals of strong autonomous territorialization envisaged by the 1999 Constitution. The promotion of the NGP, which in reference to the creation of indigenous territorial units implies a reorientation of the constitutional precepts, occupies a central position in MINPI's goals. From its inception, the ministry placed great emphasis on the fact that one of its fundamental tasks was the promotion of indigenous communal councils. In fact, minister Nicia Maldonado declared on several occasions that the creations of communes was an alternative route to the demarcation of indigenous lands. Immediately after its creation, Maldonado made clear that the promotion of the 'Explosion of Popular Power' (the fifth of the so-called revolutionary engines of Chávez's government) was a priority. In her early days in office, when confirming the appointment of deputy ministers, Maldonado made clear that they would have direct responsibility for the formation of communal councils.[2] The ministry's first Annual Report (*Memoria y Cuenta* 2007) presented to the National Assembly by Maldonado, contained as 'strategic objective number 1': 'To accelerate the creation of the new institutional structure of the State'. The NGP plays an indispensable role in that structure, of course. 'Strategic objective number 5' further clarified the approach: 'To accelerate the advancement in the construction of the new democratic model of popular participation'. The ministry pursued this goal through: (1) the formation of indigenous communal councils; (2) financing socio-productive communal projects; (3) the approval of strategic projects in the consultations promoted by indigenous communities; and (4) the constitution of the 'Cacique Guaicaipuro' Federation of Revolutionary Indigenous Communal Councils.[3] In the space of a year, the ministry had helped to create 1,159 indigenous communal councils (out of a total of 3,473 communities that the ministry had indentified in its census). In fact, since then many indigenous communities have enthusiastically joined in the process, forming communal councils and some communes which become centres of organization and administration of state resources – avenues for the self-managed pursuit of their enfranchisement.

The indigenous political-territorial units promoted by the NGP are inextricably linked to the original idea of fostering national productivity. Among MINPI's stated competences is 'fostering and coordinating the inclusive, protagonistic and jointly-responsible participation of indigenous peoples in the development model of the country'.

The investment and transfer of public resources towards the indigenous population is another priority for MINPI, which is guided by the productive development objective. In the run-up to Indigenous Resistance Day (12 October) in 2009, Maldonado noted the flow of economic resources to indigenous communities for their development (which by then had reportedly reached US$ 200 million) as one of the most outstanding achievements of the Bolivarian revolution in the previous ten years.[4] It should be noted that at present the majority of public financing to community projects is made through communal councils, consistent with the NGP. Since its creation, MINPI has listed an important portion of its expenditure under the concept of 'financing of indigenous communal councils'.

The historical pursuit that this project continues is the inclusion of the indigenous population in national productivity, in parallel with promoting their participation in public affairs – including at the national level. This vision constitutes an empowering, participatory development of the previous, left-leaning, indigenism advocated by Acosta Saignes in the 1940s. That notion was still proposed in the 1970s by the OCAI (Clarac 2002, p. 22), but the type of socioeconomic development promoted then is not like the socialist-leaning Bolivarian model. The key difference is that the latter is driven by a national popular movement such as *chavismo* in which indigenous activists have established effective alliances with other political forces – a strategy previously drawn up, though never achieved, by left-wing activists and proponents of the so-called 'indigenism of liberation' in the 1970s and 1980s.

Another of the guiding institutional objectives of MINPI is 'to consolidate a national system of social strategic participation for indigenous peoples in accord with the National Plan of Development'. (This was the Simón Bolívar National Project, also known as the First Socialist Plan (2007–2013) for Economic and Social Development of the Nation.)[5]

In support of the NGP, widespread identifications with socialism have been creatively cultivated and adopted by supporters of the state-supporting movement, in tune with the intensified broader association of *guaicaipusrismo* with socialism since 2005. From its inception, MINPI consistently presented this government project, and in particular the creation of communal councils and communes, as an expression and tangible example of indigeneity. For instance, speaking about the NGP and the formation of communal councils in indigenous communities during an interview on the VTV programme *Contragolpe* on 15 October 2007, Maldonado remarked that communal councils were 'the translation of indigenous organization' and that, when ministry officials had presented the proposal, in many indigenous communities people had commented: 'That is our organization'.

Characterizing this indigenous movement and the positioning of its members

Headed by indigenous activists (Nicia Maldonado until 2012, and Aloha Núñez since), MINPI illustrated the leading role that Bolivarianism had brought to indigenous peoples. The appointment of Maldonado also showed that to run the ministry the government relied on indigenous activists closely involved in the political dynamics of the *chavista* movement. This exacerbated differences with certain sectors of more traditional indigenous leadership in indigenous organizations. In fact, Maldonado confronted part of that leadership during the 2005 National Assembly elections, leading sectors of indigenous activism whose political strategy positioned them as an active part of the *chavista* movement for the advancement of indigenous interests. The extent to which the government depended on these sectors and appreciated Maldonando's work was illustrated by the fact that she remained MINPI's minister for five years, an extraordinary length of time in Bolivarian governments that have been characterized by relatively short and rotational ministerial terms.

The followers of the strategy of which Maldonado has been an important champion constitute the core support base of the state-sponsored and state-supporting indigenous movement. The structure of the ministry, which has eight deputy ministries, has brought in a large number of activists who identify with the socialism of the twenty-first century project and the way in which it approaches the integration of indigenous population into nationhood. Many of those recruits entered politics after 1999 and, besides being shaped by the polarized political scenario, have experienced the effects of the enfranchisement that the Bolivarian revolution has facilitated. Recruits whose political engagement predates this enfranchisement share with their companions a common basic position: the new avenues for participation in state structures, whatever their faults, have delivered more results than the unfulfilled expectations placed on autonomous 'civil society' organizations.

Minister Maldonado was upfront in her characterization of the ministry's priority goals, which are inscribed in the notions of empowerment of the indigenous population and in the inclusion of this population in the processes of national development and socialist change. From the outset, she had no qualms about her alignment with the government strategy of political incorporation and socioeconomic enfranchisement of the popular classes. This type of positioning was not merely opportunistic, but also part of an elaborate conceptualization of political participation:

> I am in favour of becoming more flexible in order to obtain
> better results. I respect my teachers very much, the leaders who
> represented us and created our political space. Now we move from
> representation to participation: we *indígenas* no longer need only
> a few to act in our name; we need to participate massively and
> directly in running the country through communal councils.[6]

When Maldonado stepped down from the ministry after being chosen as a candidate for the Amazonas state governorship in the 2012 regional elections, she stuck to her convictions: she publicized a summary of activity making clear that she had worked for the execution of 'Indigenous Public Policy', aiming to include indigenous peoples and communities in 'socio-political, economic and cultural terms'.[7] The achievements that she highlighted ranged from vaccinations, communal organization, housing and access to public education about land titling – the latter was certainly not presented as the top priority.

Maldonado's views are not exceptional in relation to what *indígenas* goals are for supporters of this indigenous movement and what the route to achieving them is. The sense of enfranchisement that indigenous activists participating in state structures often express is well illustrated by declarations such as this from MINPI's deputy minister for Valleys, Savannahs and Tepuys, Raúl Rodríguez: 'We believe in the participatory and protagonistic democracy that our *comandante* Hugo Chávez promoted. He always fought for the rights of indigenous communities and for their incorporation into government activity'.[8] In another illustration, asked to define Indo-American socialism, María Cauicuto, then acting deputy minister in the Delta, Mountain, Coast and Mangroves region, explained that it encompasses 'the construction of the new Indian, of the new Indian thought, where we the *indígenas* of this period and of this era are going to write our own history'. This encapsulates the sense of empowerment and incorporation into national life that is part and parcel of the understanding of indigeneity among indigenous actors that support and participate in this indigenous movement.

Political mobilization

MINPI currently channels a mass incorporation of the indigenous population into government activity. But the ministry's operations and the programme of activities it implements also activate a form of collective action that, far from being enclosed in the realm of bureaucracy, can be identified as social movement activity. It includes political rallies and workshops run partly outside institutional channels for political participation.

Since its creation, in addition to participating in the implementation of policy, MINPI has organized and sponsored various types of political activity in which indigenous activists and organizations gather in collaboration with, and often with the leadership of, MINPI officials and/or members of the PSUV such as indigenous MPs. These activities often mobilize hundreds and even thousands of people in demonstrations against imperialism and capitalism, and/or in favour of forms of socialism.[9]

Characteristic elements of social movements are present in the ministry's activities. They reveal the existence of working networks among individual and collective indigenous actors from spheres such as political parties, the state bureaucracy, communal councils and civil organizations. At some events, such as those organized by the ministry to commemorate the International Day of Indigenous Peoples, international activists have also been present, from countries such as Bolivia, Ecuador, Colombia and Brazil. The activities of this movement thus connect it with actors and political struggles in other parts of the continent as well. To give one example, at the Seventh Social Summit for Latin American and Caribbean Unity (*VII Cumbre Social por la Unión Latinoamericana y Caribeña*), held in Ciudad Bolívar on 26–27 September 2008, there were recurrent chants against the separatist referendum that was being proposed by the so-called '*medialuna*' elites in Bolivia. Throughout the event, several speeches from participants focused on reiterating support for Evo Morales's government, and banners carried legends such as 'With Evo and Chávez towards Indo-American socialism'. The same event included workshops for the discussion of topics such as 'ALBA: the new platform for the construction of Indo-American socialism' and 'Indigenous autonomy before the separatism of regions'. Among the facilitators of these workshops were members of MINPI and the FIEB, and indigenous deputies such as José Poyo, representing the PSUV.

Generative tensions

Participation in the state-sponsored and state-supporting movement does not preclude criticism of the government. These political differences and demands tend to be channelled institutionally, but are also sometimes presented through contentious and occasionally extra-institutional activity.

Examples of the ways in which participants in this movement channel complaints and demands through institutions are to be found in meetings between organizations' representatives and government officials. For instance, at one such meeting held at the the National Assembly's Permanent Commission of Indigenous Peoples, representatives of organizations from Zulia (ORPIZ), Delta Amacuro (UCIW), Monagas and Bolívar (FIEB) met with the then vice-president of PSUV for the southern region, Yelitza Santaella, José Luis González (a National Assembly indigenous representative), and Yaritza Aray (CLEB indigenous representative), among others. The former complained about the inefficient implementation of some projects carried out by MINPI, such as unfinished work in the areas of health and housing.

In another example, Noelí Pocaterra, who has been strongly linked to the *chavista* bloc from its inception and has occupied various institutional positions in state organs including an indigenous representation seat in the National Assembly, nonetheless publicly recognizes that in many respects legislation does not translate rapidly into tangible form. Discussing the Law of Indigenous Languages in an interview two years after its 2008 approval, Pocaterra acknowledged its limited practical reach. Referring to the law's stipulation that indigenous representatives holding public office should be bilingual (knowing both their own indigenous language and Spanish), she complained that the law had not been implemented and also that some NA members did not even support such regulation. In 2010 she also criticized the fact that the National Institute of Indigenous Languages, required by law as an addition to the Ministry of Education, had not yet been created. This type of complaint from members of the state-supporting movement is the source of creative tensions within the *chavista* movement that are often used to reorient government policy. It is significant, for instance, that following the complaints voiced by Pocaterra, the Institute of Indigenous Languages was finally inaugurated in 2014.

Social movements in relation to the current expression of popular power in Venezuela

The activity of this state-supporting and state-sponsored movement is best understood against the background of the government's general approach to relations between the state and social movements. From 1999 onwards, Chávez's governments, and Bolivarian actors in general, emphasized the importance of community organization and participatory democracy, but that principle has undergone several theoretical and practical adjustments. Initially, the concept of 'civil society organization' (as distinct from 'political society') was explicitly used as a reference point for those adjustments. When, around 2005, the government orientation shifted towards a socialist-leaning model, there were noticeable changes in government praxis. The concept of 'civil society' vanished from governmental guidelines, as the six-year national development plans clearly illustrate. The Economic and Social National Development Plan 2001–2007 appealed emphatically to the important role to be played by 'organized civil society' in the national development project, and explicitly mentioned 'civil society' eight times. Yet in its successor, the Simón Bolívar National Project, the concept of 'civil society' completely disappeared from sight. By then, the praxis of 'popular power' and 'communal power' was emerging as the source of new legitimacies to reorganize and amalgamate relations between 'political society' and 'civil society'. This political shift came along with the launch of the aforementioned new 'five engines of the revolution' in 2007, which included communal power and the promotion of communal councils and communes as areas for the construction of that power.

There are other significant expressions of this phenomenon. With the Constituent Assembly, when CONIVE was sanctioned as an institutional interlocutor at the national level, state organs considered the strengthening of 'civil society' organizations a government task. In 2005, when the LOPCI was passed, this was still the case. That law created the INPI for the coordination and execution of public policies addressing indigenous peoples and communities (Article 145). The competences given to the INPI established that, for the development of public policies it drew up, efforts should be coordinated with *organizations of indigenous peoples and communities* as well as with other state organs (Article

146.3, my emphasis). In short, the institute was obliged by law to consult and coordinate with (and even, on some issues, ultimately conform to) indigenous organizations (Article 146.16). This situation was drastically redefined at the beginning of 2007 with the creation of MINPI.

The practical expression of political participation goals, popular power and state structures are epitomized by the government's reorganization of its branches. In 2009, the Ministry of Communes and Social Protection was launched, but in 2013 its name was changed in line with overarching government dynamics in relation to popular organization to Ministry for Communes and Social Movements.

Conclusion

There is an indigenous movement in Venezuela that can be best characterized as state-supporting and state-sponsored. This movement did not exist before the *chavista* bloc; on the contrary, it is a result of the dynamizing forces activated by this political bloc, particularly since it started to gain a share of state power in 1998.

The growth of this movement was stimulated by the participatory mechanisms associated with the government policies that have, over the past 16 years, targeted socioeconomic enfranchisement. These mechanisms facilitated the recruitment and mobilization of the supporters of this movement, whose consolidation took place in close relation with branches of the state's executive power. Specifically, the creation of MINPI was a springboard for mass incorporation of the indigenous population into government activities, while also focusing the efforts of the indigenous movement that feeds into such activity.

Through their actions, the members of this movement have prioritized direct political participation in state politics and the consolidation of access to socioeconomic rights over those of self-determination. Socioeconomic rights were and remain central to indigenous demands, and the advances in their implementation explains why this stream of collective action has received mass support from the indigenous population.

This indigenous movement has developed and currently operates in synergy with political parties, particularly the PSUV, and with members of state organs. It is, however, not defined by its bureaucratic aspects, but by combining these with a capacity for extra-institutional mobilization and political activism. There is also an important convergence between the collective action deployed by this movement and that undertaken in the electoral arena by indigenous supporters of the *chavista* bloc.

This movement's contentiousness is against unbridled capitalism and imperialism, rather than against the state. But this does not preclude its members criticizing government policy, or particular state agents or organs. Indeed, this type of criticism and the creative tensions it generates are a constituent part of the *chavista* bloc, whose overall orientation is determined by internal conflict as well as opposition to external forces.

SIX

Contentious collective action in the margins of and outside the *chavista* bloc

There is a type of indigenous collective action that takes place outside the electoral sphere and the state-sponsored indigenous movement. Its main distinctive characteristics are, first, its range of activity, which includes direct action such as land reoccupation and contentious protest directed against state agents or organs, and, second, the peripheral position that, in practice, it occupies in relation to the *chavista* bloc.

Despite its difficult and often contentious relations with some government and state agents, this type of collective action is not as a whole situated within the opposition bloc, and there are in fact some important synergies between this movement and groups of activists within the *chavista* bloc. Nor does this stream fully constitute a 'social movement against the state' in terms of the demands it expresses. While it prioritizes land demarcation and titling, and advocates autonomy in terms of its political decisions, most of the demands it mobilizes are addressed to the state to fulfil existing commitments (as reflected in legislation), or for it to act against other sources of actual power that challenge the (already fragile) monopoly of legitimate violence that the state is supposed to sustain.

We shall also see that the tense relations between members of this movement and state agents are strongly conditioned by the polarized configuration of the political scenario in the country, and further complicated by external interference in Venezuelan politics. Let me begin the analysis of this very complex panorama by recalling a significant episode.

Humans, their NGOs and Indians as heritage of humanity

In 1993, in a place known as Haximú, 16 Yanomami were killed by *garimpeiros* (illegal miners) in a terrible example of the logic of dispossession that has gone hand in hand with the search for riches in Amazonia for centuries. For one reason or another, these Yanomami had become an obstacle to the miners' goals, and as mere physical obstacles their lives were expendable. The massacre, an indelible memory for survivors and their relatives, dramatically exemplified the vulnerability of some indigenous groups in the face of the private forces of development. To this day, this massacre remains a mobilizing symbol for many advocates of indigenous rights, both in Venezuela and worldwide.

Two decades later, in early September 2012, a rumour spread that Yanomami in the south of Venezuela had been victims of a new massacre. This was said to have taken place at Irotatheri, in July that year. Triggering memories of the Haximú massacre, the news rapidly sparked a response among indigenous and non-indigenous human rights advocates inside and outside Venezuela. Social media swiftly activated support networks, mobilizing people in pleas for government intervention and investigation of the event. For several days, various messages and emails spread the news and condemnation via mailing lists. Different versions circulated, most of them noting that eye-witness accounts (or at least information) from Yanomami was available. Commercial media in various countries soon joined in circulating the news.

As tends to happen in Venezuela with events that make news (or indeed with fabricated news that becomes events), the case became the setting for a political confrontation: on the one hand, critics of the government suggested that it epitomized the government's inefficiency and its disregard for indigenous rights; on the other, government supporters suggested that the story was another fabrication that aimed to destabilize the government and affect the outcome of forthcoming elections. It was indeed a politically sensitive period: the 2012 presidential elections were due in October, and regional ones in December.

In these circumstances, various members of the government and the military publicly declared that a surveillance operation (*Operación Centinela 2012*) had been carried but found no evidence of the massacre. On 7 September 2012, President Chávez felt it necessary to confirm publicly that investigations were continuing in order to clarify what had happened. He also reported that the 'media of the bourgeoisie' were using the case to create discontent prior to the October elections.

After a few days with contradictory information still in circulation, the government sent a special commission of civil and military representatives to Irotatheri itself, where they interviewed people without finding any evidence of the alleged massacre that by then had made headlines around the world. The allegations proved to be nothing more than rumours, though evidence was found that Brazilian *garimpeiros* had been, and probably still were, working nearby.

In addition to other political considerations, what ensued around the Irotatheri crisis illustrated some central dynamics around indigenous politics in the polarized Venezuelan scenario: events automatically become dragged into the whirlwind of the national struggle. But this crisis also triggered some other responses fixed in a realm that, as happens with indigenous politics, became strongly associated with 'civil society' activism during the multicultural shift of the 1990s.[1] For some people, this realm remains the natural arena of NGOs, and among them expert credentials and moral authority in indigenous affairs stems automatically from membership of a (*any*) 'civil society' platform.

NotiMujer, a CNN Spanish-language programme broadcast from Miami, was among many in the commercial media to cover the Irotatheri crisis outside Venezuela (on 3 September 2012). The programme's presenter, Mercedes Soler, announced that she had tried without success to interview MINPI staff, but relied on an NGO expert who was herself indigenous: Patricia Velásquez. The latter, interviewed from Los Angeles, is a Wayúu model and actress also involved in a foundation (Wayúu Tayá) that implements philanthropic programmes among Wayúu and other Latin American indigenous peoples. Velásquez's statements that day epitomized a particular way of understanding rights, politics and humanitarianism that still lingers in many advocates of 'civil society' initiatives for the protection of Indians: she explained that 'In that area [Irotatheri] there are Yanomami, Piaroa and Hoti populations; those populations do not have much contact with humans, with us ... hum ... with us'.[2] Velásquez continued commenting on the alleged killings and declared that it was 'not at all a political question, it is a question that has to do with human rights, it is a universal question, because the Yanomami *indígenas* are patrimony of humanity'. To further dispel any potential suspicion that her concern for this patrimony could be read as an attack on the government in the run-up to elections, she clarified: 'The Yanomami do not care about the forthcoming elections on 7 October, what the Yanomami want is to be heard'.

Perhaps the Yanomami should be very grateful that they have been able to count on the NGOs of 'human beings' to help them over the years. Perhaps they also take elections with a pinch of salt, despite it being well documented that an increasing number of them do take part in elections and organize themselves to influence elected officials (Carrera 2011; Kelly 2011, p. 26). Yet one cannot help wondering if the Yanomami actually want rely much longer on NGOs and 'humans' who want them to remain 'as "patrimony of humanity"'.

The engagement with regional and national government structures, and with the new avenues of political participation open to the Yanomami and indigenous peoples in general in Venezuela, is indeed challenging and will surely be marked by both positive and negative experiences. This is unavoidable. However, it is without question that this participation becomes a source of learning and indispensable experience for groups who seek to organize and build a collective political voice. Indeed, this seems to be the case for the Yanomami. In a recent analysis of their current political engagement based on extensive fieldwork in the region, anthropologist Javier Carrera argued that it 'is being taken [by the Yanomami themselves] as a real practical school of political training' (2011, p. 226). The learning processes of which Carrera talks might be slow and perhaps disappointing, but it is difficult not to think that these processes will help to empower participants far more than the protection proposed by 'Yanomami-as-patrimony' NGOs.

There are, however, other important political reasons why Bolivarian governments have shown distrust before political organizations that present themselves under the banner of 'civil society', as we will see next. These reasons are closely related to the protection of sovereignty that has been a guiding principle of the Bolivarian revolution since its inception.

Sovereignty and civil society in the context of the Bolivarian revolution

In June 2006, when the National Assembly was debating the first draft of a law to establish state regulation of the process of international cooperation funding, PSUV deputy Iris Varela (now a member of the Cabinet) contended that 'it is necessary to control the activity of a group of organizations that, with the façade of defending human rights, are dedicated to receiving financial support from the United States ... in order to pursue political objectives'.[3] Such comments supporting state supervision of international cooperation projects have been interpreted by critics of the Venezuelan government (and indeed of other current Latin American left-wing governments) as an expression of alleged authoritarian tendencies within the governing bloc. From that perspective, regulation is always seen as an erosion of the 'civil society' sector, a deceptively depoliticized term through which enemies of these governments conceptualize political opposition – and the hopes of ousting elected governments.[4] It is also significant that similar criticisms have been levelled against other governments, such as those of Evo Morales in Bolivia and Rafael Correa in Ecuador – governments that firmly position themselves in the orbit of the socialisms of the twenty-first century and within the new sovereign and anti-imperialist regionalist movements (Anderson 2014). The construction of the socialism of the twenty-first century is a process sustained by a strong belief in sovereignty as an essential, indispensable principle of a just and balanced international society. In Latin America, this principle is heavily invested with a progressive tradition of anti-colonial sentiment. In Venezuela in particular, progressive forces have always considered the recovery of sovereignty as a driving political goal. And, among other things, it was one of the reasons the 1915 Law of Missions was, throughout the twentieth century, a target for those forces in their approach to recasting relations between the state and indigenous rights.

Concrete concerns bring about the sovereignty principle in relation to the establishment of a minimum of regulation over the flows of international cooperation addressing 'civil societies' in the continent. It is not news that this cooperation has often been used by the US and other governments to mask support for political groups opposing left-wing or merely sovereignty-seeking governments in Latin America. In the past, appeals to human rights and humanitarianism have often been used to justify direct military intervention in the continent; as Fabricant and Postero recently reminded us (2014, p. 395), and at present, appeals to certain conceptions of civil society seem to play a key role in justifying the transfer of massive resources to political organizations that oppose left-wing governments.

In Venezuela, it is well documented that the amount of donations by agencies linked to the US government to so-called 'civil society' groups have increased exponentially over the past few years, and also that some of those organizations have embarked in overt political destabilization (Golinger 2006). In 2001, the National Endowment for Democracy (NED) started a massive intensification of its financial support for organizations opposed to Hugo Chávez's government: its annual budget quadrupled. These funds were channelled to organizations directly involved in the 2002 coup against Chávez. Moreover, after the coup, the NED created a special fund in which an additional US$ 1 million would be made available to precisely those organizations that had participated in planning the coup (Golinger 2005). This situation is not exceptional, and US 'cooperation funds' are similarly criticized in other parts of the continent for seeking the weakening and destabilization of elected governments.

US officials continue to publicly criticize Latin American governments that seek to strengthen their sovereignty. This occurs even when those governments act in accordance with widely supported international guidelines such as the Paris Declaration on Aid Effectiveness, which basically states that donors should adapt their programmes to the priorities of recipient countries. An illustrative recent example was the proposals of Rafael Correa for the management of USAID funds in Ecuador. According to cables published by WikiLeaks, the US ambassador to Ecuador, Header Hodges, considered that 'asserting Ecuador's sovereignty, rejecting foreign interference, and ensuring state control of strategic assets and the national security apparatus' were 'grandiose ideas', while suggesting that a US agency like USAID should not support them (Pearson 2014, p. 17).

Returning to the Venezuelan case, sovereignty principles and distrust of certain civil society organizations certainly condition and complicate relations between members of the government and certain groups of indigenous activism. Some groups in the orbit of the collective action I address in this chapter have occasionally been placed in the category of 'destabilizing organizations'. For instance, in June 2014 Diosdado Cabello, president of the National Assembly and a PSUV strongman, in his programme *Con el mazo dando* on public television (VTV), accused the most prominent figure in a group supporting Yukpa land claims (which will be examined below) of conspiring against the government. The finger was pointed at Lusbi Portillo who, among others, has been very critical of the government's approach to the handling of land demarcation and titling in the Perijá area in particular; he responded publicly to Cabello through media channels such as Aporrea.org, an online news portal that identifies itself as part of the *chavista* bloc, in what constituted an example of the top-down and bottom-up political dynamics that make up the bloc.[5]

The position adopted by Lusbi Portillo and *some* sympathisers of the Yukpa movement aims to sidestep the polarized national picture in pursuit of their demands. Their strategy can be summarized in statements such as 'we divide the country between those who are and those who are not in favour of indigenous rights and indigenous people',[6] a division that in principle crosses the main political boundary currently demarcating the national struggle. In fact, some supporters of this movement pursue cooperation, without distinction, with people and organizations aligned with the *anti-chavista* or the *chavista* bloc. In the Venezuelan scenario, this is an awkward and difficult position, not just because of the virtual absence of political space beyond the *chavista/anti-chavista* polarization that dominates national life. A crucial obstacle for this position is that, while discursively dividing the political arena between those in favour of indigenous rights and those who are not, in practice it ignores the fact that 'indigenous rights' are actively defined and pursued by a large proportion of the indigenous population via a different stream of collective action (one that crystallizes in the state-supporting and state-sponsored indigenous movement).

In any event, it is also important to emphasize that different branches of the state apparatus and even different members of the government respond differently to the contentious collective action undertaken by groups such as supporters of the Yukpa movement (which, as we will see next, is both an epitome of and a meeting point for the type of collective action being discussed here). That range of responses is in part an expression of the state's ultimately undefined directionality, and also of the fact that, as I noted in the Introduction, the Bolivarian state is driven by conflict – a result of the heterogeneous and not always harmonious demands that constitute the *chavista* bloc, and of the extra-institutional action of sections of the opposition. An example is the ramifications of the case summarized above: while Cabello made public declarations against supporters of the Yukpa movement, other members of the government met with them in person, sometimes through formal channels (such as the National Assembly's Permanent Commission for Indigenous Peoples) and sometimes in direct and personal confrontation of contentious action. We will see below cases that illustrate this situation, but let us first learn a little more about the Yukpa movement.

The Yukpa movement as epitome and symbol of this type of collective action

The movement surrounding the Yukpa struggle for land in the Perijá mountains of Zulia state has become an epitome and a point of convergence for the type of collective action I discuss in this chapter. In general terms, this movement prioritizes the demarcation and titling of lands and defends organizational autonomy, but understanding how it works and the position it occupies in the national panorama requires some context.

The situation of the Yukpa (and the neighbouring Barí) had already been considered dramatic in the early 1970s. Significantly, it was reported at the First Congress of Indians, held that decade. Conflict over territory in the region had intensified in previous decades, when indigenous groups sought to stop dispossession and to recover land from which they had been displaced. The effective territorial dispossession of indigenous communities in this part of the country, stimulated by development-driven expansion during Pérez Jiménez's dictatorship, had started relatively late, but sparked a conflict that remains unresolved.

Over the years, some indigenous communities in the region have reoccupied lands and gone through direct confrontation with non-indigenous landowners, at the cost of many *indígenas* lives. Among these was Sabino Romero, leader of the movement and symbol of indigenous land struggles in the country. Sabino Romero was assassinated on 3 March 2013 (incidentally two days before the death of Chávez). Violence targeting activists did not stop with Sabino's death.[7]

The Yukpa movement has become a converging point for supporters of various autonomist and indigenous demands that distrust party politics and the state-sponsored indigenous movement. It has developed its own synergies with other actors that, within or outside the *chavista* bloc, support those demands and share tactics, including some groups involved in environmental activism. In general terms, the environmental activism that converges here advocates an end to mining, which in this area is primarily for coal. This activism has developed links with some of the indigenous communities in the region, whose opposition to mining is not only an environmental issue, but also a crucial defence of their livelihoods and sustenance, which is basically dependent on agricultural production that would not be viable if the territory was further degraded by mining.

Other advocates of indigenous and pluricultural rights have also joined with the Yukpa movement, on a more intermittent basis. In fact, the contentious activities of this movement spurred on the legalization of the special indigenous jurisdiction, a right foreseen in the CRBV. In October 2009, Sabino Romero was involved in a conflict between members of different indigenous communities in Perijá that resulted in fatalities. Sabino was imprisoned and charged with homicide along with two other fellow *indígenas*, undergoing a very long and heavily criticized trial in the general judiciary that mobilized supporters of the movement around demands for an indigenous jurisdiction. Sabino was eventually acquitted, and also subsequently exculpated in a process involving traditional authorities. When the Law of Indigenous Jurisdiction was being debated in the National Assembly, indigenous members and representatives specifically pointed to the case of Sabino and his companions as an example of what could be avoided in future if such jurisdictions were in place.[8]

Members of the Yukpa movement, and in general those who participate in the type of collective action for which the movement is an epitome, have been and remain very critical of state agents and the state-sponsored movement centred on MINPI. In the Perijá region, the ministry has nevertheless built up direct contacts with members of some Yukpa communities who take an active part in the state-sponsored movement. Members of the Yukpa movement consider this to be interference in their demands for autonomy and an obstacle to their legitimate territorial rights, given MINPI's emphasis on communal council territorialization.

However, Yukpa members of this movement are not outright anti-statists. They do report bureaucratic shortcomings and abuses of state power, but they also largely rely on state forces to protect them against paramilitary activity in the region, and seek and benefit from state credits and resources. Indeed, the communities of some of those who oppose the MINPI proposals in Perijá have sought and received funding through communal councils, despite the fact that this does not resolve all the local demands. That is the case, for instance, of the Río Yaza community.[9] It is nevertheless the case that most of the state credits and resources for indigenous communities in the region have been directed towards so-called 'pilot centres' in the largest six indigenous communities in the area that are administered by *'caciques mayores'*. The latter are figures of authority recognized by part of the local population and legitimized by state agencies, yet denounced as illegitimate and artificial by some of the Yukpa that have reoccupied land in the area.[10] In this respect, this area exemplifies the political consequences stemming from the different priorities and means among the indigenous population that are channelled by the three forms of collective action I analyze in this book.

But there are also some synergies at work between the Yukpa movement and institutional state actors, often activated by a specific conflict. Let me next recall a significant instance of contention that illustrates those synergies. This event actually forced the establishment of formal contacts between activists and members of the government.

A hunger strike

In October 2010, the late José María Korta, a Jesuit and one of the founding forces behind the Indigenous University of Tauca (UIT), set up a temporary camp in front of the National Assembly building in Caracas and began an eight-day hunger strike.[11] Although he was a non-indigenous activist, his action fed directly into the stream of indigenous activism that has not joined the state-sponsored movement or engaged in the electoral sphere.

Korta released a statement setting out his motivation. This began with an acknowledgement of the historical significance of the CRBV and of Chávez's demonstrated commitment to the well-being of the indigenous population. It then complained that 'for eleven years, [Chávez's] Revolutionary Government has failed to to implement the rights in Chapter VIII of the Constitution, due to lack of knowledge about how to do it or because [this Chapter] was not properly understood'. Korta argued that 'indigenous public policies "from below"' were needed, as well as a 'destatization of the indigenous [*lo indígena*]'. Central to his concern was the fact that the demarcation of indigenous territories – 'which is but the right to the land' – had not come about, and he went on to explicitly link the figure of the late Yuka leader Sabino Romero (by then imprisoned, as already mentioned, on a charge of homicide), to Guaicaipuro: 'It was the president's decision to give Guaicaipuro a place in the National Pantheon. Today, Guaicaipuro lives again, and is among us in the libertarian struggle of Venezuelan indigenous peoples in the person of Sabino Romero Izarra'.[12]

The hunger strike had significant public repercussions and received media coverage both in Venezuela and beyond. Within the country, it generated debate between different factions of the *chavista* bloc (including members of the state-sponsored indigenous movement). Despite the fact that the state media paid hardly any attention to it, a variety of community media and activist networks did. This conflict operated as a creative tension within *chavismo*, and a series of contacts between members of the government, the hunger-striker, and indigenous activists and supporters soon ensued. Korta ended his hunger strike on 25 October, justifying this by explaining that 'in view of the dialogue that we have had with different government members, we consider that the principal issue behind the strike has received a response'.

Subsequently, a colleague from the UIT declared that the Ministry of the Environment had sent a document according to which the processes of demarcation of indigenous territories would be restarted, with the support of a parliamentary commission and with the participation of indigenous representatives. In addition, and in response to the fact that the demand for a special indigenous jurisdiction had become another demand of Korta's supporters during the hunger strike, the Supreme Court undertook to 'look again in detail' at the case of Sabino Romero and his fellow imprisoned *indígenas* (Alexander Fernández and Olegario Romero), for them to be judged according to traditional justice. This accelerated the ordinary justice trial against Sabino who, as noted above, was eventually acquitted.

This event exemplified the sensitivity shown by the Bolivarian state and members of its government towards conflict identified with popular demands. During the hunger strike, Korta was also visited by minister Nicia Maldonado, among other government officials. This constituted a face-to-face confrontation of contentious action by high-ranking state actors that is far from exceptional in the current context of Bolivarian politics – and which is somewhat rare, not to say unthinkable, in other democracies (how many ministers in your country would try to establish personal and direct dialogue with protesters *during* a protest?). Vice-president Elías Jaua met with Korta after the hunger strike, agreeing to receive a 'roadmap' that various organizations and actors supporting Korta's demands were drafting as a basis for negotiations with government representatives. On 8 November, a small deputation of activists personally delivered the finalized roadmap to the vice-presidency offices, after a group of supporters marched from Plaza Bolívar.

In subsequent months, Jaua and other government representatives accompanied Korta on visits to indigenous communities in Apure and Zulia states. In 2013, after the dramatic assassination of Sabino Romero, Jaua personally received another Yukpa delegation and undertook to accelerate the payment of expropriations that had paralyzed the granting of titles for some of the Yukpa communities in the Perijá region.[13] While obviously such commitments are always dependent on subsequent implementation (which needs to be assessed separately), the process from which they resulted illustrated the way in which conflict, in contemporary Venezuela, forms a central part of the dialectics through which state and society build and transform each other, a relationship that Thomas Muhr (2012) has rightly pointed out as pivotal in the current stage of the Bolivarian revolution.

Let us next analyze a different snapshot of the complex politics surrounding indigenous collective action in Venezuela, and specifically the stream that I discuss in this chapter.

A protest at the courts

In November 2013 I was in Caracas, and very early on the morning of the 8th I received a text message from a friend: around 9 a.m. there was to be a demonstration at the Courts of Justice in support of continuing the investigation into who was behind Sabino's assassination. The trial for that case was ongoing and, although five people had been arrested, members of the Yukpa movement and groups of supporters considered that these people were only the perpetrators of a crime commissioned by local landowners, probably in connivance with members of the local security forces – some of the suspects were in fact linked to a municipal police force.

My friend, a *caraqueño* photographer and self-declared *chavista*, has for years been involved in a variety of groups advocating indigenous rights and is an example of the range of profiles that, as pointed out above, converge around the Yukpa movement. I went to support the demonstration along with another friend from Ciudad Bolívar, a university professor at the Bolivarian University, and we arrived at the courts shortly after 9 a.m. As we approached, we could see a group of some 15–20 people gathered at the entrance with banners and posters. There were a few Indians there too, one of them wearing the same sort of outfit that Sabino sometimes wore, which identified him as a *cacique*. This was the gathering we were after, we both thought.

It did not take us long to realize that it was not. These people were protesting in *support* of those arrested in connection with Romero's assassination. They contended that the detainees were innocent, and held banners blaming some recognized figures in the groups supporting the Yukpa movement 'for causing all the problems in Perijá'.

The Yukpa movement supporters started to arrive later, and took up their position on the other side of the entrance to the courts. Banners were displayed, and chanting began. 'We are all Yukpa, Yukpa we all are' [*Todos somos Yukpa, Yukpa somos todos*] was one of the slogans chanted. Most of the people on our side were not *indígenas*, and people in the other group started to shout: 'See, none of them are *indígena*'. A woman among them (non-indigenous, judging by appearances) lifted the arm of one of her companions in protest and said: 'This one [a man dressed in *cacique* attire] really is *indígena*, not you; you know nothing about Perijá'.

Reporters from community media such as Barrio TV and Aporrea TV – both self-identified members of the *chavista* bloc that advocate popular struggle and often criticize state bureaucracy – arrived to cover the demonstrations. The Aporrea reporter in particular was not well received by the supporters of the arrestees, as they recognized her as a Yukpa sympathizer. When the reporter from Barrio TV interviewed some of the suspects' supporters, the latter argued, among other things, that the land (re)occupations that Sabino and others had carried out had only benefited a few families, and that he had not thought of 'other Yukpa'. They were also portraying the detainees as scapegoats. Some of these protesters also identified themselves as *chavistas* and revolutionaries, and one of them even sported a t-shirt with the PSUV logo and the slogan *'pa'lante comandante'* ('go ahead, comandante') – a slogan popularized during Chávez's convalescence from the illness that eventually killed him.

On the side of the Yukpa movement supporters, one activist took the megaphone to say that even though some people were trying to divide the movement in support of Sabino (in reference to the accusations against him) they would never achieve it. Several people in our group commented that those in the other group could not be true *chavistas*, who would always be on the side of the disenfranchised and the revolutionaries, as Sabino was. It was clear that the two groups had little common ground, and the verbal exchanges between them appeased and gradually transformed into shouted monologues. Each of the two groups remained on different sides of the courts entrance with banners on display.

Conclusions

Both the protest at the courts and the hunger strike help us to understand and characterize the workings of the type of indigenous collective action that positions itself outside electoral politics and the state-sponsored movement. I argued that the Yukpa movement is an epitome of this collective action, and also showed how it became the converging point for a variety of non-indigenous activist groups that joined in the Yukpa struggle.

What mainly distinguishes this movement is, as we have seen, its repertoire of actions, primarily contentious, and, in political terms, the fact that, while some of its supporters discursively negate the validity of the *chavista/anti-chavista* division of the national political playing field for the advancement of their interests, this avenue of collective action has developed important synergies with non-indigenous sectors of activism that position themselves firmly within the *chavista* bloc. That is why this stream occupies a peripheral position in relation to that bloc, despite clear differences with some of its members – including declared antagonisms with the members of the state-sponsored and state-supporting indigenous movement, and particularly with MINPI officials and structures.

The contentious action deployed by this stream of collective action and the tensions it generates are in fact an example of the dialogue that at this stage of the Bolivarian revolution characterizes the relationship between state and society. In the cases analyzed in this chapter, open conflict stemming from social activism was precisely what activated contacts between government members and indigenous activists and supporters, and what changed state praxis on several fronts – from legislative powers to the judiciary and executive powers.

The Yukpa movement cannot be defined as anti-statist, as some people argue in comparative overviews of indigenous struggles on the continent. And in Venezuela this statement extends to other indigenous components of the route of collective action of which the Yukpa are a part. Members of the Yukpa movement do criticize and often confront state officialdom, but in turn they ultimately rely on state forces to protect them in the face of para-military activity in the region, one in which the state is far from having the monopoly of legitimate violence. In the absence of the state, the Yukpa would be even more vulnerable to violence, dispossession and exploitation. In addition, we saw that, in pursuit of basic infrastructural and productive projects on which their livelihood depends, members of that movement seek, and have benefited from, credits and resources that the Bolivarian state currently dispenses as part of its redistributive policies.

I also showed why the tense relations between activists involved in this type of indigenous collective action and state agents are aggravated by external interference in Venezuelan politics, and particularly by the fact that under the label of 'international cooperation' there has been a massive transfer of resources from the US government to 'civil society' organizations that barely hide their political agitation against Bolivarian governments. This situation does not, of course, imply that all those civil society organizations that in Venezuela present contentious positions to the government are covert coup plotters but, among members of the government (and indeed many supporters of the *chavista* bloc), it nevertheless generates a high degree of distrust and automatically opposed responses.

Finally, looking at the situated events I described above reinforces another crucial caveat that I have already advanced in the Introduction and will further discuss next: in reading our complex social texts and their politics, it is no longer possible (if it ever was) to take for granted what the demands of collective subjects characterized as identity groups are. This impossibility includes simplistic generalizations about indigenous peoples and their 'indigenous struggles'. In the next chapter I will further elaborate on this point, reflecting in particular on the demonstrated possibility that those struggles become inscribed in the promotion of (indigenous) capitalism, and on the implications of this for the analysis of Venezuelan and global politics.

SEVEN

Indigenous peoples, capitalism and the political economy of the socialisms of the twenty-first century in Latin America

Both indigenous collective action and state transformation in Venezuela are conditioned by structural economic factors – by political-economic factors, more specifically. These factors help to explain why Bolivarian governments have favoured the model of political organization, productive development and indigenous territorialization associated with the New Geometry of Power, but also why central parts of indigenous collective action have supported it. This model has been compatible with, and indeed has facilitated, the socioeconomic and political enfranchisement prioritized by the state-supporting and state-sponsored indigenous movement as a galvanizing goal steering collective action. However, on the foundations of minimum convergence bounded by those goals, a heterogeneous landscape of demands and social horizons continues to be projected by the indigenous population – such as happens among supporters of the *chavista* bloc in general. Against the background set by preceding chapters, I will next elaborate on this fundamental question, which adds uncertainty to forecasting the directionality of the Boliviarian process but also acts as a stimulating platform from which to discuss Venezuelan and global politics. Let me start by looking at the broad picture.

Socialisms of the twenty-first century: economic foundation

Despite the radical transformations in certain aspects of political participation and some steps in the promotion of socialism, the core driving goals of the socialisms of the twenty-first century in Venezuela have undoubtedly been socioeconomic development and the consolidation of sovereignty. These have operated as converging points for a large set of democratic demands that were initially mobilized and brought to an 'equivalential chain' (Laclau 2007, p. 37) within the *chavista* bloc. With *chavismo* as an overarching movement, those fragmented but quite heterogeneous demands found a platform where they were portrayed as occupying an 'equivalent' position in the national arena – initially a position defined by the way in which the previous political system had situated them as unsatisfied demands. The effectiveness in materializing those core goals to a minimum degree subsequently facilitated the maintenance of 'equivalences' among different demands, as socioeconomic development and sovereignty are shared as converging points among such demands.

However, these core goals also operate as limiting boundaries in response to any demand stemming from within the bloc: its dominant forces can ignore or displace demands whose satisfaction is (politically) deemed to compromise the fulfillment of the core goals. This generates internal tension when neglected demands retain strong organized support.

Given the current economic structure of the countries in which the socialism of the twenty-first century project is being advanced, the short-term achievement and long-term consolidation of the core goals mentioned above requires a significant degree of economic revenue and development. They are indispensable to facilitating access to social services (i.e. to bring about socioeconomic human rights), promoting productive diversification and guaranteeing some degree of sovereignty that translates into reduced economic dependence on foreign interests (at least, foreign interests that directly impose conditions inimical to the maintenance of the project's core political directionality; foreign credit from China or Russia, for instance, has been sought by countries such as Venezuela along these pragmatic terms).

Unavoidably, this conjuncture creates enormous political challenges in countries where the economy is still fundamentally dependent on extractive industries. On the one hand, when the governments of these countries pursue projects of national-level development and sovereignty, tensions will emerge between centralizing/decentralizing and representative/participatory forms of decision-making and policy implementation. Any demand for political autonomy that includes a territorial dimension exacerbates these tensions. In Latin America, this type of demand takes on forms as diverse as those related to indigenous self-determination and those spurred by regional oligarchies seeking to exercise direct control over resource exploitation at the expense of potentially redistributive national-level, state-supported projects (recall the so-called '*Media Luna*' crisis in Bolivia[1]). Against this backdrop, one can better understand why in Venezuela titling of indigenous territories in the spirit established by the 1999 Constitution was displaced by a form of (weak) indigenous territorialization that, in line with the NGP, makes national-level planning compatible with degrees of local and regional autonomy and political organization – e.g. indigenous communal councils and some communes.[2]

It is also important to emphasize that national territorial integration was one of the first projects defined by Bolivarianism (Buxton 2009, p. 63). This sought to address historical problems of territorial fragmentation in the Republic, but also to contribute to the socioeconomic development of rural areas of the 'interior'. In Venezuela, the oil-based economy translated throughout the twentieth century into a gradual reduction in the contribution of agriculture to national product, and diversification of manufacturing never took off either. This process was accompanied by migration to the country's capital and some other (mostly coastal) cities, concentrating population and economic activity in an export-oriented (and import-dependent) extractive model. Though Bolivarian governments have successfully addressed the most acute symptoms of poverty and disenfranchisement that the model generated, they have not been able to reverse this process to an extent that sees the expansion and consolidation of an internal diversified production.

Extractivism thus remains at the core of the Venezuelan economy, as it does in other Latin American countries pursuing the socialism of the twenty-first century. In addition to the aforementioned tensions that this created between centralizing/decentralizing and representative/participatory forms of decision-making and policy implementation, other enormous challenges arise from this situation. One, with repercussions beyond national borders, is that of sustainability. More accurately, this should be called a challenge to the principles of *just* sustainability, a concept that brings to the fore the politics of (in)equality and (in)justice that underpin the apparently depoliticized connotations of 'sustainability' (Agyeman 2013).

As soon as we touch on the subject of sustainability, the extraction of non-renewable resources – which is at the core of the socialism of the twenty-first century – looks like a poisoned chalice. Current global (unequal) levels of both consumption of resources and of pollution are reaching what experts describe as a 'tipping point' of no return, and extractivism certainly brings this point ever closer. But this takes place in a way in which countries such as Venezuela, Ecuador and Bolivia should not be singled out as responsible for global problems, or put at the top of the list of suspects. Extractivism is a global phenomenon, and global responsibility for it is widespread and overlapping. It not only involves the countries in which extractivism takes place and those in which the finance for it originates: it also involves all those countries whose population, through the consumption of goods, foods and services, sustain the economic demand for hydrocarbons, minerals and other non-renewable resources.

This global phenomenon creates worldwide (if unequally shared) responsibilities, but it has winners and losers too. From the perspective of sustainability, *everyone* loses out, needless to say. No wall will be high enough and no border secure enough to protect anyone, including the most powerful elites and nations, from the consequences of an irreversibly degraded planet. Yet on the death row into which, as it were, the current mode of production methods are transforming the spaceship *Planet Earth*, we find different classes of inmate: there are some whose lavish last wishes are plentifully fulfilled, while others wait for the fatal day in misery. The latter cry out for some degree of justice in the intervening period, even at the expense of an ideal of sustainability whose achievement, after all, does not depend on the sacrifice imposed upon them.

Against this backdrop, 'extractivist' countries where the popular classes (including indigenous ones) were for decades structurally affected by severe levels of poverty and low degrees of social development should not be denied the right to a dignified end – an end whose script is largely written elsewhere. And still less so those countries where governments are demonstrating a commitment to alleviating the poverty and disenfranchisement that was borne by the majority of their population. In this light, such countries appeal for the right to euthanasia, as it were. And it appears as legitimate in the face of rights actually exercised in other countries – such as the right to live well above one's own biocapacity,[3] as happens in the so-called developed world.

Let me make very clear that I am far from celebrating the insane route to global degradation towards which global capitalism is leading us, in which extractivism plays a central part. I actually subscribe to the arguments of those who advocate a shift towards genuinely (and just) sustainable societies, which, among other things, would imply important degrees of collective planning in production, a change in forms of consumption, and of course a move towards renewable sources of energy. Yet this is only achievable with structural changes at a global level, and until these occur I consider it unethical to put the blame on those countries which are only weak links in a global chain, and particularly so when those countries are effectively trying to do something about social justice – even if, admittedly, they are doing as little as the so-called developed countries in terms of global sustainability.

Political digestion of this unpalatable entrée might not be easy. But let us try to process it as best we can, because the meal is not over and, alas, heavy main courses are on the menu. Let me further explore the political implications of this situation, starting with a comment on criticisms that in relation to extractivism are often directed at countries such as Venezuela.

The politics of criticism of neo-extractivist countries and 'indigenous movements' debates

Some analysts argue that there is nothing substantially different between the socialisms of the twenty-first century and the neoliberal extractivist models they replaced. It has been suggested, for instance, that labelling countries such as Bolivia and Ecuador as 'post-neoliberal' is misguided (see, for example, Bebbington and Bebbington 2011), and that what we are witnessing in a country such as Bolivia is little more than a reconstitution of neoliberalism (see, for example, Webber 2013). While stemming from different political angles, these criticisms lead to political condemnation of the socialisms of the twenty-first century and have some basic common traits. First, they sidestep a range of socioeconomic indicators that reveal a situation in which neoliberal policy is on the back foot. Second, they tend to present 'social movements', allegedly opposed to the governments of these countries, as the depositories of the anti-neoliberal antidote.

On the first point, to suggest that, for instance, there is not something at least 'post-' in the 'neoliberalism' of Correa's government seems to be a rather whimsical proposal. A government that, just to name a few (but telling) examples, has audited and defaulted foreign bonds illegitimately contracted by previous governments, has increased public expenditure on health and education threefold, and has improved revenue collection while raising taxes among the most wealthy (Becker 2013b) surely deserves, at the very least, some sort of prefix to distinguish it from its immediate neoliberal predecessors. In the case of Bolivia, we similarly find abundant evidence to argue that Evo Morales's government is a fairly unorthodox pupil of the market-oriented Chicago Boys (see, for instance, García Linera 2010, pp. 24–7; Fuentes 2014, pp. 109-10), with increased state (public) participation in the economy and a re-direction of economic surplus towards national productive actors that, accompanied by a redistributive social policy, has translated into improved socioeconomic indicators for the popular classes. In Venezuela, the anti-neoliberal orientation of government policy in many respects cannot be questioned. In this book I have outlined traits of this policy, particularly in the way in which it has benefited and been supported by the indigenous population. The current level of enfranchisement experienced by this population derives from a solid social-democratic (in its antineoliberal connotation) orientation of policy, and is inseparable from the forms of collective action analyzed in previous chapters: that action has supported and helped to guide the state structure that facilitated it.

Particularly from the left of the political spectrum, criticism of neo-extractivist governments is sometimes based on systemic and global-system perspectives. Authors such as Petras and Veltmeyer (2007, p. 372) present the view that a 'capitalist state, regardless of its internal political formation or ideological complexion, necessarily operates in the interest of capital'. This is so because, in aggregate terms, their labour, production and marketing regimes do not alter the process of capital accumulation, despite partial reforms with a progressive appearance. This type of analysis is sometimes applied to the Venezuelan government and deserves comment.

While the fact that Venezuela is not outside capitalism cannot be questioned, in 'all or nothing' analyses of state politics one is always left wondering how, when and where a non-capitalist state is going to originate. And this relates to the second question pointed out as a common trait in criticisms of neo-extractivist countries. These criticisms often invoke 'social movement' activity as the source of political solutions (and, let it be said, as a source of immaculate political purity). When invoked in the name of the Left, that activity is normally associated with class struggle, while when coming from the Right it tends to be framed as part of a sort of civil society redemption. Yet these criticisms never present convincing evidence of how one or the other become mass-mobilizing engines in a way that effectively translates into a democratic seizure of power to undertake and sustain the transformation of the state. Unsurprisingly, this often leads to labelling disdainfully as 'populist' the governments of countries that remain within capitalism despite progressive political and economic policies.

These analyses present two major difficulties: on the one hand, they do not recognize the potential of political blocs that, by achieving shares of state power through elections, can transform that power into a mobilizing, creative force; on the other, they struggle to acknowledge the existence of social movements that incorporate themselves into those blocs as state-supporting movements. In this book I have been demonstrating that these two questions are a reality, and that, even if it is uncertain whether they will lead to post-capitalist structures, they have at least proved effective in keeping neoliberalism on the back foot.

Class struggle indeed exists, and the indicators that tell us of the unresolved contest between capital and labour (and between different types of labour) are everywhere to be seen. Yet many have been there for over two centuries, waiting for the magic recipe that translates them into subjectively-led mobilization – particularly, though not exclusively, in democracies sustained by electoral competition. What the political processes in countries such as Venezuela demonstrate is that this mobilization can initially take place through 'populist' tactics. These are but the tactics deployed by national-popular movements along the lines theorized by Ernesto Laclau (2007), which should not be rejected out of hand as a constituent dimension of politics. The political directionality of the blocs that emerge from these logics is unpredictable and never predetermined. They appear as 'movements against' a previous order of things, and it is only by analyzing their actions once they gain shares of state power that one can check their credentials and assess the direction they take – which can, of course, be to the right or the left.

In relation to the main theme of my discussion, let me focus on the way in which 'indigenous movements' have been brought into the debate about the extractivist countries in the orbit of the socialisms of the twenty-first century. The questioning of the leftist credentials and achievements of governments such as those of Maduro (and previously Chávez), Correa or Morales is often accompanied by the cliché that among the forces that they have clashed with are precisely 'indigenous movements'. This is presented as the ultimate demonstration that those governments would have drifted away from their progressive promises, at the same time betraying a sector of the population that had played a central role in their rise to power. Iconic (and indeed serious) conflicts over projects such as that of the *Territorio Indígena y Parque Nacional Isiboro–Secure* (TIPNIS, Isiboro–Sécure National Park and Indigenous Territory) in Bolivia and Perijá in Venezuela, or CONAIE's disputes with Correa's government in Ecuador, are highlighted as evidence that those governments are playing to the tune of the upper classes and international oligarchies – ultimately, of global capitalism. This type of argument, however, is questionable, first in its overall premise: as I argued above, there is strong evidence to clearly distinguish neoliberalism-as-usual from what these governments are implementing. But the argument is also questionable in its presentation of the cliché that 'indigenous movements' oppose these governments because of the latter's class and 'anti-indigenous' politics.

In the case of Venezuela, I have shown in this book that key segments of the indigenous population endorse the government's aims, which has considerably improved the political strength of the popular classes and their socioeconomic conditions – including that of the indigenous population. In fact, important segments of this population have been actively involved in the formation of a (state-supporting and state-sponsored) indigenous movement. This latter point needs to be noted, particularly in the light of other frequent criticisms of the government shaping the socialisms of the twenty-first century.

Admittedly, the existence of active political engagement between members of indigenous movements and state agents and structures has occasionally been recognized, but this engagement tends to be presented as evidence of continuing attempts at 'co-opt-and-rule' among (only apparently) progressive states (Hogenboom 2012, p. 123). Facilitating participation in the social programmes that these states implement to the benefit of the popular sectors is consequently interpreted as a co-optive strategy. These perspectives express a conception of the state that one could call the 'state as lobotomist'. This is an understanding of institutional state politics as a sphere unavoidably subjected to an all-powerful and all-pervasive co-option of political subjects. Without further qualification of the origin or the consequences of the co-optive forces, two political implications necessarily flow from these analytical perspectives: first, the equation of the politics of right-leaning and left-leaning projects of state transformation; and second, a complete negation of indigenous agency and politics. Active engagements with government and state agencies are thus negated as a conscious political choice – a conceptualization that in the case of indigenous politics is further sealed by the teleological understanding of the politics of indigeneity as 'anti-statist'. Given the current state of affairs across the world, one cannot help thinking about a logical if counter-intuitive expansion of these arguments: if helping to materialize the people's demand for socioeconomic enfranchisement (that is, for socioeconomic human rights) while broadening political participation is co-option, perhaps it is 'co-opting democracies' that so many people around the world, including indigenous people, are nowadays actively striving for.

Returning to the implications of the 'indigenous movements' debates in connection with extractivism, in the Latin American scenario we see that indigenous protests are not necessarily projected against it, or against the 'modernization' principles that underpin the orientation of the governments in the orbit of the socialism of the twenty-first century. Below, I will further illustrate this question as it relates to Venezuela, but well-founded, empirically supported research has already demonstrated this point as it relates, for instance, to the situation in Bolivia.

In that country one can certainly find protests among miners, including indigenous ones, who oppose not extractivism as such, but rather the conditions of state regulation upon it, as these affect various organized labour groups (Fuentes 2014). One can also learn, for instance, that the protests over TIPNIS, which had international echoes, mobilized indigenous groups both in support and against Morales's government. Furthermore, we learnt that some of the protests against the TIPNIS project, rather than expressing outright opposition to the government's construction of a road through the national park, sought changes to its route (in order to optimize its benefits for the local population) and criticized the lack of informed consent in the process (McNeish 2013). Against this background, we can move to look in more detail at the situation of indigenous peoples and their goals in Venezuela.

Indigenous peoples and communities in the Venezuelan political economy

From the outset I pointed out that the indigenous population in Venezuela occupies quite different positions in the country's economic structure. This fact may not have fully determined, but has certainly influenced, the shaping of the range of political interests and goals behind the various forms of indigenous collective action discussed in preceding chapters. There are, for instance, groups, such as the Warao mentioned in the Introduction, that have undertaken temporary or permanent migrations to cities to sell arts and crafts and beg as part of their subsistence strategies, after being dispossessed of land and impacted by environmental change driven by development projects. In a comparable structural position one also finds, for instance, Guahibos from the Venezuelan and Colombian *llanos* (plains) who, displaced by the advancing agricultural frontier (in this case, cattle and agriculture), temporarily migrate to cities such as Ciudad Bolívar, Ciudad Guayana and Puerto Ayacucho, where they adapt traditional subsistence activities to occupy modern-day marginal economic niches such as gathering and recycling garbage, living in dreadful, insanitary conditions for months at a time (Ortiz 2002). There are, however, communities that, because of the incomplete and uneven development of capitalism in Venezuela, have maintained semi-subsistence economies. This has been facilitated by their *de facto* control over significant extensions of (border) territory, which has also granted them significant degrees of political autonomy. This is the case of, for example, some Ye'kuana, Hoti, Yanomami, Sanema and even Pemon communities.[4] In these communities, integration into the regional and global markets is to a considerable extent voluntary and temporary, and they produce a significant proportion of what their members consume. In theoretical terms, this fits in the category of groups with 'market participation', which is the opposite of 'market dependence' (Wood 2002; Byres 2006; Patterson 2009): the latter occurs when communities *must* participate in the market as they have lost access to subsistence goods outside it.

On the other hand, some communities are totally integrated in the market. Among these one can find those whose members have been fully proletarianized and those whose members have preserved or created a productive platform from which to integrate themselves in those markets with a degree of control and ownership over the means of production. This might range from actual ownership of natural resources gained through campaigns for territorial rights to some forms of the commodification of culture or identities that, in part, have been facilitated by the struggles for cultural rights (for a discussion of these variants see, for instance, Comaroff and Comaroff 2009). One of the platforms through which a few indigenous communities have avoided dispossession and displacement (and have integrated themselves in the market from a more advantageous position) has been mining – of gold and diamonds in particular. Let us see in what context this has unfolded in Venezuela.

Small-scale mining of gold and diamonds has taken place without interruption since the first half of the nineteenth century. At present, it continues strongly in Amazonas, Bolívar and part of

Delta Amacuro states (such as Yocoima *municipio*) in the Guayana region. The majority of sites at which gold and diamonds are exploited are in territories in which there is a continuing presence of indigenous communities.

Current estimates of gold reserves in the Guayana region vary according to the source. They range between 8,000 metric tons (3,000 of which would only be exploitable through underground mining; source CVG, 1986) through 4,636 mt (Ministry of Basic Industries and Mining (MIBAM), 2011) to 3,817 mt (PDVSA, 2013) (see Milano 2014, p. 219). MIBAM was created in 2005 to coordinate policy in the mining sector, by extending the mining remit of the CVG. PDVSA (*Petróleos de Venezuela S.A.*, the state oil company) replaced MIBAM in the control of gold extraction after gold reserves were declared a public utility in 2013. In January that year, the industrial branch of PDVSA launched the *Corporación Venezolana de Minería* (CVM) (Venezuelan Mining Corporation).

While small-scale mining is estimated to produce 1.7 per cent of national mining production, it is very extensive in geographical terms as well as important in the creation of employment and revenue. This small-scale mining, which includes artisanal activity[5] along with small and medium-sized private companies, is considered by some unofficial sources to systematically evade fiscal liabilities, despite adding to an estimated 40 per cent of national production (Milano 2014).

Mining has indeed been exploitative, and often directly criminal on the part of miners against indigenous groups. Most renowned cases such as the Haximú massacre are only the tips of icebergs, salient moments in a continuum of exploitation and displacement that in general has accompanied the mining enterprise. However, some indigenous people and even entire communities have been actively involved in artisanal and small-scale mining too. This engagement is not to be explained by these communities being less 'environmentalist' than those that oppose mining in, for instance, the Perijá region in Zulia state, where members of the Yukpa movement are active against coal mining. A crucial factor to explain these different positions on mining is that, in the latter areas, mining (of coal, for instance) is extremely capital-intensive: this excludes indigenous inhabitants from its exploitation and also increases external interests, led by investors and their local agents, in dispossessing local people of land and displacing them. In this respect, indigenous opposition to mining, even when accompanied by environmental discourse, can be read as an instance of what Martínez-Alier (2002) stimulatingly called the 'environmentalism of the poor': in environmental terms, that opposition certainly has the positive implication of potentially blocking an extremely polluting and predatory industrial activity, but this goes hand-in-hand with the defence of the local community's own means of sustenance and reproduction. Coal mining in the Perijá region is both a direct threat to the possibilities for sustaining peasant indigenous forms of social (re)production and an inaccessible economic enterprise for them.

In locations where direct and, on occasion, self-managed engagement in mining has developed among the indigenous population, the relatively easy access to gold and diamonds has enabled some locals to acquire equipment for extraction. They thus operate and control small extractive teams that can be integrated into community economies to a greater or lesser degree. Sometimes, young people (principally men) from indigenous communities located far from mining sites also travel there for temporary work.[6] In some cases, such engagements of indigenous communities or people have been regulated through traditional authorities that allocate shifts for participation in the activity (Milano 2014), but in many other cases there is no community authority or institution in place to regulate the activity.

The thirst for precious minerals, subject to continuing international demand, remains unfortunately too strong and tempting an economic force.[7] It is also sometimes the only economic activity that generates sufficient levels of employment and revenue in indigenous territories. The engagement of indigenous communities and people in mining activities can therefore be read as a means to avoid proletarianization. These people and communities obviously oppose external threats of dispossession and displacement that, in connection with the continuation of mining, come through illegal (mining invasions) or legal means (such as concessions given by state authorities to companies or individuals that exclude the local population from substantial participation in the ventures). In this scenario, indigenous territorial rights, in addition to other political goals, also become a tool for the protection of extraction rights.

I previously noted that, of the 21 indigenous land titles granted to indigenous communities in 2013, the largest in terms of area (597,983 hectares) was granted to Pemon communities in the Ikabarú sector (Bolívar state). This is a very important mining area. While those titles were accompanied by funding for the diversification of productive activities, it is unrealistic to think that in the medium term mining will completely stop in the area. There is a drive towards regulating mining, rather than completely halting it. In 2014, a Presidential Commission for the Protection, Development and Integral Promotion of Lawful Mining Activity in the Guayana Region was created. Significantly, Nicia Maldonado, the former minister of Indigenous Peoples, was then appointed Minister of State for the Guayana Strategic Integral Development

Region. In this scenario, it is reasonable to presume that one of the possible effects of demarcation in areas such as Ikabarú is that the local indigenous population regains control over extractive activities – or, at least, more direct participation in the management of them.

Conflicts over small-scale extractivism in indigenous communities and the rights at stake

Expectations of the (hyperreal) indigenous population have often been too high (in the sense that it would not and should not participate in economic activities considered not only polluting, but also particularly un-indigenous). However, direct indigenous participation in mining, which as I have been arguing can be read as part of a strategy to stop proletarianization and dispossession, is far from new in Venezuela and other parts of Latin America. Decades ago, these processes were already very well developed. In Venezuela in particular, throughout the 1990s it was common to find both reports of the activities of unauthorized foreign miners in indigenous territories (see, for example, Colchester and Watson 1995, p. 26) and evidence that mining was often seen as an economic alternative within indigenous communities. This is what a Pemon from El Abismo (near El Paují, not far from the Ikabarú area) said to the press in 1993:

> They forbade us from mining because they say that mining destroys the river and destroys the forest ... We left the mines alone. But now who can explain why [foreigners] went into the Abismo, the great forest, with much more destructive machines than our mining pans? Why do they take Indians out of the mines, Venezuelan Indians? Why, after excluding the Indians, do they permit foreigners to exploit that which they forbid us? (Quoted in Colchester and Watson 1995, p. 23)

These complaints were being made in the 1990s, but very similar ones can be found today, and occasionally give rise to open conflict. An example erupted in February 2013, when organized members of several communities in the Urimán sector of Gran Sabana kidnapped 43 members of the Venezuelan military in protest at the latter's alleged abuses. With the intention of controlling illegal mining and smuggling, the military had suspended the authorizations for private small aircraft that, according to the members of those communities, were used to supply the communities with food and medicine, as well as to transport ill people to Santa Elena or Ciudad Bolívar when necessary. At the time, the *capitán* of San Miguel de Caroní, one of the communities involved, argued that they were not against the military's intervention against illegal gold mining, but also noted that it needed to be understood that this was the economic sustenance of those communities.[8] This type of action was in fact not exceptional: in October 2011 a similar incident took place in which 22 members of the Navy and Army were kidnapped, accused of allowing illegal mining in connivance with outside miners. In both the 2011 and 2013 cases, there were also reports that members of the military were involved in various forms of corruption, such as illegally extracting fees from local miners for them to work and to permit the delivery of supplies.

February 2013 saw a very interesting example of what was at stake in these conflicts. In this particular case, it was again revealing of the concerns and sources of argument of indigenous people engaged in mining activities, but also of the way in which conflict is incorporated into the dynamics that guide the Bolivarian state. At the time, a video was circulated through various networks and media in which a Pemon woman in Urimán confronted a high-ranking National Guard officer, Division General Clíver Alcalá

Cordones.[9] The two were surrounded by a large group of members of the community, which had direct stakes in the mining industry. Among the remarks that the woman directed at the general was: 'This land is ours, and you are not going to take it away from us. What do you want, to give it to the Chinese, the Russians,[10] for them to come and damage the land of the Pemon?'

Alcalá Cordones's visit to Urimán was part of a long dispute. The National Guard had previously suspended flights to the community from Ciudad Bolívar and Puerto Ordaz in a renewed attempt to control illegal mining. *Capitanes* of the Pemon communities of the sector travelled to those cities in order to complain to civil and military authorities about these measures, arguing that the suspension of flights was strangling the economy of the area, which largely lives off mining and is basically dependent on market trade: most of their food and basic consumer supplies depend on air transport to reach the area, which is quite inaccessible via land and requires very long journeys by river. In the video, one can hear how the woman angrily recalled that, in their visits to regional authorities when trying to explain their problems, Alcalá Cordones in particular and other officers had ignored and offended them. 'And [now that you are in our community] if we want to take you hostage we will do so, because here we Pemon Indians are in charge, just as you said in Puerto Ordaz', the woman threatened; 'it is your fault, everything that is happening here'. The general, who had stoically been listening to the torrent of criticism (just watch the video), finally responded: 'I admit it and apologize'.

This video, which, as usual in Venezuela, was circulated and politicized as part of the communication wars at play in the country, was initially launched as an attack on the government: comments on the video variously presented it as an example of inept military and state bureaucracies, and as an instance of the way in which the government undermined indigenous rights. However, this event was also an interesting example of the way in which agents of the Bolivarian state often face conflict and are the targets of various forms of contentious action. Can the reader think of many countries in which a very senior officer of the military or police force would be willing (or ordered) to go to a protest to listen to the participants and, moreover, to publicly take responsibility on the spot and apologize before protesters? I cannot. Beyond the colourful exceptionalism of the event, it is an expression of the dialectics that develop between state agents and diverse forms of social mobilization (including extra-institutional ones) in a country where protest and the contentious demands of organized popular forces are also considered a source of political creativity.

In terms of the discussion outlined above, these events also have analytical and political implications. In particular, they cause us to reflect on the heterogeneous landscape of demands and social horizons that exists among the indigenous population. Preconceived ideas about 'indigenous struggles' and indigenous rights do not always work well, and assumptions about the character and finality of land rights illustrate this point very well. These rights, intimately associated with indigenous struggles, indeed remain key to modifying historical processes of dispossession and exploitation. Yet while formally based on one-fits-all legal principles, they are nonetheless in practice linked by their potential holders to a variety of political and economic projects. These might range from the extreme of self-managed conservationism to, say, that of self-managed extractive activity, with quite different points in between. In order to understand these struggles and their goals it is crucial to separate their abstract conceptualization from teleological preconceptions and analyze them in context as potentially changeable projects. This requires a detailed knowledge of specific struggles. The amount of scholarship addressing the processes of dispossession and de-territorialization of indigenous groups is understandably far greater than the studies and theorization of their various current incorporations into the capitalist world system. Yet the latter are equally necessary if one aims to understand the contemporary dynamics of indigenousness and its diverse connections with global capitalism (Li 2010). It is important to understand that those incorporations vary substantially between different parts of the world, both in their present configuration and in the political directionality that they reveal: the positioning in relation to capitalism and state politics, for instance, is far from always being the same in the local struggles for indigenous rights in, say, Bolivia, New Zealand, Venezuela or the US. Let me further elaborate on this point and its implications by bringing in ongoing debates about indigenous rights as these are framed by some analysts.

Indigenous capitalisms?

Discursive identifications of indigeneity with anti-capitalism, collectivism or environmentalism are still very common and part of conventional wisdom in many parts of the world. In this book I have examined the creative discursive elaboration through which indigeneity has been associated in Venezuela with socialism by members of the *chavista* bloc, including indigenous actors.[11] However, this does not of course imply that, as a matter of principle, there is any natural connection between socialism and indigeneity, and indeed there is nothing necessarily anti-capitalist in the implementation of indigenous rights, including territorial rights.

In a sense this was underscored in the well-known discussions on the idea of the 'permitted Indian' and the way in which neoliberal governance and capitalist adjustment are perfectly compatible with the reinforcement of a certain framing of indigenous identities and rights (see, for example, Hale 2002; Hale and Millamán 2004). And this compatibility is currently producing new and very coherent organic theorizations from within (a certain type of) indigenous struggles. A typical example is centred on the concept of 'indigenous capitalisms'.

This concept is being theorized with the explicit objective of using it as an index of self-determination and an expression of the political strength of indigenous peoples seeking to avoid cultural dissolution (e.g. Bunten 2011). The suggestion is that the latter goals will be (and are being) realized by determined indigenous groups whose economic ventures successfully exploit capitalism without reproducing its anti-humanist goals. Let us see if that is the case, or if on the contrary we are facing a bold and sparkling celebration of triumphant capitalist logics and ideology.

An actual case that this organic intellectuality uses to illustrate indigenous peoples' current stakes in global capitalism is an Alaska Native corporation called Chenega. This corporation, we are informed, exemplifies 'culturally appropriate' participation in global capitalism, one rooted in 'indigenous value systems' (Bunten 2011, p. 207). Chenega, and indigenous corporations in general, would possess distinctive features that set them apart from what the author herself qualifies as the 'antihumanist assumptions and goals that inform capitalism' (ibid.). In following this argument, one is led to believe that it is 'non-indigenous' corporations – and only them – that would share those antihumanist assumptions and goals. This line of thinking is extraordinarily striking for many reasons, but it reaches paroxysm when one learns about the type of humanism that Chenega actually cultivates through its culturally appropriate entrepreneurial activities.

The economic success of Chenega, which in 2009 produced revenue of US$ 1.1 billion, rested largely on contracts with the US federal government. So far, so good. However, those contracts had been obtained, incidentally, to participate in activities such as the reconstruction of Iraq and the securitization of the prison at Guantánamo Bay. That is, contracts for the rebuilding of Iraq's infrastructure after a bloody war launched on the basis of fabricated information (and whose dramatic consequences are still felt in a completely destabilized region, with 'Islamic State' emerging from its ashes), and for the reinforcement of security in a jail that epitomizes the way in which a country such as the US can blatantly violate international law and human rights conventions if so required according to the interests defined by its governing elites.

One can accept, for the sake of argument, that the internal management of Chenega is rooted in 'indigenous value systems' and that this might contribute to indigenous self-determination – though in fact there is not much evidence about how that translates into practice. One can even fleetingly accept, also for argument's sake, that non-indigenous corporations are all internally managed according to a homogeneous 'non-indigenous' value system – something that is of course unsustainable, the idea that capitalist corporations do not harbour diverse 'managerial cultures' in different parts of the world. Yet, even leaving all that aside, what stands out most clearly, and what the theorists of 'indigenous capitalisms' leave unsaid, is that both indigenous corporations and non-indigenous ones outwardly project exactly the same values: business is business, as it were. Ethical concerns, the subjugation or dissolution of (other) peoples and the reproduction of imperialist foreign policy should not interfere with a corporation's need to accumulate and multiply capital, regardless of the type of 'cultural values' that might pervade its internal management.

The case of Chenega is certainly particularly striking – though it has been used precisely to illustrate the existence of 'indigenous capitalisms'. What is not so exceptional is the fact that many a political and economic project can fit under the banner of indigenous self-determination. For, as I have been arguing throughout this book, indigenous struggles are not teleologically predetermined.

Often with little or no alternative, given the political contexts in which they manoeuvre, many indigenous peoples and communities across the world are actively seeking strategies to incorporate themselves into capitalism from positions of relative advantage that sometimes stem from claims to indigenous rights. This can be read as a strategy to halt a centuries-long history of dispossession, displacement and subjugation, as I have been arguing, and to that extent it is more than understandable. If no-return proletarianization and/or forced dispossession can be stopped in this way, what is the objection to those processes, given the apparent lack of alternatives? In any event, in addition to contradicting the conventional wisdom that associates indigeneity with anti-capitalism, the existence of this reality obviously demands caution in the analysis of political processes. And it also calls for renewed paradigms in approaching, for instance, the study of relations between indigenous movements and (at least some) states.

While indigenous movements have indeed very often been oriented to oppose neoliberalism and fully-fledged capitalism for the consequences that they brought upon them, in the absence of broader political projects in which to incorporate themselves these movements can also be and are steered towards other horizons, including conspicuous examples of 'indigenous capitalisms'. However, some states driven by blocs that amalgamate popular forces are capable, as this study shows, of helping to stop age-old processes of indigenous proletarianization and dispossession as part of larger political projects. These projects open the doors of socioeconomic and political enfranchisement to indigenous peoples, but in parallel catalyze anti-neoliberal forces and potentially anti-capitalist ones. In such projects there is room for the strengthening of cultural identities too, and for the achievement of increased levels of autonomy – when this is defined as leading to effective political empowerment. That is why those states generate positive synergies with indigenous channels of collective action in places like Venezuela. This collective action, unlike that of those who present capitalism as an avenue of cultural redemption, is part of larger political movements driven by the ideal that other models of social organization are not only possible, but also necessary and more just when the goal is well-being and justice for all – and not only for those who, through isolated struggles, can secure a safe place, if perhaps only temporarily, in this jungle of ours.

Closing considerations

The Venezuelan political economy imposes limits on the Bolivarian project of state transformation. Oil, in addition to other mineral resources, constitutes the wealth upon which the country rests, and for the time being no viable alternatives have been developed. Access to and control over those resources thus remains indispensable for socioeconomic development and the consolidation of sovereignty, which the revolution has so far maintained as its core goals. That requirement conditions the government's approach to state reconfiguration, which can only take place with a degree of sovereign control over the national territory and its resources. At the same time, the strength of the revolution effectively started to spread with, and has become dependent on, the facilitation of popular participation in the configuration and guidance of the state structures. This partly explains the adoption of the New Geometry of Power as a political framework that can make the centralization in the design of national-level development compatible with local and regional spheres of (relatively) autonomous organization. This framework, and the national project of transformation in general, is not compatible with demands for (absolute) autonomy that include a territorial dimension. These demands become obstacles for the national project, particularly when they spring from resource-rich areas. The model of indigenous territorialization that the government has favoured, prioritizing the creation of communal councils and communes at the expense of territorial rights as originally designed in the CRBV, is a coherent response to the challenges it faces as a result of political-economic constraints.

It would be misleading to present this as merely a state-centric move away from 'indigenous movements' and demands in the country. There are sectors of the indigenous population that do not separate their pursuit of socioeconomic and political enfranchisement from the demand for territorial demarcation and titling. Yet it is that enfranchisement, whose pursuit is deeply rooted in history, that is prioritized by major segments of the indigenous population in the country. Indeed, enfranchisement constitutes *the* galvanizing goal guiding indigenous collective action, including that of the groups that pursue it in (partial) opposition to existing state structures. Beyond that galvanizing goal, which has focused the action of the state-sponsored and state-supporting movement, a complex landscape of heterogenenous demands and social horizons exists among the indigenous population. Sectors of that population, and particularly those involved in the indigenous movement, show a determined commitment to the socialist-leaning Bolivarian project, but other sectors harbour specific demands beyond the galvanizing goal of enfranchisement that might well be compatible with, and even necessary for, business-as-usual capitalism – as long as some advantageous position can be guaranteed for them within it, for instance by gaining effective rights to manage resource extraction.

It is against this background that the Bolivarian revolution becomes the stimulus for broader discussions of indigenous movements and rights. In this process, there is an indigenous movement that supports the state and has developed synergies with its agents. This has been possible because state power has been used simultaneously to facilitate socioeconomic and political inclusion and to foster popular mobilization. Unlike models in which 'indigenous capitalisms' are boldly presented as the route to the realization of indigenous rights, the Bolivarian revolution has in this respect effectively offered an alternative in which they become empowered as part of a larger popular movement with socialist leanings. This demonstrates that indigenous peoples, as well as non-indigenous, have more than one option when it comes to shaping their future. It is clear that more and stronger capitalism is not the only possible route that indigenous peoples take in order to achieve empowerment and social justice.

The Bolivarian revolution has been criticized by some advocates of indigenous rights who struggle to recognize that, as a political project, it is strongly supported by important sectors of the indigenous population too. Those criticisms are often the result of teleological conceptions of indigenous rights and struggles that deny political agency to indigenous subjects. In addition, some of those criticisms target the Bolivarian process for its dependence on extractivism, which, when opposed by indigenous collective action, becomes another argument to prove the alleged anti-indigenous character of the revolution. In this chapter I have shown why that argument is flawed. Extractivism, which admittedly is a global problem, is legitimately opposed by *some* indigenous groups in *some* circumstances (certainly when it endangers the basis of their subsistence), but it is not an activity that as a matter of principle is excluded from indigenous demands. It is always by the detailed analysis of struggles, and not by resorting to preconceived ideas, that we can understand their causes and consider their implications. Against that reality, it is up to everyone to decide which non-indigenous and indigenous struggles are to be supported, and with what (if any) limitations.

EIGHT

Closing remarks

At certain points in history, the day-to-day events that constitute it are inexplicably transformed into everyday attempts at *making* it. It is a rare but recurrent situation. Multitudes begin to act and to interpret their actions as if driven by the sudden realization that the world is not as it should be. Wilfulness prevails, and nihilistic inclinations vanish from within the ranks of the discontented: the cry against the existing world goes hand-in-hand with the belief that a better one is indeed possible. These are forward-looking periods of intense political struggle. The definition of the future becomes the object of a contest: widespread mobilization unavoidably faces its countermovement. How long these periods will last is unpredictable, and their final outcome uncertain. They always contain the seeds of change, yet it is only with hindsight that the character of their offspring can be properly identified. The emergence, maintenance and termination of these processes can only be explained through a combined analysis of structural conditions and subjectively guided behaviours. The Bolivarian revolution, a process sustained by electoral contests, constitutes an instance of this type of phenomenon, and is ongoing. Aspects of this process are still undefined, but one can nevertheless attempt to understand how it came to be, how it achieved the changes that have actually come about and what possibilities it has opened up through the political dynamics it has activated. I undertook this task by analyzing relations between the state and indigenous peoples, which unsurprisingly have been fully enmeshed in the overall revolutionary process.

Much has been written about how this particular revolution came to be. But the undeniable importance of a generative electoral victory needs to be underscored. A movement of these dimensions cannot appear from nowhere, of course, and in order to understand its genesis both earlier struggles and structural factors must be taken into account. But those struggles disappear (or continue indefinitely as forms of localized, dispersed and limited resistance) unless they are given impetus by some power-shifting generative moment. In democracies sustained by electoral competition, this moment will normally come through an electoral victory that can translate into the seizure of significant shares of state power. Such was the case in Venezuela.

For the nascent Bolivarian bloc, the win in the 1998 presidential elections guaranteed access to shares of state power without which the revolutionary process could have never been effectively started. State power was catalytic for the political bases of that emerging bloc: previously amorphous and quite fragmented bases accelerated their crystallization as a national-popular bloc whose combined strength was much greater than the sum of its constituent political parts. By becoming part of a larger movement, and by the very motion stimulated by the exercise of state power, some previously existing foci of activism and political organization multiplied their effective strength. The dynamics created by the swift call for an assembly to draw up a new constitution were particularly generative and productive, and the way in which they impacted on the realm of indigenous organizations perfectly illustrates the point.

This initial, frantic period of the revolutionary process created some organizations as empowered actors. That is, those organizations already existed, but during this time they were qualitatively transformed into something else. At this juncture CONIVE was a languishing, weak organization, but it came out of it reinvigorated, if full of internal tensions. The organization had been invested with previously unachievable powers.

Such a dramatic transformation resulted partly from the state's requirement for a legitimate institutionalized collective actor to mediate with the indigenous constituency. Yet the more fundamental and durable effects of that empowerment sprang from the development of fluid synergies between members of this organization and other activists, political parties and organizations within the orbit of the *chavista* bloc. This brought CONIVE fully into the national contest between *chavismo* and *anti-chavismo*, and politicized the organization well beyond its particularistic demands. Internally and externally, it is now exposed to the dialogue of conflict and cohesion that drive political agents in the Bolivarian milieu.

In terms of the changes that the Bolivarian revolution has brought about, I noted that the current political and socioeconomic enfranchisement of the indigenous population is unprecedented in the country's history. I also associated the analysis of this enfranchisement with the discussion of how it came about: it cannot be separated from the forms of indigenous collective action deployed in the ongoing process of reconfiguration of the state/society complex. A particularly influential type of such action has developed into a state-sponsored and state-supporting indigenous movement. This movement has been pivotal in the facilitation of socioeconomic enfranchisement for large proportions of the indigenous population. It has been involved in the articulation of government social programmes and funds, and at the same time has empowered actors who now see themselves as active members in the national political arena.

This indigenous movement epitomizes the way in which, within the Bolivarian revolution, powerful synergies have developed between a large variety of popular actors, party politics and state organs and agents. The functioning of this movement weakens widespread preconceptions about social movement activity. In practice, it invalidates arguments about 'state' and 'society' as ontologically separated entities. Members of this movement operate on both sides of that alleged divide, and their overall political orientation firmly positions them as drivers of a state-supporting social movement − supportive of a state structure that could effectively guarantee enfranchisement in relation to the forces that have historically ignored it and broken it up.

The existence of this indigenous movement also undermines teleological preconceptions about 'indigenous struggles' as antithetical to state and party politics. Those who cultivate these preconceptions, in particular as they refer to indigenous politics, struggle to recognize what this movement has brought to light. Their reaction to the changes taking place in countries such as Venezuela is puzzling: whether they deny reality or resort to arguments that present that reality as a betrayal of truly indigenous interests and goals. It is from this second perspective that we hear the worn-out cliché about co-opting state structures neutralizing indigenous actors (or indeed any actors from subaltern classes) who decide to work within them, or in cooperation with state agents, in pursuit of their goals. This type of argument produces major difficulties for the political analysis of the contemporary world. An immediate problem is that it is incapable of distinguishing between different forms of state praxis: whether they become a champion of neoliberal reform or take a firm socialist-leaning path of reform, states are always presented as co-opting, neutralizing devices for the aspirations of subaltern classes. In this light, the Bolivarian state, the Chilean state, the Colombian state and the Mexican state (to name just a few examples) are equal in relation to indigenous struggles: all of them co-opt, and have leanings that deviate from the (teleologically defined) goals of indigenous emancipation. And, of course, in this light there is no room for indigenous goals that go beyond certain notions of self-determination. In short, these perspectives translate into a negation of politics.

However, reality is stubborn. In Venezuela, for instance, central elements of indigenous collective action have constituted themselves as a state-supporting movement. And they have done so in pursuit of what their praxis consistently reveals as their priority goals: political and socioeconomic enfranchisement. Moreover, this indigenous movement has also intentionally incorporated itself into a larger political bloc that pursues a socialist-leaning reconfiguration of the overall state/society complex – and not only of parts of that complex. In practice, the emergence of this larger political bloc echoes the theoretical proposals of Latin American activists who, from the 1960s onwards, sought to combine an understanding of the specificities of indigenous peoples and their histories with the construction of political blocs that, beyond those specificities, could bring indigenous forces into alliance with other popular sectors of society in pursuit of socialist-leaning models of state transformation. These proposals were theoretically displaced and politically condemned during the multicultural tsunami, conceptualized as deceitful deviations of real processes of indigenous emancipation. Yet those proposals, which for nearly two decades had virtually had no organic theorization, became real as soon as indigenous actors were effectively given the opportunity to join in a popular national movement. This is the possibility that in Venezuela opened up with the emergence of Bolivarianism as a national-popular bloc, and particularly after it seized shares of state power through elections.

The determined and active incorporation of the indigenous movement into the shaping and expression of the national-popular bloc does not, of course, mean that the entire indigenous population shares its political priorities and the route chosen to pursue them. There is a combative element of indigenous collective action that has maintained a contentious position towards government inefficiencies and some state organs. This demonstrates the existence of a range of interests and political priorities among the indigenous population, which occupies different positions within the structures of capitalism and nationality and is riven by a variety of structuring cleavages. These divisions help to explain why, beyond the galvanizing goals of enfranchisement that everyone pursues, a heterogeneous landscape of social horizons can be identified among the indigenous population (as well as among the non-indigenous one). These cleavages also underpin the various types of collective action that, revealing different political priorities, have unfolded in Venezuela.

For some commentators and activists, only those types of collective action that (partially) oppose state action constitute a 'social movement'. Throughout this book, I have argued why that is a misleading characterization of the complex arena of indigenous collective action in Venezuela. But this characterization is also worth an additional comment on some other political implications with which it is associated. That positioning contains echoes of the ideological condemnation of 'the state' that the neoliberal revolution (as well as the collapse of left-wing alternative projects before it) achieved on many fronts. The state, even in its welfare-oriented version, was presented as a sphere of coercion and all sorts of social and economic problems. The neoliberal Right had an antidote against it: the so-called 'civil society', an alleged social space without public power through which freedom, justice and efficiency was to be achieved. Many on the Left abandoned 'the state' (whether characterized as 'bourgeois' or as a neoliberal tool) as a potential tool for emancipatory projects, and in turn placed most of its hopes in 'social movements'. The ramifications of that dual movement against state politics are still felt. At present, for instance, a puzzling phenomenon is clearly identifiable in certain criticisms of the socialisms of the twenty-first century projects: 'civil society' and 'social movements' have come to occupy the same political niche in relation to (or rather against) 'the state' that these projects brought back in.

Leaving aside such criticisms, the political prospects for the Bolivarian project remain uncertain. For the time being, the socialism of the twenty-first century in Venezuela retains socioeconomic development and sovereignty as its core goals. And these goals are not only 'elite' or 'government' goals: they are also the galvanizing goals that guide the central elements of collective action, including indigenous collective action, that support and shape the government, as we have seen. In turn, social development in Venezuela and other countries in the region requires an important degree of economic development, which is still dependent on resource extractivism. In this respect, the socialisms of the twenty-first century have not yet demonstrated radically different relations with the environment. The dramatic effects of capitalist development, within which the socialisms of the twenty-first century structurally remain, have in some countries reached levels that, if exported to the rest of the world population, would make it literally impossible to maintain life on the planet, as discussion of so-called environmental footprints have shown. The search for alternative development models therefore remains a high priority. Yet it would be misguided and unethical to blame 'extractivism' in the countries in the orbit of the socialism of the twenty-first century for the global problem of un-sustainability. These countries are only weak links in global chains of consumption and production, and unless structural changes to those chains take place they could reasonably claim a right to euthanasia: that is, the right for their populations to have a dignified end, given the right to wait for the end living well above one's biocapacity that is claimed and effectively exercised in other parts of the world.

Finally, two comments on the lessons that can be taken from the Bolivarian revolution as a process of state reconfiguration. First, one about the particular conditions of the country where it emerged. It is often argued that this process is unique and cannot be replicated, since it rests on Venezuela's oil wealth, which provides immense resources for redistributive policy, among other things. This is indeed a unique factor. Yet the consolidation of *chavismo* as a national-popular bloc was not a natural result of those conditions. In essence, it was the product of a particular form of re-articulating and mobilizing popular forces already latent in the country. This political strategy had two pillars: first, the creation of a broad, multiclass popular movement to win elections, and, second, understanding the need to ensure shares of state power and class-oriented policy as potential engines for popular mobilization. This strategy is not dependent on oil.

The second comment relates to the debates about state power as a potential ally or irredeemable enemy of emancipation. Party structures and state organs always contain risks of excessive bureaucratization, corruption and centralization of decisions, in Venezuela and elsewhere. And it is legitimate and necessary to report those digressions in the search for social justice and wider democracy. But the political dynamics over the past 16 years in Venezuela have also demonstrated that parties and state organs can be more adaptable to popular forces and demands when government actions guide them in that direction and popular mobilization pushes in the same direction. These structures have proved to be successful in massively improving access to socioeconomic and political rights for many people in Venezuela – among them, many indigenous people. This is not a panacea for all the issues Venezuelans must deal with, but it is no small feat either, given the world we live in.

APPENDIX

Extraordinary Assembly

Here is the description of an assembly in which the politics of indigenous organizations feed into electoral politics. The assembly, which I attended, was organized by the FIEB and took place on 29 February 2004 at the La Piscina hotel in Ciudad Bolívar. Its aim was the selection of a federation-supported indigenous candidate for the Legislative Council of Bolívar state (CLEB); regional and municipal elections were due later that year. In 2000, due to a lack of coordination with the MVR, the federation failed to ensure that its candidate was elected. The assembly's dynamics illustrate the challenges and complexities of a novel and empowering political enfranchisement – challenges that indigenous actors tackle head-on.

The event was presided over by the federation's Executive Committee, made up of president Juvencio Gómez (Pemon), general secretary Yaritza Aray (Kariña) and treasurer Nicolás Betis (Pemon).[1] With them sat José Luis González (a Pemon and indigenous member of the National Assembly) and José Gregorio Cascante, the regional coordinator for indigenous political participation.

Gómez introduced the event, acknowledging the effort made by the assemblymen whose arrival in Ciudad Bolívar had entailed exhausting travel from distant communities. He confirmed that the assembly's aim was the selection of FIEB's official candidate for the Regional Legislative Council (CLEB), but that there were also other issues to be dealt with (a list of eleven separate points had been drafted).

Gómez regretted that there was no representation from the 17 indigenous peoples in Bolívar state (attendees were overwhelmingly Pemon). The president also welcomed observers and members of the media, pointing out that other invited guests included Kuyujani,[2] the Piaroa Parliament, OCIGRANSA[3] and indigenous municipal councillors from the *municipios* in Bolívar state.

Cascante explained the plan that had been designed to promote participation, emphasizing the organizational effort that the assembly implied. A quorum had been established for the legitimation of the assembly, calculated by adding up, for each of the six municipal units considered by the federation,[4] the following attendees: *capitán* and one delegate from each indigenous community within that *municipio*; *capitán general* from each sector;[5] and indigenous councillors from relevant *alcaldías* (town halls). He went on to detail the situation at the assembly, which should in principle have a qualified majority of representatives from each *municipio*. Summing up, he announced that there was no quorum for the assembly, nor for any of the six *municipios* represented.

There were no representatives at all from Heres *municipio* (where the assembly was being held) or sectors of other *municipios* (e.g. Icabarú sector in Gran Sabana *municipio*). In total, there were five *capitanes generales* and two municipal councillors; the mayor of Gran Sabana *municipio*, Ricardo Delgado, was also present. The three executive members of OCIGRANSA were not present. Tulio Gudiño, indigenous member of the Regional Assembly, had been invited, but was also a no-show.

Gómez resumed, noting the importance of the federation sticking to the rules 'like any other organization'. He said that the rules for the assembly, among them that of the quorum, aimed to produce that formal standard and thus strengthen legitimacy. Acknowledging the difficulties that these processes entailed, he nevertheless gave his opinion that if there was no quorum, the assembly should be called off. However, he recognized the effort made by those who had actually come, and wanted to know what they thought: Should a new meeting be held (hoping to obtain a quorum)? Or should they rather continue with the present assembly without a quorum and make a decision anyway? In the latter case, even if he knew that a majority of communities would support the decision, attendees would need to think about how the decisions would go down in the communities.

Gómez then requested opinions from attendees, which went on for about one hour. Three main options were expressed: 1. '*reglamentista*' (by the rules: no quorum, no Assembly); 2. 'traditionalist' (if indigenous tradition were observed, 'this type of meeting would be held with whoever was present'), which converged with the 'pragmatic' position ('let us go with what we have'); 3. 'delegative' (the assembly should choose candidates and then put those names to the communities, where, organized by sector, people could make the final selection; it was implied that a *capitán* did not have authority to decide on behalf of his or her community).

Gómez called for a vote. He summarized the options:

1. call the assembly off due to the absence of a quorum
2. make a decision there and then about the candidate for the CLEB.

Tito Poyo (Kariña, brother of José Poyo) then spoke.[6] 'We are in a learning process', he said. He suggested that the pre-established rules for decision-making should not be applied so rigidly. Claiming to speak from experience, he supported the continuation of the assembly. Moreover, he requested permission to actively participate in it, noting in anticipation of criticism that he was an *indígena* from 'outside the communities' (he had lived in Ciudad Bolívar most of his life).

Voting then took place. The question 'Do we continue with the Assembly?' was posed, and a show of hands requested. Gómez called first for those who wished to vote NO (he translated his words into Pemon). Not a single hand was raised. Then he asked who wanted to vote YES: all (literally) hands were raised.

After the vote, Gómez responded to Poyo. He asked him to what federal unit he belonged, since at a national level Poyo was representing Anzoátegui state. Gómez suggested that one could not participate in everything, and also referred to the issue of 'urban *indígenas*'.[7] Several delegates then intervened to give their opinions on the matter (three spoke in Pemon, which was then translated into Spanish). Tito Poyo was finally accepted, by acclamation rather than a vote.

Next came the reading of the candidates' profiles, prepared by the federation. The profile consisted of 13 points. The candidate should:

1. be an indigenous person
2. have a good knowledge of indigenous peoples' issues
3. be responsible, and morally recognized by indigenous communities
4. have a solid background or suitability as a social activist
5. be down to earth and humble of heart (there is, of course, no instrument to measure this, but Cascante states that 'it can be felt')

6. be discerning
7. have teamwork skills
8. be enterprising and creative in the achievement of indigenous peoples' political goals
9. be incorruptible
10. have a general knowledge about relevant matters of national and international politics
11. have a calling for service and humanism
12. be independent of political parties
13. be emotionally well balanced.

Before moving on to the selection of candidates, José Luis González gave a talk on 'political participation and strategic alliances'. He recalled Article 125 of the CRBV and linked this to the requirement to get organized and establish rules to rationalize decision-making processes.[8] González added that it was necessary to look for a candidate committed to the revolutionary process led by President Chávez and backed by Chapter VIII of the CRBV. He did not believe indigenous peoples would want to appoint representatives who were against the revolutionary process. González noted that it was the first time in the Republic's history that it was possible for indigenous people to do what they were doing in that very meeting: to elect their own representatives. He hoped that the mayor of Gran Sabana, who González used as an example of a recently elected indigenous candidate, would follow the revolutionary and Bolivarian path.[9]

González also stressed the importance of those who valued the traditional authority of *capitanes* and *capitanes generales*, but emphasized that the Extraordinary Assembly was a historic event in itself. A good number of people were attending the event, he added, and hoped that in the future there would be many more. He suggested that FIEB should keep looking for a system that enabled everyone in the communities to participate, without relying upon representatives. González ended by exhorting everyone to look for a governor of Bolívar state who would not betray indigenous rights and who was committed to the revolutionary process.[10]

Before leaving the rostrum, González explicitly referred to 'strategic alliances': 'We [*indígenas*] are fully committed to the revolutionary process', adding that indigenous representatives at the national level were trying to build support within the revolutionary bloc. He confirmed that alliances with the parties of the revolution were being sought. Ideally the indigenous organizations would like to go it alone, but could not do so under the existing electoral system. In order to attain their goals, González said they would support Chávez's candidate for the Bolívar state governorship; but also that they would demand in return that the central government supported the candidates chosen by the indigenous peoples themselves for the CLEB, *municipios* and *parroquias*.

The assembly reconvened with the introduction of nominated candidates. It was stipulated that the candidates would participate in '*planchas*' (closed lists with a principal candidate and a substitute). A representative of the CNE (Yoisi Mendoza) was then introduced, and voting took place. Candidatures were identified by numbers:

1. Juvencio Gómez and Yaritza Aray
2. José Gregorio Rodríguez and C. Esteba
3. Tito Poyo and Camilo Esteban.

(Yaritza Aray had requested the withdrawal of the candidature in which she was principal and Juvencio Gómez the substitute.)

Attendees were called to vote individually, by *municipio*. A helper was requested if the voter was illiterate. The vote was universal for all attendees and secret: the ballot papers were deposited in a cardboard box. The results were as follows:

Candidature 1: 121
Candidature 2: 9
Candidature 3: 20
Invalid: 3
Total votes: 153

Juvencio Gómez and Yaritza Aray thus became the federation's official candidates for the CLEB elections.

An Official Assembly Report was produced to be sent to the CNE, and another was produced for internal consumption.

The Extraordinary Assembly and the ordinary challenges of indigenous organization

The assembly faced several constraints (time frame, opposing views on legitimacy, internal manoeuvring, language and ethnic diversity), but achieved its principal goal: a federation-supported candidate was selected for the regional elections. Organizational challenges and political differences were overcome, but they were a constituent part of the process. Political differences stemmed not only from actors' position before the revolutionary process, which by then (2004) was already a noticeable part of the 'indigenous politics' realm; but also from the existence of diverse forms of authority and legitimacy which indigenous representatives had to negotiate (and manoeuvre within) in this type of event (representation vs direct participation; 'tradition' vs modernization).

The politics of indigeneity become part of the tactical manoeuvres in this type of event. The requirements for candidates establish that they must be indigenous, but this often creates problems of definition (which are political problems), for they translate into the inclusion or exclusion of candidates. The tension between 'urban' as opposed to community-based *indígenas* was highlighted by the case of Tito Poyo.

Notes

INTRODUCTION

1 The Warao's traditional territory is in and around the Orinoco Delta (Delta Amacuro and Monagas states). Their temporary or permanent migrations to cities, primarily for economic reasons, were exacerbated from the late 1960s onwards due to land dispossession spurred by agricultural projects and failed state-planned development that included environmental intervention. The case of Caño Mánamo, one of the Delta water channels, was crucial in this process. Closed in the mid-1960s to prevent seasonal flooding of surrounding lands deemed most suitable for agriculture, it had catastrophic socioeconomic consequences for indigenous and non-indigenous communities in the area (see, for instance, García Castro and Heinen, 1999). For an additional examination of causes and characteristics of temporary Warao migration to cities, see García Castro, 2000.

2 '*Malandro*' is a term used in Venezuela to refer generically to outlaws and/or criminals.

3 Liborio Guarulla, a Baniva, was a militant of the radical left and has been through various splits in the parties of which he has been a member. While he was initially involved in the *chavista* bloc, he left this and has developed strong links with the opposition leadership over the last few years.

4 Let me make very clear that here I use the term 'populism' not to describe a departure from democratic ideals, but rather as a concept that enables us to study and understand a constituent dimension of politics. I largely base my analytical approach to this concept on Laclau's theoretical work (2007), and have previously argued about its utility even for the analysis of international politics. Specifically, I resorted to those interpretations in order to explain the significant impact of Bolivarian politics and Venezuelan foreign policy in the international sphere (see Angosto-Ferrández 2014a and 2014d).

5 There is a large degree of convergence between the terms '*chavismo*', '*bolivarianismo*' and even 'socialism of the twenty-first century' as they apply in Venezuela: mostly as (partially meaningless) terms that facilitated collective political identification for the political bloc currently in power.

6 I use the term 'popular classes' principally in reference to the non-elite sectors of Venezuelan society, in the sense that it is normally used in the country (which

includes, among others, workers in the formal and informal economy (including social reproduction sector), peasants, indigenous groups and the unemployed. It is, of course, a vague term, but it is widely used in Latin American countries and helps to describe disenfranchized groups in quite segmented societies. For a conceptualization of the popular movement in its application to the urban sphere, see Schönwälder 2002, pp. 15–18.

7 Referring to *shares* of state power is a necessary nuance. It is not 'state power' that has been seized as a whole. The vagaries of state power are dotted with strongholds that do not respond to a single commanding force nor to a single class orientation, and in countries like Venezuela that fact was further complicated by the obsolete and often corrupt state of some state bureaucratic structures. In analysing the Bolivarian process, the prominence of executive power in the channelling of government plans partly results from that question: activating 'state power' and the state apparatus as a whole in pursuit of reform and in the implementation of policy was unthinkable. The Executive is the most agile branch of that power.

8 Struggles between different political currents of *chavismo* were particularly noticeable throughout 2014 at a time of difficulties and adjustments for the government. The Third Congress of the PSUV (*Partido Socialista Unido de Venezuela*, or United Socialist Party of Venezuela), held on 26–28 July 2014, brought to the surface some of those internal differences, which nevertheless have not so far developed into splits. In turn, the opposition, for a while grouped around the MUD (*Mesa de la Unidad Democrática*, or Democratic Unity Roundtable) platform, continues to show signs of internal fracture. By 2014, Capriles' leadership was clearly weakened, R.G. Aveledo resigned as MUD coordinator and a new platform project, the *Movimiento Independiente Democrático* (MID, Independent Democratic Movement), has recently been launched with the support of a radical section of the opposition. The situation in the *anti-chavista* bloc has worsened in 2015. In preparation for the 2015 National Assembly elections, it has been working on the election of unitary candidates in a process that created new divisions, due to the lack of strong leadership and organic structure. Claims of a lack of transparency and democractic mechanisms have been widespread, and have alienated several regional leaders. Within the *chavista* bloc, one external factor greatly facilitated a regrouping of forces: President Obama's Executive Order of 9 March 2015 declaring Venezuela an 'extraordinary and unusual threat to the national security and the foreign policy of the United States of America' sparked a strong nationalist reaction in Venezuela and smoothed over internal differences within the *chavista* bloc. On top of the primary elections that the PSUV within this bloc has introduced to choose unitary candidates for the forthcoming elections, the US action has further strengthened *chavismo* in this electoral year.

9 In this sense, I want to highlight the difference between the 'contortionism' and 'transformism' of the state. The latter term, with Gramscian roots, is used to talk about gradual recomposition of forces during processes of change that nevertheless end up excluding subaltern classes from effective participation (see Hesketh and Morton 2014 for an application of this concept in discussing current Bolivian politics). With the term 'contortionism' I emphasize the current lack of definition

in the process of change in Venezuela, still argued over by antagonistic forces. Throughout the book I will be arguing against understanding this process of change as one of co-option of subordinate forces.

10 The so-called 'Five Engines of the Revolution' had been launched by this stage, articulating tactical guidelines for the government after Chávez's presidential victory in 2006, his first win after his explicit call to build the 'socialism of the twenty-first century'.

ONE

1 For an accessible overview of the material bases of pre-colonial economic and social organization and its subsequent colonial transformations in contemporary Venezuela, see Sanoja Obediente 2011.
2 Part of this sub-section is taken from my article 'From "café con leche" to "o café o leche": national identity, mestizaje and census politics in contemporary Venezuela' (2014), published by the *Journal of Iberian and Latin American Research* (JILAR).
3 As written, asking if one belongs to an '*etnia*' could be misinterpreted – an '*etnia*' includes all those who are not 'indigenous'. A better wording would have been: '*¿Pertenece a algún pueblo o etnia indígena?*', with the adjective '*indígena*' applying both to the 'people' and the ethnic group.
4 While some analysts have referred to these categories as ethnic, the way in which they were formally presented, with a direct association between physical features and culture, corresponds with a racial conceptualisation. For a detailed discussion of this question, see Angosto-Ferrández 2014c.
5 Up to the 1942 census, the relative percentages have been calculated considering the indigenous population as already integrated in the national population numbers. From 1950 to 1992, indigenous censuses were conducted separately from general censuses, so the relative percentage has been calculated by adding the indigenous population to the national one in order to obtain a national total.
6 The general census was conducted in 1981 and the indigenous census in 1982.
7 The general census was conducted in 1990 and the indigenous census in 1992.
8 The states were Amazonas, Anzoátegui, Apure, Bolívar, Delta Amacuro, Monagas, Sucre and Zulia.
9 Directorate of Indigenous Cults and Affairs (DICA), by 1974 ascribed to the Ministry of Justice. The number of peoples resulted from a study that DICA commissioned from an academic department of the *Universidad Central de Venezuela*, in the absence of an indigenous count in that census round (Angosto-Ferrández 2012b, p. 227).
10 Basic Law of Indigenous Peoples and Communities (LOPCI), passed in 2005. This included a list of recognized indigenous peoples, and held open the possibility of further future recognitions.
11 Not that there was absolute agreement on the matter. In his 1975 book *El indígena venezolano en pos de su liberación definitiva*, Esteban Mosonyi identified 23 peoples (Madero 2010, p. 36).
12 For a full listing of indigenous peoples recognized by censuses from 1974 onwards, see Angosto-Ferrández 2012b, pp. 255–6.

13 E.g. the document 'Indigenous peoples in Venezuela', circulated by MINPI at the Fourth Bolivarian Congress Young Indo-America – Against Capitalism, War and for Socialism (which ended on 9 August, a month before the start of the 2011 census).
14 For a history of the Vicariate written from within the Capuchin order, see Gutiérrez 2006a and 2006b.
15 This is a US-based evangelical Christian organisation with a long history of proselytization and missionary work in Latin America.
16 New Tribes were formally expelled by Resolution 427 of the Ministry of Home Affairs and Justice (*Gaceta Oficial de la República Bolivariana de Venezuela* no. 38, 313, 14 November 2005).
17 In Heinen and Coppens (1986) the change is said to have occurred in 1951.
18 *Junta de Gobierno* is the name that the post-1948 coup *Junta Militar* received after the assassination of its leading figure, Delgado Chalbaud, and the subsequent appointment of Germán Suárez Flamerich as president.
19 In 2003, I still had to go through this bureaucratic process supervised by the DAI when preparing my fieldwork in Gran Sabana.
20 Under the colonial regime, *resguardos* were lands granted to indigenous communities by the Spanish crown through titles that permitted collective usufruct.
21 Rubber exploitation and mining had already taken place, with dramatic consequences, but the scale of the projects was restricted by the remoteness of the project. See, for instance, Coppens (1972, pp. 4–5); Arvelo-Jiménez (2000).
22 Other important movements were those against the influence of religious proselytisers such as New Tribes.
23 The *Declaración de Barbados* included Venezuelan participants, such as Nelly Arvelo and Esteban Mosonyi who, along with scholars such as Gerard Clarac, González Yáñez and Jacqueline Clarac were in those circles of support.
24 During the early 1970s, the National Agricultural Institute (IAN) contained a faction identified with 'new indigenism' who, due to their differences over the 'Conquest of the South' and their sympathies towards some indigenous claims, were labelled as a 'communist' and subversive group.

TWO

1 For a well-documented overview of the gestation of this movement, with its roots in the *Ejército Bolivariano 200* (later the *Movimiento Bolivariano Revolucionario* [MBR]*200*) and with connections in a variety of civilian branches of left and revolutionary activism, see Raby 2006, pp. 145–58.
2 Along with the *Movimiento Quinta República* (MVR), the mass political party created in 1997 as an electoral tool for the MBR200 and their allies, the *Polo Patriótico* gathered the Communist Party (PCV), *Patria Para Todos* (PPT – a splinter group from *La Causa R*, which turned to the right with previously left-leaning Andrés Velásquez), and part of *Movimiento al Socialismo* (MAS).
3 During this period, CONIVE was competing with a number of organizations with which it had no previous affiliation, and which in some cases were being

openly promoted by political parties such as AD. It is significant that, for the July meeting, the CNE had agreed to block the participation of organizations that had been created after 1 March 1999 – a sign of the craze of organizational manoeuvring across the country during the constituent period.

4 Part of this discussion has been published in my article 'Pueblos indígenas, multiculturalismo y la nueva geometría del poder en Venezuela' (Angosto-Ferrández 2010).

5 This Mixed Special Commission, which brought together the Security and Defence Commission and the Indigenous Peoples Commission, was created *ad hoc* after the controversy that followed the first drafts of the indigenous rights chapter.

6 Interview available at www.analitica.com/constituyente/articulos/e08.asp, accessed 21 September 2009.

7 The LOPCI was finally passed in 2005.

8 Discussion of conservationism in parts of the Amazon territory in the 1980s were shrouded in similar controversy. For instance, there was heavy pressure from the Permanent Secretary of the National Security and Defence Council (SECONASEDE) to stop projects that proposed the creation of a biosphere reserve in Yanomamo territory, using the argument that it posed a threat to sovereignty (Arvelo-Jiménez 2001, pp. 37–8).

9 Bocaranda was later to become one of the intellectual leaders of the opposition. He currently has more than 1.94 million followers on Twitter and is characterized by his alignment with the most radical critics of the government.

10 See Arvelo-Jiménez (2001, p. 33) for a discussion of the contents of this book, in which she highlighted as one of its objectives 'the defence of the economic interests of the business group to which the author belongs'.

11 Other notable examples are the sculptures of Francisco Narváez and the murals of César Rengifo at the Centro Simón Bolívar.

12 The 'whitening' project involved ideals of a population shaped by values of 'modernization', rather than merely based on ideals of phenotypical lightening.

13 This was, for instance, the case in Ciudad Bolívar in 2009, attended by members of the country's government.

14 There had been earlier debates in the National Assembly about including Guaicaipuro in the Pantheon, but they had never come to anything. It was only under Chávez's governments that it took place.

15 Famous representations of Guaicaipuro had existed for a long time. Among emblematic representations are the sculpture erected in Los Teques in 1915 by Andrés Pérez Mujica and the mural containing Guaicaipuro's figure, created by Pedro Centeno Vallenilla, at the headquarters of the Central Bank of Venezuela.

16 Simón González, 'Caracas celebra el 12 de octubre sin Cristóbal Colón ni indígenas', *El Nacional*, 11 October 2009 (*Ciudadanos Caracas*).

17 This referendum defeat was the first, and so far the only, for the Bolivarian bloc in a national-level vote.

18 Interview broadcast on '*La Noticia*', VTV, 20 December 2007.

19 'Chávez lamentó no haber tenido un gobernador revolucionario en el Zulia', *Nueva Prensa*, 20 November 2006, p. A8.
20 See Karem Racines Arévalo, 'Comenzó la "indigenización" de sectores y avenidas en Vargas', *El Nacional*, 19 October 2008, p. 2 (*Ciudadanos Caracas*).
21 In other examples, he also noted his *mestizo*-ness, mentioning his black and white forbears, in addition to his indigenousness. This was done on important political occasions, which demonstrated the tactical importance that Chávez attributed to this type of positioning in the public domain. For instance, at the XVII Ibero-American Summit of Heads of State and Government held in Santiago de Chile in 2007, he declared in one of his speeches: 'I am half Indian, half black, and a little bit of white'. See also 'Indigeneity, empty labels, and electoral competition' in Chapter 3.
22 See www.un.org/News/briefings/docs/2003/Indigenous_PC.doc.htm, accessed 15 August 2006.
23 See '*El Archivo*' section, *El Nacional*, 12 October 2007, p. 2 (*Nación*).
24 'Premio al genocidio en Maracaibo', 2 September 2014; available at http://www.aporrea.org/regionales/a194258.html, accessed 29 June 2015.
25 For an interesting study of the role of these independent media in the shaping of world news, see Serrano 2009.
26 'El "bautismo" chavista', *El País*, 26 December 2009, p. 24.
27 'Proyecto de Ley de Jurisdicción Indígena espera por aprobación del Parlamento', *Correo del Orinoco*, 10 August 2010, p. 5.
28 Franchesly Liberto, 'La Asamblea Nacional realizó sesión especial', *El Luchador*, 6 July 2009, p. 7.

THREE

1 In October 2013, a draft Law of Education of Indigenous Peoples was completed, and the National Assembly Permanent Commission of Indigenous Peoples predicted that it could be formally passed before the end of the year (*El Tiempo*, 2 October 2013). The same commission is currently working on the draft Law of Coordination of the Special Indigenous Jurisdiction, essential to express constitutional principles (Article 260) and LOPCI statutory frameworks for such jurisdictions (Articles 130 to 136). The preparation of the latter law was encouraged by one of the most controversial episodes in the realm of indigenous peoples' policy of the past decade. In 2009, prominent leaders of a Yukpa movement involved in the struggle for traditional land around the Perijá mountains (Zulia state) were arrested, jailed and tried under ordinary jurisdiction. After nearly two years in prison and a long and convoluted trial, they were acquitted. This case and the campaigning of Yukpa supporters helped bring to light some of the legal contradictions in the process of indigenous recognition framed by the 1999 Constitution.
2 See 'Gobierno ha entregado 74.6% de títulos de tierras solicitados por comunidades indígenas', Avn.info.ve, available at http://www.avn.info.ve/contenido/gobierno-ha-entregado-746-t%C3%ADtulos-tierras-solicitados-comunidades-ind%C3%ADgenas, accessed 6 May 2013.

3 These six-year plans are: (1) Economic and Social Development Plan of the Nation 2001–2007; (2) Simón Bolívar National Project (First Socialist Plan) for Economic and Social Development Plan of the Nation 2007–2013; and (3) Plan for Bolivarian Socialist Management 2013–2019.
4 See directives 5 and 6 of the MINPI annual report (*Memoria y Cuenta*) 2011. Available at http://minpi.gob.ve/minpi/images/stories/enlaces/memoria2011.pdf, accessed 28 September 2013.
5 For instance, question 8 of Section III ('services in the community'), specifically focused on access to *misiones*, listing 14 of them, while questions 11 to 13, related to health services, mentioned *Misión Barrio Adentro* only as one type of health service provision that can reach communities.
6 Section III in the 2001 questionnaire addressed 'services in the community' with questions very similar to those in 2011 (but without the focus on *misiones*, of course), so it is possible to develop some direct comparisons regarding access to social services at the beginning and towards the end of Chávez's governments.
7 See United Nations data on 'Venezuela (Bolivarian Republic of), International Human Development Indicators', available at http://hdrstats.undp.org/en/countries/profiles/ven.html.
8 See http://www.rlc.fao.org/es/paises/venezuela/noticias/reconocimiento-de-la-fao-a-venezuela, accessed 30 October 2014.
9 'Resumen de Gestión Periodo Legislativo 2012', Comisión Permanente de Pueblos Indígenas, Asamblea Nacional, República Bolivariana de Venezuela, 2012, p. 10.
10 Government investment in social housing has been enormous over the past three years. In April 2015, the government publicized the handover of the 700,000th house since the launch of *Misión Gran Vivienda*. Some indigenous communities have also benefited from this programme. To give one example, in February 2014, in the middle of the toughest period of the violent protests that had emerged in Venezuela, MINPI minister Aloha Núñez announced that more than 2,000 houses were being built in Amazonas state as part of this *misión*, including projects for the Yanomami of Maroa, Manapiare and Río Negro (see 'Aprobados Bs 198 millónes para proyectos socioproductivos en comunidades indígenas', Aporrea.org, 26 February 2014).
11 This is the case with the *municipios* of Cedeño and Gran Sabana in Bolívar state, for instance, and Pedernales and Antonio Díaz in Delta Amacuro state. Amazonas state, the only one with an indigenous majority, presents an ambiguous case. See Angosto-Ferrández 2014b, pp. 139–41.

FOUR

1 See 'Declaran con lugar recurso electoral presentado por comunidad indígena Chaima', Tsj.gov.ve, 8 July 2005. http://www.tsj.gov.ve/informacion/notasdeprensa/notasdeprensa.asp?codigo=2238(http://www.tsj.gov.ve/decisiones/selec/Julio/79-060705-000020.htm), accessed 27 October 2010.
2 It is important to note that the leadership of the opposition is disputed, and that

there are signs of fracture that make it difficult to argue that there is any united coordination of this political bloc.
3 In the Spanish original: '*Si queríamos establecer igualdad, entonces establezcamos ciudadanos iguales completamente*'. See 'Henrique Capriles Radonsky: no vine a la política a enriquecerme, mi vocación es el servicio público', Analítica.com. http://www.analitica.com/constituyente/articulos/e08.asp, accessed 25 April 2013.
4 Nicolás Maduro, the *chavista* candidate, won the elections with 50.78 per cent of the vote.
5 For an extraordinarily informed account of these events, see Villegas 2009.
6 An ad hoc opposition platform created to counter the Bolivarian movement.
7 It is a constitutional right in Venezuela that voters can, through a referendum, recall elected officials after they have completed the first half of their mandate (see Article 72 of the CRBV). In 2004 Hugo Chávez was brought to such a referendum, in which the continuation of his mandate received majority support.
8 There would be a split in the revolutionary bloc that would translate into PODEMOS and its legislators moving over to the opposition.
9 The constitutional referendum consisted of two proposals: 'A', amendments to 33 articles proposed by Chavez and 13 by the National Assembly; and 'B', amendments to 23 articles, proposed by the NA alone. Proposal A was rejected by 50.7 per cent of the valid votes, and B by 51.05 per cent.
10 '*La Salida*' plan was linked to the *guarimbas*. '*Guarimbas*' was the term used to describe the street protests, some of them violent and orchestrated to destabilize the country, which after the launch of '*La Salida*' occurred for nearly three months in various parts of the country – primarily in neighbourhoods and cities with a high concentration of upper-middle class or middle-class opposition voters. They caused major economic losses in the country and left a serious number of deaths, including civilians and members of the military and the police. Many of these deaths are still being investigated. An interesting report – which, however, cannot be considered a substitute for official information – was written in April 2014 by a Venezuelan journalist on Albaciudad.org. It can be found at http://albaciudad.org/wp/index.php/2014/04/conozca-los-26-fallecidos-a-un-mes-del-inicio-de-las-protestas-opositoras-la-gran-mayoria-son-victimas-de-las-barricadas, accessed 27 April 2015.
11 In early 2014, the opposition showed clear signs of a split, with the MID emerging as a parallel alternative opposition platform. In the run-up to the National Assembly elections due in 2015, the selection of unitary candidates within the opposition bloc, which the MUD has attempted to coordinate, is proving to be a source of internal tension. Complaints about a lack of transparency and internal democracy have been continuous among regional leaders of the opposition, whose leadership decided to hold primary elections only in a minority of states, leaving the appointment of remaining candidates to a 'consensus' method that seems to be generating anything but.
12 A dual system exists for elections to legislative bodies: the list-vote (i.e. votes for lists of candidates drawn up by political parties); and the nominal vote (i.e. votes

for individual candidates). Where data on the list-vote were not available, for the purpose of comparison I resorted to the results in gubernatorial elections, as in this case the electoral register coincides with the register used to elect indigenous candidates.

13 See Angosto-Ferrández 2011 and 2014b for detailed tables with all relevant electoral data.
14 For a full list of these indigenous organizations and communities, see Angosto-Ferrández 2011, pp. 24–5. I noted that the CNE data presented a few cases that invite us to consider the possibility that the same community was registered with a slightly different name in two elections, but even taking such cases into account and assuming that some or all of them in fact refer to the same community, the total number of indigenous organizations and communities that participated in the elections would still be enormous, ranging from 151 to 171. In fact, there may have been even more: the CNE has not published online all the relevant data for the 2005 municipal elections.
15 Data from the 2011 census are available (see Chapter 1) but, since I am examining elections held up to 2010, I use the official census data available during that period (that is, from 2001).
16 The *Universidad Indígena de Tauca* was created in 2000 with the support of Causa Amerindia Kiwxi, linked to the Jesuits and under the leadership of the late José María Korta. It finally gained recognition from the National Council of Universities in 2010, although state support has been uneven since.
17 See 'CONIVE rechaza declaraciones de ex directivo', http://www.abrebrecha.com/73252_CONIVE-rechazadeclaraciones-de-ex-directivo.html, accessed 20 February 2014.
18 See 'Bolívar: COINKA convoca a la renovación del movimiento indígena en Venezuela', Abrebrecha.com, 2 August 2010, available at http://abrebrecha.com/82924_Bol%C3%ADvar:-COINKA-convoca-a-la-renovación-del-movimiento-ind%C3%ADgena-en-Venezuela-.html, accessed 20 February 2014.
19 See 'Diputado indígena José Poyo promueve plan en defensa del Caura y ratifica su candidatura', Aporrea.org, 12 July 2010, available at www.aporrea.org/actualidad/n161144.html, accessed 12 March 2014.
20 This column shows the number of federal states (out of the eight in which regional indigenous deputies and councillors are elected by law) in which these organizations have taken part in regional and municipal elections.
21 Lauriz Zamora, 'Fieb presentó equipos políticos', *El Luchador*, 29 May 2011, p. 7.
22 There are a total of 14 legislators on this regional legislative council.
23 This is the term given to an electoral tactic by which candidates of a given party are nominated by different platform in the voting list and in the nominal vote, so that they are formally released from the requirements of the CNE. In the 2008 regional elections, CLEB candidates of the Bolivarian bloc were backed by the PSUV in the voting list, while in the nominal vote they were backed by the *Unión de Vencedores Electorales* (UVE).
24 That is, representation characterized by demographic and sociological similarities between elected positions and those represented.

25 See 'Pueblo de Amazonas recibió al candidato de la Patria Maduro: la burguesía está enchufada con el amor al dinero', Vtv.gob.ve, 8 April 2013. Available at http://www.vtv.gob.ve/articulos/2013/04/06/pueblo-de-amazonas-recibe-al-candidato-de-la-patria-nicolas-maduro-7837.html, accessed 9 April 2013.
26 *Caprichito* ['little whim'] is a play on Capriles' name that Maduro coined during the election campaign.
27 He had already held a mass event in Puerto Ayacucho on 19 May, and on 1 October, the same day that he visited San Félix (Bolívar state), he held an event to close his campaign.
28 Images and audio available at http://www.aporrea.org/actualidad/n212337.html.
29 'Proponen incluir el método D'Hont en la ley electoral', El Universal.com, 9 June 2009, available at http://www.eluniversal.com/2009/06/09/pol_art_proponen-incluir_1423769, accessed 15 April 2012.

FIVE

1 Along with deputy ministries in regions with 'traditional' indigenous population, MINPI had a deputy ministry for the indigenous population in urban areas.
2 See, for instance, the case of Bernardo Araya in Bolívar state: 'Juramentado viceministro indígena para Bolívar', *Nueva Prensa*, 26 March 2007, p. A5.
3 Available on the MINPI website: http://mail.minpi.gob.ve/minpi/images/stories/enlaces/memoria2007.pdf, accessed 19 October 2010.
4 The summary of these declarations can be consulted at www.abn.info.ve/noticia.php?articulo=202569&lee=1, accessed 22 November 2009.
5 This plan contained the following objectives: the new socialist ethic, supreme social happiness, revolutionary democracy first, the socialist productive model, the new national geopolitics, Venezuela as a world energy power, and the new international geopolitics. The new national geopolitics is linked to the strengthening of popular power, which in turn is linked to the formation of indigenous communal councils and the creation of communes.
6 See Esperanza Castillo, 'Una yekuana desobediente: Nicia Maldonado', Venezuelareal.zoomblog.com, 7 March 2007, available at http://venezuelareal.zoomblog.com/archivo/2007/03/08/una-Yekuana-Desobediente-Nicia-Maldona.html, accessed 25 April 2015.
7 See 'Logros históricos de los pueblos indígenas de Venezuela', Aporrea.org, available at www.aporrea.org/actualidad/a152765.html, accessed 23 October 2012.
8 See http://asambleanacional.gov.ve/noticia/show/id/3556, accessed 4 November 2013.
9 Events organized by MINPI include the 'First International Encounter of Anti-imperialist Indigenous Peoples of Abya Yala' and the 'First "Young Indo-America" Bolivarian Congress of indigenous warriors against misery and imperialism', at which attending *indígenas* declared their allegiance to the socialist process with t-shirts reading 'Indigenous socialist warrior, *a la carga*! ["charge!"]', or banners such as 'Indigenous socialist warriors from Amazonas, *presentes* ["present"]'.

SIX

1 The strengthening of 'civil society' governance was, of course, well underway, and not only in connection with identity politics. In Latin America in particular, the debt crises of the 1980s and the accompanying wide-ranging spread of neoliberal reform set the stage for 'civil society' to become a politically and financially oriented goal for the supranational organizations that supported and promoted that reform (Petras and Veltmeyer 2001). In the context of these changes, the governments of 'underdeveloped' countries in this and other parts of the world were displaced as recipients of financial support for development projects: financing 'civil society' organizations was at the heart of new paradigms of development and political reform.
2 The programme can be viewed here: http://www.youtube.com/watch?v=uy9QNJS1s00, accessed 17 October 2014.
3 'Donaciones de Chávez no seran reguladas', *El Nacional*, 17 May 2009, p. 2 (*Siete Días*).
4 This meaning was summed up well, as Edgardo Lander has noted, in a document circulated on 12 April 2002, during the coup against Chávez, in which opposition actors celebrated the event with the slogan: 'Civil society salutes the rebirth of the Venezuelan Republic' (Lander 2007, p. 115).
5 See 'Lusbi Portillo responde a acusaciones de Diosdado Cabello y denuncia asesinato de Yukpa', available at http://www.aporrea.org/desalambrar/n253410.html, accessed 27 January 2015.
6 Lusbi Portillo at the Venezuelan National Congress of Anthropology in November 2013 (Maracaibo).
7 In June 2014, Cristóbal Fernández, another son of Carmen Fernández, the mother of one of Sabino Romero's companions-in-arms (Alexander Fernández, also killed), was assassinated, allegedly by members of the National Guard who were said to support the local oligarchy.
8 See 'Proyecto de Ley de Jurisdicción Indígena espera por aprobación del Parlamento', *Correo del Orinoco*, 10 August 2010, p. 5. The indigenous jurisdiction is starting to be applied, causing some controversy in particular cases. For instance, the Constitutional Branch of the Supreme Court annulled the verdict that had condemned an adolescent Warao to 20 years' prison for murder (Ricardo Márquez, 'TSJ anuló condena a un warao adolescente', *Últimas Noticias*, 8 August 2011, p. 28).
9 'La montaña es un lugar sagrado', *El Nacional*, 12 October 2008, p. 3 (*Siete Días*).
10 Edgar López, 'Promesa incumplida', *El Nacional*, 12 October 2008, pp. 1–3 (*Siete Días*).
11 Korta died in a car accident in 2014, while working on the development of the Indigenous University of Tauca.
12 See 'Razones de la huelga de hambre del hermano jesuita José Korta', available at http://sicsemanal.wordpress.com/2010/10/19/razones-de-la-huelga-de-hambre-del-hermano-jesuita-jose-korta.
13 See 'Hijo de Sabino Romero: en mayo entregan territorio Yukpa demarcardo',

Albaciudad.org, 26 March 2013, available at http://albaciudad.org/wp/index.php/2013/03/hijo-de-sabino-romero-en-mayo-entregan-territorio-yukpa-demarcado, accessed 14 April 2013.

SEVEN

1 In 2008, the *prefectos* of the rich-in-resources eastern departments of Santa Cruz, Tarija, Beni and Pando, with the support of local oligarchies, radicalized their political opposition to Evo Morales's government with a number of acts of sabotage and violence, in the midst of demands of autonomy and threats of secession.
2 The 'communal state' project in Venezuela rests partly on an understanding of these tensions. This project, in tune with conceptions of popular power, would lead to increased degrees of political and economic decentralization and autonomy by reconfiguring state structures through cumulative introduction of local and regional organization. For a comment on the political principles before the project, see Azzellini 2013.

Yet this project is still very limited in its actual reach, particularly on the crucial economic front, and the prospects for its realization continue to be uncertain. It therefore does not alter, for the time being, the essence of the aforementioned tensions in the case of Venezuela.
3 Here I use this term as it has been conceptualized by the Global Footprint Network, which defines it as 'the capacity of ecosystems to produce useful biological materials and to absorb waste materials generated by humans, using current management schemes and extraction technologies'. For a more detailed definition, see http://www.footprintnetwork.org/en/index.php/GFN/page/glossary, accessed 24 June 2014.
4 For example, during 2004 I lived and worked in a Pemon community in which the economy was one of semi-subsistence. At that time, only two people there received regular salaries (the two schoolteachers), while the rest of the community was primarily sustained by working in their relatively small slash-and-burn cultivations and occasional integration into regional market activities (selling arts and crafts during peak tourist seasons, for instance). This is, however, not common to all Pemon communities, some of which are fully integrated in the market.
5 This is defined by Article 82 of Decree 295 of 5 September 1999 (*Ley de Minas*) as: 'Personal and direct labour in the exploitation of gold and alluvial diamonds, through simple and portable manual equipment. This can only be exercised by natural persons of Venezuelan nationality'.
6 Through my fieldwork in Gran Sabana, I personally know of young men who travelled for cash-in-hand work from communities in the central Apanwoao river course (where there is no significant mining) to mines in the Ikabarú and the so-called Km 88 (Sifontes *municipio*) areas, for months at a time. The absence of alternative local sources of income lies behind such choices.
7 It is significant that, during the global financial crisis, gold in particular was viewed yet again as an apparently secure deposit of wealth, more so than the fragility and volatility of monetary deposits.

8 'Indígenas de Urimán en Bolívar detienen y desarman a 43 militares', *El Universal*, 8 February 2013, available at http://www.eluniversal.com/nacional-y-politica/130208/indigenas-de-uriman-en-bolivar-detienen-y-desarman-a-43-militares, accessed 27 January 2015.
9 The video can be viewed at https://www.youtube.com/watch?v=WoUSXrzRLoI, accessed 24 July 2015.
10 This was a reference to the fact that some large mining concessions in the Guayana region had passed into foreign hands. The reference to China and Russia – which are, of course, not the only countries whose companies and finance are involved in mining in Venezuela – could also be taken as a comment on world geopolitics, given current relations between those two countries and Venezuela and other Latin American countries.
11 I argued that the identification of indigeneity with socialism in contemporary Venezuela is a manifestation of the characteristic widespread dynamics that help to galvanize the *chavista* bloc as a collective political subject, in the context of populist movements (Laclau 2007). This does not imply that this bloc is 'socialist', despite including socialist forces. If one looks at the achievements of its politics, this bloc remains within the parameters of social democracy, though admittedly this might be a confusing concept at present, when it is already separated not only from its Marxist roots but also – given the sweeping force of the neoliberal revolution – even from its welfare-state contents. The model in Venezuela, with its distinctive characteristics and some of the forces it harbours, can in this context be called socialist-leaning despite the fact that the revolutionary process remains undefined, and driven by conflict.

APPENDIX

1 Aray was also the indigenous representative for Bolívar state in the National Commission for the Demarcation of the Habitat and Lands of Indigenous Peoples and Communities.
2 Indigenous organization from the Caura Basin; it is basically Ye'kuana, with some Sanema involvement.
3 Organization of Indigenous Communities of the Gran Sabana (Pemon).
4 Of the eleven *municipios* in Bolívar state, only six were enlisted for the event. Caroní, El Callao, Piar, Roscio and Padre Chien are more urbanized areas, with no significant indigenous 'community population'.
5 The federation divided some *municipios* into different *sectores* for organizational purposes. The *sectores* concentrate the largest number of indigenous (Pemon) communities in the whole federal unit.
6 He was Executive Secretary of CONIVE and the indigenous (Kariña) representative for Anzoátegui state in the National Commission for the Demarcation of Habitat and Lands of Indigenous Peoples and Communities.
7 This continues to be an issue, in spite of the self-attribution criterion that the national census has recognized and despite the statutes of the FIEB itself, Article 9

of which states that any *indígena* shall be able to join the federation if they show a desire to do so, even if they 'do not live in the indigenous communities'.
8 He did not use these exact words, but González did use as an example (to be avoided) the possibility that communities closer to centres of decision-making become over-represented.
9 These comments were making a veiled allusion: Delgado, the first indigenous mayor in the *municipio*, was known to have 'turned his back' on Chávez in the immediate aftermath of the 2002 coup, which in time led to Delgado's ostracism in the 2004 local elections (which he lost to the MVR-supported candidate, a *criollo*).
10 Another pre-electoral allusion, in this case to the federal governor of the time, Rojas Suárez, who had also been labelled a traitor to the cause after the position he took in the 2002 coup, when he 'recognized' the *de facto* government.

Bibliography

Aguilar, V. and L. Bustillos (2007) *Transversalización de la política (pública) para pueblos indígenas: hacia una definición del Ministerio del Poder Popular para los Pueblos Indígenas de la República Bolivariana de Venezuela*, GTAI, Consejo de Publicaciones de la Universidad de los Andes, Mérida.

Agyeman, J. (2013) *Introducing Just Sustainabilities: Policy, Planning and Practice*, Zed Books, London.

Albro, R. (2006) 'The culture of democracy and Bolivia's indigenous movements', *Critique of Anthropology*, Vol. 26, No. 4, pp. 387–410.

Allais, M.L. (2004) '*La población indígena en Venezuela según los censos nacionales*'. Paper presented at the Segundo encuentro nacional de demógrafos y estudiosos de la población, Caracas, 24–26 November.

Amodio, E. (1999) *Los Resguardos Indígenas en la Legislación Republicana de Venezuela (1810–1852)*, Montalbán, pp. 212–29.

—— (2007) 'La república indígena: pueblos indígenas y perspectivas políticas en Venezuela', *Revista Venezolana de Economía y Ciencias Sociales*, Vol. 13, No. 3, pp. 175–88.

Anderson, P. (1976) 'The antinomies of Antonio Gramsci', *New Left Review*, No. I/100, pp. 5–78.

Anderson, T. (2014) 'Chávez and American integration', in L.F. Angosto-Ferrández (ed.) *Democracy, Revolution and Geopolitics in Latin America: Venezuela and the International Politics of Discontent*, Routledge, New York, pp. 13–46.

Angosto-Ferrández, L.F. (2008) 'Pueblos indígenas, guaicapurismo y socialismo del siglo XXI en Venezuela', *Antropológica*, No. 110, pp. 9–33.

—— (2010) 'Pueblos indígenas, multiculturalismo y la nueva geometría del poder en Venezuela', *Cuadernos del Cendes*, No. 73, pp. 97–132.

—— (2011) 'La competencia por la representación indígena en las elecciones venezolanas (2004–2011)', *Cuestiones políticas*, Vol. 27, No. 46, pp. 13–54.

—— (2012a) 'Participación y representación indígena en los procesos electorales venezolanos', *América Latina Hoy*, Vol. 60, pp. 153–82.

—— (2012b) 'National censuses and indigeneity in Venezuela', in L.F. Angosto-Ferrández and S. Kradolfer (eds) *Everlasting Countdowns: Race, Ethnicity and National Censuses in Latin American States*, Cambridge Scholars, Newcastle Upon Tyne, pp. 221–63.

—— (2014a) 'Democracy, revolution and geopolitics in Latin America: Venezuela and the international politics of discontent', in L.F. Angosto-Ferrández (ed.) *Democracy, Revolution and Geopolitics in Latin America: Venezuela and the International Politics of Discontent*, Routledge, New York, pp. 1–12.

—— (2014b) 'Indigenous peoples, populist logics and polarization: understanding the pivotal role of indigeneity in Venezuelan elections' in L.F. Angosto-Ferrández (ed.) *Democracy, Revolution and Geopolitics in Latin America: Venezuela and the International Politics of Discontent*, Routledge, New York, pp. 119–46.

—— (2014c) 'From "café con leche" to "o café, o leche": race, ethnicity and national identification in contemporary Venezuela', *Journal of Iberian and Latin American Research*, Vol. 20, No. 3, pp. 373–98.

—— (2014d) 'Ordering discontent: domestic and international dynamics of the Bolivarian revolution', in L.F. Angosto-Ferrández (ed.) *Democracy, Revolution and Geopolitics in Latin America:Venezuela and the International Politics of Discontent*, Routledge, New York, pp. 177–94.

Angosto-Ferrández, L.F. and S. Kradolfer (2012) 'Race, ethnicity and national censuses in Latin American states: comparative perspectives', in L.F. Angosto-Ferrández and S. Kradolfer (eds) *Everlasting Countdowns: Race, Ethnicity and National Censuses in Latin American States*. Cambridge Scholars Publishing, Newcastle Upon Tyne, pp. 1–40.

Aporrea (2007) 'Ministra PP de Pueblos Indígenas Nicia Maldonado: "implementaremos el socialismo originario"'. Available at www.aporrea.org/ideologia/n94253.html (accessed 28 April 2009).

Arvelo-Jiménez, N. (1982) 'The political struggle of the Guayana region's indigenous struggles', *Journal of International Affairs*, Vol. 36, No. 1, pp. 55–71.

—— (1990) *Indigenismo y el debate sobre desarrollo amazónico: reflexiones a partir de la experiencia venezolana*, Palestra no Seminário do Departamento de Antropologia da UnB, Brasília, 9 October.

—— (2000) 'Three crises in the history of Ye'kuana cultural continuity', *Ethnohistory*, Vol. 47, No. 3-4, pp. 731–46.

—— (2001) 'La saga de los yanomamö: reflexiones en torno al libro Darkness in El Dorado', *Interciencia*, Vol. 26, No. 1, pp. 32–8.

Assies, W., G. van der Haar and A. Hoekema (2000) 'The challenge of diversity: indigenous peoples and reform of the state in Latin America', Thela Thesis, Amsterdam.

Azzellini, D. (2013) 'The communal state: communal councils, communes, and workplace democracy', *NACLA Report on the Americas*, Vol. 42, No. 2, p. 26.

Barié, C.G. (2005) 'La cuestión territorial de los pueblos indígenas en la perspectiva latinoamericana', in Friedrich Ebert Stiftung–Instituto Latinoamericano de Investigaciones Sociales (eds) *Visiones indígenas de descentralización*, Plural, La Paz.

Barreto, D. (1995) 'Identidad, etnicidad, antropología', *Boletín Americanista*, No. 45, pp. 7–21.

—— (2011) 'The indigenous question: winning and losing with Bolivarian socialism', *Dialectical Anthropology*, No. 35, pp. 261–3.

Bastidas Vallecillos, L. (1997) 'Una Mirada ethnohistórica a las tierras indígenas de Mérida (I, época colonial)', *Boletín Antropológico*, No. 41.
—— (1998) 'Una Mirada ethnohistórica a las tierras indígenas de Mérida (II, siglos XIX e inicios del XX)', *Boletín Antropológico*, No. 43, pp. 5–51.
Bebbington, A. and D. Bebbington (2011) 'An Andean avatar: post-neoliberal and neoliberal strategies for securing the unobtainable', *New Political Economy*, Vol. 16, No. 1, pp. 131–45.
Becker, M. (2011) *Pachakutik: Indigenous Movements and Electoral Politics in Ecuador*, Rowman and Littlefield Publishers, Lanham, MD.
—— (2013a) 'The stormy relations between Rafael Correa and Social Movements in Ecuador', *Latin American Perspectives*, Vol. 40, No. 3, pp. 43–62.
—— (2013b) 'Ecuador's *buen vivir* socialism', in R. Burbach, M. Fox and F. Fuentes (eds) *Latin America's Turbulent Transitions: the Future of Twenty-First Century Socialism*, Zed Books, London, pp. 99–113.
Bello, L.J. (2005) *Derechos de los Pueblos Indígenas en el Nuevo Ordenamiento Jurídico Venezolano*, IWGIA, Copenhagen.
—— (2011) 'El reconocimiento constitucional de la existencia de los pueblos y comunidades indígenas y de los derechos originarios sobre las tierras que ocupan: proceso de demarcación de hábitat y tierras indígenas y garantía del derecho a la propiedad colectiva', in L.J. Bello (ed.) *El estado ante la sociedad multiétnica y pluricultural: políticas públicas y derechos de los pueblos indígenas en Venezuela (1999–2010)*, Wataniba/IWGIA, Caracas, pp. 35–86.
Beltrán Acosta, L. (2002) *El pensamiento revolucionario del cacique Guaicaipuro*, Ediciones Akurima, Caracas.
—— (2003) *El pensamiento revolucionario del Cacique Guaicaipuro*, Akurima, Caracas.
Bengoa, J. (2009) '¿Una segunda etapa de la emergencia indígena en América Latina?', *Cuadernos de Antropología Social*, No. 29, pp. 7–22.
Bobes, V.C. (2010) 'De la revolución a la movilización: confluencias de la sociedad civil y la democracia en América Latina', *Nueva Sociedad*, No. 227, pp. 31–50.
Bowie, K.A. (2005) 'The state and the right wing: the village scout movement in Thailand', in J. Nash (ed.) *Social Movements: an Anthropology Reader*, Blackwell, Malden (MA), pp. 46–65.
Brubaker, R., Loveman, M. and Stamatov, P. (2004) 'Ethnicity as cognition', *Theory and Society*, Vol. 33, pp. 31–64.
Brysk, A. (2000) *From Tribal Village to Global Village: Indian Rights and International Politics in Latin America*, Stanford University Press, Stanford, CA.
Bunten, A. (2011) 'A call for attention to indigenous capitalisms', *New Proposals: Journal of Marxism and Interdisciplinary Inquiry*, Vol. 5, No. 1, pp. 60–71.
Buxton, J. (2001) *The Failure of Political Reform in Venezuela*, Ashgate, Aldershot.
—— (2009) 'Venezuela: the political evolution of Bolivarianism', in G. Lievesley and S. Ludlam (eds) *Reclaiming Latin America: Experiments in Radical Social Democracy*, Zed Books, London.
Byres, T.J. (2006) 'Differentiation of the peasantry under Feudalism and the transition to capitalism: in defence of Rodney Hilton', *Journal of Agrarian Change*, Vol. 6, No. 1, pp. 17–68.

Caballero, H. (2007) 'La demarcación de tierras indígenas en Venezuela', *Revista Venezolana de Economía y Ciencias Sociales*, Vol. 13, No. 3, pp. 189–208.

Carrera, J. (2011) 'Participación política y cambios culturales en el pueblo Yanomami', in L.J. Bello (ed.) *El estado ante la sociedad multiétnica y pluricultural: políticas públicas y derechos de los pueblos indígenas en Venezuela (1999–2010)*, Wataniba/ IWGIA, Caracas, pp. 218–27.

Chávez, H.R. (2007) *Poder popular: alma de la democracia revolucionaria. [Transcripción de la Juramentación del Consejo Presidencial para la Reforma Constitucional y del Consejo presidencial del Poder Comunal. Teatro Teresa Carreño (Miércoles 17 de enero de 207)]*, Impreso en la República Bolivariana de Venezuela, Caracas.

Checkel, J.T. (1998) 'The constructivist turn in international relations theory', *World Politics*, Vol. 50, pp. 324–48.

Choudry, A. and E. Shragge (2011) 'Disciplining dissent: NGOs and community organizations', *Globalizations*, Vol. 8, No. 4, pp. 503–17.

Ciccariello-Maher, G. (2013) *We Created Chávez: a People's History of the Venezuelan Revolution*, Duke University Press, Durham, NC, and London.

Clarac, J. (2001) 'Análisis de las actitudes de políticos criollos e indígenas en Venezuela (de los años sesenta hasta el 2001)', *Boletín Antropológico*, No. 53, pp. 335–72.

—— (2002) 'La política indigenista venezolana a través del tiempo. Contactos y conflictos interétnicos en Venezuela: el eterno problema. Los problemas recientes', *Cenipec (Mérida)*, Vol. 21, pp. 11–44.

Clark, A. (1998) 'Race, "culture", and mestizaje: the statistical construction of the Ecuadorian nation, 1930–1950', *Journal of Historical Sociology*, Vol. 11, No. 2, pp. 185–211.

Colchester, M. and F. Watson (1995) *Venezuela: Violations of Indigenous Rights – Report to the International Labour Office [sic] on the Observation of ILO Convention 107*, Forest Peoples Programme, Chadlington, England.

Comaroff, J.L. and J. Comaroff (2009) *Ethnicity, Inc.*, University of Chicago Press, Chicago.

Combellas, R. (2003) 'El proceso constituyente y la Constitución de 1999', *Politeia*, Vol. 30, No. 30, pp. 183–208.

Conklin, B. (1995) 'The shifting middle ground: Amazonian Indians and eco-politics', *American Anthropologist*, Vol. 97, No. 4, pp. 695–710.

Coppens, W. (1971) 'La tenencia de tierra indígena en Venezuela: aspectos legales y antropológicos', *Antropológica*, No. 29, pp. 1–37.

—— (1972) *The Anatomy of a Land Invasion Scheme in Yekuana Territory*, Venezuela, International Work Group for Indigenous Affairs (IWGIA), Copenhagen.

Coronil, F. (1997) *The Magical State: Nature, Money, and Modernity in Venezuela*, University of Chicago Press, Chicago.

Cox, R. (1999) 'Civil society at the turn of the millennium: prospects for an alternative world order', *Review of International Studies*, Vol. 25, No. 1, pp. 3–28.

Crabtree, J. (2005) *Patterns of Protests: Politics and Social Movements in Bolivia*, Latin America Bureau, London.

Cunill Grau, P. (1987) *Geografía del Poblamiento Venezolano en el Siglo XIX*, Ediciones de la Presidencia de la República (Three TOMOS), Caracas.

Cunin, E. and O. Hoffmann (2012) 'De la dominación colonial a la fabricación de la naci{oact}n. Las categorías étnico-raciales en los censos e informes y sus usos políticos en Belice, siglos XIX–XX', *Secuencia*, Vol. 82, pp. 153–74.

Dangl, B. (2010) *Dancing with Dynamite: Social Movements and States in Latin America*, AK Press, Oakland, CA.

Declarations of the Venezuelan Federations of Indians (1980), in Y. Martene (ed.) *The Indian Awakening in Latin America, Friendship Press*, New York. Available at http://www.nativeweb.org/papers/statements/materne/2venezuela.php[MR1], accessed 24 July 2015.

Diani, M. (1992) 'The concept of social movement', *The Sociological Review*, Vol. 40, No. 1, pp. 1–25.

Díaz Polanco, H. (2005) 'Los dilemas del pluralismo', in P. Dávalos (ed.) *Pueblos indígenas, estado y democracia*, Claco, Buenos Aires, pp. 43–66.

—— (2009) *Elogio de la diversidad: globalización, multiculturalismo y etnofagia*, Monte Ávila, Caracas.

Dorling, D. and S. Simpson (1999, eds) *Statistics in Society: The Arithmetic of Politics*, Arnold, London.

Edelman, M. (2005) 'When networks don't work: the rise and fall and rise of civil society initiatives in Central America', in J. Nash (ed.) *Social Movements: an Anthropology Reader*, Blackwell, Malden (MA), pp. 29–45.

El Nacional (2008) 'Comenzó la "indigenización" de sectores y avenidas en Vargas"'. *El Nacional*, Caracas, Venezuela, 10 October, Section c, p. 2.

El Tiempo (2013) 'El proyecto de Ley de Educación de los Pueblos Indígenas se podría aprobar la segunda semana de este mes, estimó el integrante de la Comisión Permanente de Pueblos Indígenas de la AN, César Sanguinetti'. 2 October. Available at http://eltiempo.com.ve/venezuela/parlamento/el-proyecto-de-ley-de...permanente-de-pueblos-indigenas-de-la-an-cesar-sanguinetti/109530, accessed 6 October 2013.

Ellner, S. (2006) 'Las estrategias "desde arriba" y "desde abajo" del movimiento de Hugo Chávez', *Cuadernos del Cendes*, Vol. 23, No. 62, pp. 73–93.

—— (2011) 'Venezuela's social based democratic model: innovations and limitations', *Journal of Latin American Studies*, Vol. 43, No. 3, pp. 421–49.

Ellner, S. and M. Tinker Salas (2007) 'The Venezuelan exceptionalism thesis: separating myth from reality', in S. Ellner and M. Tinker Salas (eds) *Venezuela: Hugo Chávez and the Decline of an 'Exceptional Democracy'*, Rowman and Littlefield Publishers, Plymouth, pp. 3–15.

Fabricant, N. and N. Postero (2014) 'Performing the "wounded Indian": a new platform of democracy and human rights in Bolivia's autonomy movement', *Identities: Global Studies in Culture and Power*, Vol. 21, No. 4, pp. 395–411.

Fernandes, S. (2010) *Who Can Stop the Drums? Urban Social Movements in Chávez's Venezuela*, Duke University Press, Durham, NC.

—— (2013) 'Barrio women and popular politics in Chávez's Venezuela,' in J.R. Webber and B. Carr (eds) *The New Latin American Left: Cracks in the Empire*, Rowman and Littlefield, Lanham, MD.

Fernández Buey, F. (2007) 'Sobre el movimiento de movimientos', *Revista de Estudios de Juventud*, No. 76, pp. 21–36.

BIBLIOGRAPHY 273

Figueroa, C. (2005) *Pataamunaanü'nin: nuestras tierras son de nosotros*, Ediciones El Pueblo, Caracas.

Finnemore, M. (1996) *National Interests in International Society*, Cornell University Press, Ithaca.

French, J.D. (2009) 'Understanding the politics of Latin America's plural lefts (Chávez/Lula): social democracy, populism and convergence on the path to a post-neoliberal world', *Third World Quarterly*, Vol. 30, No. 2, pp. 349–70.

Fuentes, F. (2013) 'Venezuela's twenty-first century socialism', in R. Burbach, M. Fox and F. Fuentes (eds) *Latin America's Turbulent Transitions: the Future of Twenty-First Century Socialism*, Zed Books, London, pp. 49–76.

—— (2014) '"Bad Left Government" versus "Good Left Social Movements"? Creative tensions within Bolivia's process of change', in S. Ellner (ed.) *Latin America's Radical Left: Challenges and Complexities of Political Power in the Twenty-First Century*, Rowman and Littlefield, Lanham, MD.

García, J. (2007) 'Indígenas luchando por su territorio', *Venezuela Misionera*, No. 626, pp. 31–4.

García, M.E. (2005) *Making Indigenous Citizens: Identities, Education, and Multicultural Development in Peru*, Stanford University Press, Stanford, CA.

García Castro, Á. (2000) 'Mendicidad indígena: Los warao urbanos', *Boletín Antropológico*, No. 48, pp. 79–89.

García Castro, Á. and D. Heinen (1999) 'Planificando el desastre ecológico: impacto del cierre del caño Manamo para las comunidades indígenas y criollas del Delta Occidental (Delta del Orinoco, Venezuela)', *Antropológica*, No. 91, pp. 31–56.

García Gavidia, N. (2003) 'Iconos y símbolos indígenas en la invención de la identidad nacional', in C. Alès and J. Chiappino (eds) *Caminos cruzados: ensayos en antropología social, etnoecología y etnoeducación*, IRD/ULA GRIAL, Mérida, Venezuela.

García Linera, Á. (2010) 'El estado en transición: bloque de poder y punto de bifurcación', in A. García Linera, R. Prada, L. Tapia and O. Vega Camacho, *El estado: campo de lucha*, La Paz, Muela del Diablo Editores.

Goldberg, D.T. (1997, ed.) *Racial Subjects: Writing on Race in America*, Routledge, New York.

Golinger, E. (2005) *El código Chávez: descifrando la intervención de Estados Unidos en Venezuela*, Monte Ávila, Caracas.

—— (2006) *Bush vs Chávez: la guerra de Washington against Venezuela*, Editorial José Martí, Havana.

Griffiths, T. (2010) 'Schooling for twenty-first-century socialism: Venezuela's Bolivarian project', *Compare*, Vol. 40, No. 5, pp. 607–22.

Gustafson, B. (2009) *New Languages of the State: Indigenous Resurgence and the Politics of Knowledge in Bolivia*, Duke University Press, Durham, NC.

Gutiérrez, E. (2011) *La interculturalidad en el Estado venezolano: los derechos humanos de los pueblos y comunidades indígenas*, Defensoría del Pueblo/Fundación Juan Vives Suriá, Caracas.

Gutiérrez, M. (2006a) *80 años sembrando evangelio: la iglesia por las tierras de la Gran Sabana, Guayana y Delta Amacuro*, Vol. 1, Vicariato del Caroní/CVG-Edelca, Caracas.

—— (2006b) *80 años sembrando evangelio: la iglesia por las tierras de la Gran Sabana, Guayana y Delta Amacuro*, Vol. 2, Vicariato del Caroní/CVG-Edelca, Caracas.

Hale, C. (2002) 'Does multiculturalism menace? Governance, cultural rights and the politics of identity in Guatemala', *Journal of Latin American Studies*, Vol. 34, No. 3, pp. 485–532.

Hale, C. and R. Millamán (2004) 'Rethinking indigenous politics in the era of the "indio permitido"', *NACLA Report on the Americas*, Vol. 38, No. 2, pp. 16–21.

Hardt, M. (1995) 'The withering of civil society', *Social Text*, No. 45, pp. 27–44.

Harnecker, M. (2002) *Hugo Chávez Frías: un hombre, un pueblo*, Desde Abajo, Caracas.

Heinen, D. and W. Coppens (1986) 'Indian affairs', in J. Martz and D. Myers (eds) *Venezuela: the Democratic Experience* (revised), Praeger, New York.

Heinen, H. and H. Seijas (1998) 'La actual coyuntura indígena en Venezuela', *Interciencia*, Vol. 23, No. 3, pp. 158–62.

Hellinger, D. (2000) 'Understanding Venezuela's crisis', *Latin American Perspectives*, Vol. 27, No. 1, pp. 105–19.

—— (2012) 'Venezuela: movements for rent?', in G. Prevost, C. Olivia Campos and H.E. Vanden (eds) *Social Movements and Leftist Governments in Latin America: Confrontation or Co-optation?* Zed Books, London.

Henley, P. (1982) *The Panare: Tradition and Change on the Amazonian Frontier*, Yale University Press, New Haven, CT.

Hesketh, C. and A. Morton (2014) 'Spaces of uneven development and class struggle in Bolivia: transformation or *trasformismo*?', *Antipode*, Vol. 46, No. 1, pp. 149–69.

Hill, J.D. (1994) 'Alienated targets military discourse and the disempowerment of indigenous Amazonian peoples in Venezuela', *Identities Global Studies in Culture and Power*, Vol 1, No. 1, pp. 7–34.

Hogenboom, B. (2012) 'The return of the state and new extractivism: what about civil society?' in B. Cannon and P. Kirby (eds) *Civil Society and the State in Left-Led Latin America: Challenges and Limitations to Democratization*, Zed Books, London.

Irvine, J., I. Miles and J. Evans (1979, eds) *Demystifying Social Statistics*, Pluto, London.

Jackson, J. and K. Warren (2005) 'Indigenous movements in Latin America, 1999–2004: controversies, ironies and new directions', *Annual Review of Anthropology*, Vol. 34, pp. 549–73.

Juncosa, J. (comp.) (1991) *Documentos indios: declaraciones y pronunciamientos*, Abya-Yala, Quito, Ecuador.

Kelly, J.A. (2011) *State Health and Yanomami Transformations: a Symmetrical Ethnography*, University of Arizona Press, Tucson.

Kertzer, D. and D. Arel (2002) *Census and Identity: The Politics of Race, Ethnicity and Language in National Censuses*, Cambridge University Press, Cambridge.

Kirby, P. and B. Cannon (2012) 'Globalization, democratization and state-civil society relations in left-led Latin America', in B. Cannon and P. Kirby (eds) *Civil Society and the Estate in Left-Led Latin America*, Zed Books, London, pp. 3–16.

Laclau, E. (2007) *On Populist Reason*, Verso, London.

Lander, E. (2002) 'Sociedad civil: ¿un espacio democrático de los movimientos sociales y del movimiento popular?' *Utopía y Praxis Latinoamericana*, Vol. 7, No. 18, pp. 109-15.

—— (2007) 'El Estado y las tensiones de la participación popular en Venezuela', *OSAL*, Vol. VIII, No. 22, pp. 65-86.

Lauer, M. (2006) 'State-led democratic politics and emerging forms of indigenous leadership among the Ye'kwana of the Upper Orinoco', *Journal of Latin American Anthropology*, Vol. 11, No. 1, pp. 51-86.

Laurent, V. (2005) *Comunidades indígenas, espacios políticos y movilización electoral en Colombia, 1990-1998: motivaciones, campos de acción e impactos*, ICANH/IFEA, Bogotá.

Lehman, K. (2014) 'The right to information: indigenous media and the Bolivarian revolution', in L.F. Angosto-Ferrández (ed.) *Democracy, Revolution and Geopolitics in Latin America: Venezuela and the International Politics of Discontent*, Routledge, New York, pp. 87-118.

Li, T.M. (2010) 'Indigeneity, capitalism, and the management of dispossession', *Current Anthropology*, Vol. 51, No. 3, pp. 385-414.

Lievesley, G. (2009) 'Is Latin America moving leftwards? Problems and prospects', in G. Lievesley and S. Ludlam (eds) *Reclaiming Latin America: Experiments in Radical Social Democracy*, Zed Books, London, pp. 21-36.

Linares, J.G. (2011) *América indígena comunitaria y el nuevo socialismo: veintiún principios que orientan el socialismo en Nuestra América*, Fondo Editorial Ipasme, Caracas.

López Maya, M. (2000) *Protesta y cultura en Venezuela: los marcos de acción colectiva en 1999*, CLACSO, Buenos Aires.

Luzardo, A. (1988) *Amazonas: el negocio de este mundo: investigación indigenista*, Ediciones Centauro, Caracas.

Madero, A. (2010) *Esteban Emilio Mosonyi: identidad nacional y pasado indígena*, El perro y la rana, Caracas.

Madi, I. (1998) *Conspiración al sur del Orinoco*, Copy Press, Caracas.

Maingón, T. (2006) 'El estado de bienestar social en Venezuela: el caso de las misiones', *Ágora: revista de ciencias sociales*, No. 14, pp. 31-72.

Mansutti, A. (2006) 'La demarcación de territorios indígenas en Venezuela: algunas condiciones de funcionamiento y el rol de los antropólogos', *Antropológica*, No. 105-106, pp. 13-38.

Mansutti-Rodríguez, A. (1986) 'Integración política y cambio social: los congresos Piaroa', *Boletín Antropológico*, No. 10, pp. 63-75.

—— (1999) 'Crónicas indigenistas desde el Consejo Nacional Electoral en Venezuela: por una representación legítima de los pueblos indígenas venezolanos en la constituyente', *Boletín Antropológico*, No. 46, pp. 135-50.

—— (2000) 'Pueblos indígenas y cambios constitucionales: El caso de Venezuela', *Boletín Antropológico*, No. 50, pp. 79-98.

—— (2010) 'Walter Coppens (1937-2010)', *Antropológica*, Tomo LIV, No. 114, pp. 5-16.

Marroquín, A.D. (1977) *Balance del indigenismo: informe sobre la política indigenista en América*, Instituto Indigenista Interamericano, Ediciones Especiales (76), México.

Martens, R. (2011) 'La demarcación del habitat y tierras de comunidades y pueblos indígenas del estado Bolívar, entre el desarollo nacional y la identidad cultural', *Boletín Antropológico*, No. 82, pp. 132–62.

Martí i Puig, S. (2006) *Un estudio prospectivo sobre la presencia y la relevancia de los partidos indigenistas en América Latina*, CIDOB, Barcelona.

Martínez, B. (2005) 'Una advertencia a los intelectuales venezolanos', Voltairenet.org. Available at http://www.voltairenet.org/article123221.html, accessed 6 October 2013.

Martínez, C., M. Fox and J. Farrell (2010) *Venezuela Speaks! Voices from the Grassroots*, PM Press, Oakland.

Martínez Alier, J. (2002) *The Environmentalism of the Poor: a Study of Ecological Conflicts and Valuation*, Edward Elgar, Cheltenham.

Martínez Novo, C. (2013) 'The backlash against indigenous rights in Ecuador's Citizen's Revolution', in T.A. Eisenstadt, M.S. Danielson, M.J. Bailón Corres and C. Sorroza Polo (eds) *Latin America's Multicultural Movements: the Struggle between Communitarianism, Autonomy, and Human Rights*, Oxford University Press, Oxford, pp. 111–31.

Mato, D. (2010) 'Las iniciativas de los movimientos indígenas en la educación superior: un aporte para la profundización de la democracia', *Nueva Sociedad*, No. 227, pp. 102–19.

Mayhall, M. (2005) 'Modernist but not exceptional: the debate over modern art and national identity in 1950s Venezuela', *Latin American Perspectives*, Vol. 32, No. 2, pp. 124–46.

McNeish, J.A. (2013) 'Extraction, protests and indigeneity in Bolivia: the TIPNIS effect', *Latin American and Caribbean Ethnic Studies*, Vol. 8, No. 2, pp. 221–42.

Milano, S. (2014) 'Venezuela', in C. Heck and J. Tranca (eds) *La realidad de la minería ilegal en los países amazónicos*, Sociedad Peruana de Derecho Ambiental (SPDA), Negrapata, Lima.

Montiel, N. (1992) *Movimiento indígena en Venezuela*, Secretaría de Cultura Gobernación del Zulia, Maracaibo.

Morales, J.C. and L. Morales (2003) 'El derecho a la participación de las minorías indígenas venezolanas dentro del marco legal de 1999', *Frónesis*, Vol. 10, No. 2, pp. 9–29.

Mosonyi, E. (1975) *El indígena en pos de su liberación definitiva*, FACES, Caracas.

—— (1992) 'Prólogo', in N. Montiel (ed.) *Movimiento indígena en Venezuela*, Secretaría de Cultura Gobernación del Zulia, Maracaibo, pp. 7–11.

—— (2008) 'Universidad Indígena de Venezuela', in D. Mato (coord.) *Diversidad cultural e interculturalidad en educación superior: experiencias en América Latina*, IESALC-UNESCO, Caracas.

—— (2009) 'Balance general de los diez años del proceso bolivariano: pueblos indígenas', *Revista Venezolana de Economía y Ciencias Sociales*, Vol. 15, No. 1, pp. 155–72.

Muhr, T. (2010) 'Counter-hegemonic regionalism and higher education for all: Venezuela and the ALBA', *Globalisation, Societies and Education*, Vol. 8, No. 1, pp. 39–57.

—— (2012) 'Reconfiguring the state/society complex in Venezuela', in B. Cannon and P. Kirby (eds) *Civil Society and the State in Left-Led Latin America: Challenges and Limitations to Democratization*, Zed Books, London.
Muhr, T. and A. Verger (2006) 'Venezuela: higher education for all', *Journal for Critical Education Policy Studies*, Vol. 4, No. 1, pp. 160–94.
Nash, J. (1992) 'Interpreting social movements: Bolivian resistance to economic conditions imposed by the International Monetary Fund', *American Ethnologist*, Vol. 19, No. 2, pp. 275–93.
Nixon, J.W. (1960) *A History of the International Statistical Institute: 1885–1960*, International Statistical Institute, The Hague.
Nobles, M. (2000) *Shades of Citizenship: Race and the Census in Modern Politics*, Stanford University Press, Stanford, CA.
OCEI (Oficina Central de Estadística e Informática) (1993) *Censo Indígena de Venezuela 1992: nomenclador de comunidades y colectividades*, Taller Gráfico de la OCEI, Caracas.
Olivera, O. and T. Lewis (2004) *¡Cochabamba! Water War in Bolivia*, South End Press, Cambridge, MA.
Ortiz, B. (2002) 'Los nuevos recolectores: los guahibos recicladores de basura en Ciudad Bolívar', *Boletín Antropológico*, No. 54, pp. 483–98.
Patterson, T.C. (2009), *Karl Marx, Anthropologist*, Berg, Oxford.
Pearson, L. (2014) 'How USAID undermined sovereignty', *Green Left Weekly*, No. 1028, p. 17.
Petras, J. (2007) 'The development state in Latin America: whose development, whose state?' *The Journal of Peasant Studies*, Vol. 34, No. 3–4, pp. 371–407.
Petras, J. and H. Veltmeyer (2001) *Globalization Unmasked: Imperialism in the 21st Century*, Madhyam Books, New Delhi.
—— (2005) *Empire with Imperialism*, Zed Books, London.
—— (2007) 'The "development state" in Latin America: whose development, whose state?' *The Journal of Peasant Studies*, Vol. 34, No. 3–4, pp. 371–407.
—— (2008) *América Latina: movimientos, cambios y gobiernos de centroizquierda*, Monte Ávila, Caracas.
Postero, N. (2009) *Ahora somos ciudadanos*, Muela del Diablo, La Paz.
Postero, N. and L. Zamosc (eds) (2005) *La lucha por los derechos indígenas en América Latina*, Abya Yala, Quito.
Poulantzas, N. (1978) (trans. Patrick Camiller) *State, Power, Socialism*, NLB, London.
Prevost, G., C. Oliva Campos and H.E. Vanden (2012) 'Introduction', in G. Prevost, C. Oliva Campos and H.E. Vanden (eds) *Social Movements and Leftist Governments in Latin America: Confrontation or Co-option?* Zed Books, London, pp. 1–21.
Quispe, M.T. and D. Moreno (2011) 'La educación intercultural bilingüe en un contexto de transformación social', in L.J. Bello (ed.) *El estado ante la sociedad multiétnica y pluricultural: políticas públicas y derechos de los pueblos indígenas en Venezuela (1999–2010)*, Wataniba/IWGIA, Caracas, pp. 118–27.
Raby, D. (2006) *Democracy and Revolution: Latin America and Socialism Today*, Pluto, London.
—— (2014) 'Brief hypothesis on the state, democracy, and revolution in Latin America

today', in S. Ellner (ed.) *Latin America's Radical Left: Challenges and Complexities of Political Power in the Twenty-First Century*, Rowman and Littlefield, Lanham, MD.

Ramos, A.R. (1994) 'The hyperreal Indian', *Critique of Anthropology*, Vol. 14, No. 2, pp. 153–71.

Resultados Población Indígena, XIV Censo de Población y Vivienda (2011) Instituto Nacional de Estadística. Available at http://www.ine.gov.ve/documentos/Demografia/CensodePoblacionyVivienda/pdf/ResultadosBasicos_11-03-14.pdf, accessed 24 July 2015.

Rodríguez, O. (1991) *Contribución a la crítica del indigenismo*, Sovar-Abre Brecha, Caracas.

Roldán Ortega, R. (2005) *Manual para la formación en derechos indígenas. Territorios, recursos naturales y convenios internacionales*, 2nd ed. Abya-Yala, Quito.

Samudio, E. (1996) 'De la propiedad comunal a la propiedad privada: los resguardos indígenas de Mérida del siglo XIX', in R. Giacalone (comp.) *Mérida a través del tiempo: siglos XIX y XX*, Consejo de Publicaciones Universidad de los Andes, Mérida.

—— (2005) 'La propiedad territorial de las comunidades indígenas en la política agraria de Venezuela a finales de lo siglos XVIII y XIX', in G. Cardozo and A. Urdaneta (eds) *Colectivos sociales y participación popular en la independencia hispanoamericana*, Ediciones de la Universidad de Zulia, Maracaibo.

Sanoja, M. (1991) 'Presentación', in O. Rodríguez, *Contribución a la crítica del indigenismo*, Sovar-Abre Brecha, Caracas.

Sanoja Obediente, M. (2011) *Historia sociocultural de la economía venezolana*, Banco Central de Venezuela, Caracas.

Schiller, N. (2011) 'Catia sees you: community television, clientelism, and the state in the Chávez era', in D. Hellinger and D. Smilde (eds) *Venezuela's Bolivarian Democracy: Participation, Politics and Culture under Chávez*, Duke University Press, Durham, NC, pp. 104–30.

Schönwälder, G. (2002) *Linking Civil Society and the State: Urban Popular Movements, the Left, and Local Government in Peru, 1980–1992*, Pennsylvania University Press, University Park, PA.

Serbín, A. (1980) 'La autogestión desde la perspectiva antropológica: modelos y realidades', in O. González Ñañez and A. Serbín (comps) *Coloquio sobre indigenismo y autogestión (Ciudad Bolívar, Mayo 1976)*, Monte Ávila, Caracas.

Serrano, P. (2009) *Desinformación: cómo los medios ocultan el mundo*, Península, Barcelona.

Sevilla, V. (1997) *El régimen de excepción y los derechos humanos indígenas*, Capatárida, Buchivacoa, Venezuela.

Shaw, M. (1994) 'Civil society and global politics: beyond a social movements approach', *Journal of International Studies*, Vol. 23, No. 3, pp. 647–67.

Sieder, R. (2002) 'Introduction', in R. Sieder (ed.) *Multiculturalism in Latin America: Indigenous Rights, Diversity and Democracy*, Palgrave, New York.

Silva, N. (2007) 'Los derechos territoriales de los pueblos indígenas en Venezuela. Situación actual y perspectivas', in L. Meneses, G. Gordones and J. Clarac (eds) *Lecturas antropológicas de Venezuela*, Editorial Venezolana, Mérida.

Silva, N. and A. Mansutti-Rodríguez (1996) 'Situación de los Pueblos Indígenas de Venezuela', *Journal de la Societé des Americanistes*, Vol. 82, pp. 348–58.
Simpson, S. and D. Dorling (1999) 'Conclusion: statistics and "the truth"', in D. Dorling and S. Simpson (eds) *Statistics in Society: The Arithmetic of Politics*, Arnold, London.
Skerry, P. (2000) *Counting on the Census: Race, Group Identity, and the Evasion of Politics*, Brookings Institution Press, Washington.
Skocpol, T. (1979) *States and Social Revolutions: a Comparative Analysis of France, Russia, and China*, Cambridge University Press, Cambridge.
Spanakos, A. (2011) 'Citizen Chávez: the state, social movements, and publics', *Latin American Perspectives*, Vol. 38, No. 1, pp. 14–27.
Sutherland, M. (2013) 'Aumento del 894% en la importación estatal', Rebelion.org. Available at http://www.rebelion.org/docs/174961.pdf[MR2], accessed 24 July 2015.
Terhorst, P., M. Olivera and A. Dwinell (2013) 'Social movements, left governments, and the limits of water reform in Latin America's left turn', *Latin American Perspectives*, Vol. 40, No. 4, pp. 55–69.
Thompson, E.P. (1991 [1963]) *The Making of the English Class*, Penguin, London.
Tierney, P. (2000) *Darkness in El Dorado: How Scientists and Journalists Devastated the Amazon*, WW Norton, New York.
Tillet, A. (2011) 'La implementación del derecho a la salud integral de los pueblos indígenas y el reconocimiento de la medicina tradicional', in L.J. Bello (ed.) *El estado ante la sociedad multiétnica y pluricultural: políticas públicas y derechos de los pueblos indígenas en Venezuela (1999–2010)*, Wataniba/IWGIA, Caracas, pp. 132–62.
Trouillot, M.R. (2001) 'The anthropology of the state in the age of globalization: close encounters of the deceptive kind', *Current Anthropology*, Vol. 42, No. 1, pp. 125–38.
Últimas Noticias (2009) 'Descartan, por ahora, cambio de nombre y día del estado', *Últimas Noticas*, Caracas, Venezuela, 22 April, Section *Pulso Regional* (Vargas), p. 34.
Uzcátegui, C. (1995) 'Una aproximación al estudio de la política indigenista venezolana en el siglo XIX', *Montalbán*, Vol. 28, pp. 195–207.
Uzcátegui, F. (2007) 'Análisis de la evolución de las políticas públicas en comunidades indígenas venezolanas (1836–1959)', *Revista Venezolana de Ciencia Política*, No. 32, pp. 11–22.
Van Cott, D.L. (2000) *The Friendly Liquidation of the Past*, University of Pittsburgh Press, Pittsburgh.
Van Cott, D.L. (2002) 'Movimientos indígenas y transformación constitucional en Los Andes: Venezuela en perspectiva comparativa', *Revista Venezolana de Economía y Ciencias Sociales*, Vol. 8, No. 3, pp. 41–60.
—— (2003a) 'Andean indigenous movements and constitutional transformation: Venezuela in comparative perspective', *Latin American Perspectives*, Vol. 20, No. 1, pp. 49–69.
—— (2003b) 'Cambio institucional y partidos étnicos en Sudamérica', *Análisis Político*, Vol. 16, No. 48, pp. 26–51.

—— (2005) *From Movements to Parties in Latin America: the Evolution of Ethnic Politics*, Cambridge University Press, New York.
—— (2008) *Radical Democracy in the Andes*, Cambridge University Press, Cambridge.
Villalón, M.E. (1985) *Aspectos fundamentales de la problemática indígena del estado Bolívar: tenencia de la tierra, salud, educación, evangelización y política indigenista*, Comisión para el Estudio de la Situación Indígena del estado Bolívar, Informe al Ejecutivo Regional, Gobernación del Estado Bolívar, Dirección de Cultura, Ciudad Bolívar.
—— (1994) *Educación para indígenas en Venezuela: una crítica razonada*, Documento de Trabajo No. 9, Centro Venezolano de Investigación en Antropología y Población (CEVIAP), Caracas.
—— (2011) 'Los idiomas indígenas oficiales', in L.J. Bello (ed.) *El estado ante la sociedad multiétnica y pluricultural: políticas públicas y derechos de los pueblos indígenas en Venezuela (1999-2010)*, Wataniba/IWGIA, Caracas, pp. 22–34.
Villegas, E. (2009) *Abril, golpe adentro*, Editorial Galac, Caracas.
Vivas Ramírez, F. (2001) 'Tributación y reorganización del trabajo indígena en Venezuela (1687-1697)', *Anuario de Estudios Americanos*, Vol. LVIII, No. 2, pp. 437-47.
Webber, J. (2011) *From Rebellion to Reform in Bolivia: Class Struggle, Indigenous Liberation, and the Politics of Evo Morales*, Haymarket Books, Chicago.
—— (2013) 'From left-indigenous insurrection to reconstituted neoliberalism in Bolivia: political economy, indigenous liberation, and class struggle, 2000-2011', in J. Webber and B. Carr (eds) *The New Latin American Left: Cracks in the Empire*, Rowman and Littlefield, Lanham, MD, pp. 149-89.
Wood, E.M. (1990) 'The uses and abuses of "civil society"', *Socialist Register*, Vol. 26, pp. 60-84.
—— (2002) 'The question of market dependence', *Journal of Agrarian Change*, Vol. 2, No. 1, pp. 50-87.
Wright, W. (1990) *Cafe con Leche: Race, Class, and National Image Venezuela*, University of Texas Press, Austin.
Yashar, D. (2005) *Contesting Citizenship in Latin America: the Rise of Indigenous Movements and the Postliberal Challenge*, Cambridge University Press, Cambridge.

Index

Acosta Saignes, Miguel, 41–2, 44, 62, 177
'Act of Compromise with History', 88
AD (Acción Democrática), 44, 56, 64, 80
agriculture, importance diminished, 51
alternative development models, search for, 244
Amazonas state, 4, 75, 111–12, 145, 151, 221; governorship, 179; Salesian missionaries, 52
American Indigenous Parliament, 147
AN (National Assembly), 42, 131, 137, 175, 183; elections 2005 and 2010, 136, 143–4, 178
ANC (National Constituent Assembly 1999), 9, 14, 72, 74–5, 78, 85, 105, 134, 184; catalytic effects of, 22, 71; CONIVE transformation, 73; land titling debate lack, 82; multiculturalism differences, 77; neoliberal weak presence, 80; referendum, 73–4; Security and Defence Commission, 81; universalist argument absence, 79
anti-chavismo, 10; attitude shift, 134; heterogeneous, 135
Aporrea.org, 195
Apure state, 112, 202
Aray, Yaritza, 152, 182
'areas of traditional indigenous occupation', 130
Arreaza, Jorge, 109

Arvelo-Jiménez, Nelly, 46, 65–6, 68
'autonomy', -'centralization' creative tension, 87; definitions of, 15
Azpurua, Carlos, *Yo hablo a Caracas*, 61

Baniva people, 5
Barreto, Daysi, 121
Barreto, Juan, 93
Basic Law of Public Administration 1976, 43
Batallón 51, 120
'Battle of Boyaca', Bolivar victory, 101
Berlin Wall, fall of, 171
Bernal, Freddy, 93
black and indigenous peoples, depiction, 91
'Black Friday' 1983, 8
Blanco, Guzmán, state modernisation project, 27
Bocaranda, Nelson, 84
Bolívar, Simón, 89
Bolívar state, 4, 111, 124, 126, 221; Gran Sabana, 114, 157, 226; national park, 54
Bolivarian bloc, 1998 presidential election, 238
Bolivarian Congress Young Indo-America, 100
Bolivarian constitution 1999, 4, 16, 23, 27, 38, 42, 88, 92, 105; approval of, 34; Chapter VIII, 77, 81–2, 200; differentiated indigenous right, 127; referendum for, 74

INDEX

Bolivarian revolution, 72, 100, 239; election success sustained, 237; powerful synergies, 240
Bolivarian Schools project, 117
Bolivarian University, (UBV), 119, 203; Coordination of Indigenous Peoples, 118
Bolivarianism, 100; national-popular bloc, 242; pluricultural element, 89
Bolivia, 2, 67, 79, 192, 212, 214, 229; economic surplus re-directed, 215; 'Media Luna' crisis, 210; miners, 219; multicultural reform, 13; 'plurinationalism, 15; separatist elites, 181
Brazil, 79, 181
Briceño, A., 78

Cabello, Diosdado, 194, 196
Cabrujas, José Ignacio, 17
'Cacique Guaicaipuro' Federation of Revolutionary Indigenous Community Councils, 176
Cacique Nigale, 117
Caldera, Rafael, government of, 41, 52, 59
Campins, Herrera, government of, 8
capital accumulation, 215
Capriles, Henrique, 11, 80, 98, 109, 137, 159, 16; political shift, 134
Capuchin order, 39; state convention with 1922, 40
Carmona, Pedro, 83
Carrera, Javier, 191
Cascante, José Gregorio, 153–4
Castro, Fidel, 10–11, 66
CAT (High Technology Centres), 119
Cauicuto, María, 180
CDI (integrated Diagnostic Centres), 119
Centeno Vallenilla, Pedro, 91
censuses: 'arithmetic of politics', 28; creational power of, 30, 38; political tools; 29; supranational coordination of design, 31; Venezuela, 27, 32, 36–7, 130, 201
Cerro Autana, 6
Chávez, Adán, 79

Chávez, Hugo, 10, 42, 78, 81, 101–2, 147, 153–4, 159, 161, 172, 180, 189, 200; death of, 143; Indian identity claim, 96, 160; 1998 election victory, 9, 20, 22, 69, 71; 2002 coup against, 83, 135, 193; 2006 landslide victory, 136, 172
Chavista movement/*chavismo*, 8, 92, 10; bloc, 87, 209, 239; electoral discipline of, 148; emergence of, 21; indigenous activist dynamism, 178; indigenous activists gravitating to, 162; indigenous movement creation, 102; tensions within, 24, 83, 200, 209
Chenega, Alaska Native corporation, 230, 232; economic success of, 231
Chile, state, 241
China, credit from, 210
Christopher Columbus statues: El Calvario removal, 93; Plaza Venezuela pill-down, 94
CIN (National Commission for Indigenous Affairs), 44
cinematic production, 122
Ciudad Bolívar, 102; bus station, 5; indigenous migration to, 220
Ciudad Guayana, indigenous migration to, 220
'civil society', 243; agencies of, 15; concept disappearance, 184; NGO-ism, 190
class struggle, 216
CLEB (Bolívar state legislative council), 152, 154, 182
clientelist relations, non-explanatory, 167
CNE, (National Electoral Council), 73, 75–6, 127, 131–2
'co-option', sweeping accusation, 218, 241
coal mining, Yukpa movement against, 223
COINKA (Kariña Indigenous Communities), 147
Colombia, 67, 79, 181, 220; state, 241
Committee for the Defence of Guajiro, Zulia, 57
communal property, extinction, 51

INDEX 283

communities, services access, 114
community media, 121; indigenous community use, 167, 204
CONAIE (Confederation of Indigenous Nationalities of Ecuador), Correa government disputes, 217
Confederation of Venezuelan Indigenous Peoples, 58
Congress of Cúcuta, 50
Congress of Indians (First), 57
Congressional Decree for Indigenous *Resguardos*, 49
CONIVE (National Council of Venezuelan Indians), 75-6, 78, 85-7, 89, 139-40, 146-8, 150, 169, 184; Chavista bloc positioning, 149; creation of, 63; divisions in, 73, 145; institutionalisation of, 74; internal differences, 73; -PSUV relation, 170; transformation, 65, 239
'Conquest of the South' project, 52-3, 66
conservationist policy, 53
Constitutions 1811, 49; 1947, 47; 1961, 47, 57; *for 1999 see also* CRBV
Constitutionalism, Latin American, 13, 82
Consultorios Populares, 119
COPEI(Social Christian Party), 56, 59, 64
Coppens, Walter, 61
Cordones, General Clíver Alcalá, Urimán dispute, 227
Coronil, Fernando, 17
Correa, Rafel, 192, 194, 217; socialist policies, 214
communal councils, funding of, 123
coups, 1992, 9; 2002, 83, 135, 193
CRBV (Bolivarian constitution 1999), 4, 16, 23, 27, 38, 42, 88, 92, 105, 173, 198, 200, 234; approval of, 34, 55; Chapter VIII, 77, 81-2, 200; differentiated indigenous right, 127; referendum for, 74;
(Seventh) Temporary Provision, 127
Cuba, 120
Cuiva people, 96
cultural diversity, neo-liberal version, 14

Cumaná Assembly, 147
Cumanagoto community, 109
CVG, 53; bureaucratic expansion, 47; mining remit, 222

DAI (Directorate for Indigenous Affairs), 45; Extraordinary Congress of Venezuelan Indigenous People support, 75
Declaration of Barbados 1971, 133
Declaration of the First National Council of Venezuela, 63
Delta Amacuro state, gold and diamonds, 222
Delgado, Ricardo, 156-7
Delta Amacuro state, 124, 126, 151
demands, chavista 'equivalential chain', 209
Democratic Coordinator, anti-Chavista, 135
'descriptive representation', 157
DGAI (Directorate General for Indigenous Affairs), 37
diamonds, 221, 223; indigenous land, 222

Economic and Social National Development Plan, 184
economic crisis 1980s, 8
Ecuador, 2, 67, 79, 181, 192, 212, 214, 217; multicultural reform, 13; plurinationalism, 15; sovereignty, 194
education: indigenous access to, 43, 48, 115-16 participatory programmes, 117; right to, 118
El Carazaco protests, 9
ELAM, Cuban, 120
electoral politics, 5; constituencies design, 129; indigenous organizations and communities, 125, 143; indigenous pragmatism, 128, 132; importance of, 16, 23; mobilizing force, 161, 216; regional, 139; transformative power of, 11; victory importance, 238
environmental activism, 197; 'of the poor', 223;

284 INDEX

Escalanate, Bernarda, 61
ethnic consciousness, 62
Evolucíon, 149
extractivism, 244: critiques directed, 213; dependence on, 210; global phenomenon, 212; importance of, 25; indigenous movements' connection, 219,224

Fabricant, Nicole, 193
Fedecámras, 83
federal legislative councils, 129
Felipe, Negro, 91
Fernández, Alexander, 201
Fernández, Noly, 120
FIEB (Indigenous Federation of Bolívar State), 63, 152, 153, 182 -PSUV chavista bloc alliance, 151, 154
Finnemore, Martha, 31
Finol, Yldefonso, 79, 97
First Congress of Indians, 197
First Pemon Congress, Kavanayén 1983, 61
First Piaroa Congress of Caño Grulla, 62
First Warao Congress, 61
Fondo Editorial Ipasme, 100
'Fourth Republic', 8, 10, 47, 116; collapse of, 14; political parties of, 60
FUNDACIDI, 145-6
FUNDAFACI, 65

Gallegos, Rómulo, coup against, 44, 56, 90
García Gavidia, Nelly, 90-1
garimpeiros, 188
global capitalism, 229
Globovisión, 85
Gómez, Juvencio, 152, 154-6
Gómez, Juan Vicente, dictatorship of, 56, 90
gold, 221, 223; mining, 226
González, José Luis, 75, 85-7, 146-7, 182
Gramsci, Antonio, 171-2
Gran Misión Vivienda, 123
Gran Sabana, 157; military kidnapping, 226

grass roots organizations, -state synergies, 120
Guahibos, displaced, 220
Guaicaipuro, 91, 93, 95, 101; Municipal Council, 96
Guaicaipurismo, 89-90, 92, 94, 100, 158; Bolivarian mix, 101, 177
Guantanamo Bay, Chenega business with, 231
Guarulla, Liborio, 5, 7
Guatemala, 67; indigenous mobilization, 15
Guevara, Guillermo, 75, 145
Gutiérrez, Mariano, 40
Gutiérrez, Freddy, 80
Guyana region: gold reserves, 222; Strategic Integral Development Region, 224
Guzmán Blanco, President, 50

Haximú massacre 1993, 188, 222
health services, access to, 119
'historical debt' discourse, 77-8, 81, 88
Hodges, Header, 194
Hoti people, 190, 221
'Hyperreal Indian', the, 15, 162; expectations of 225

IAN (national Agricultural Institute), 59, 66; 'communist' accusation, 52
identity formation, 102
Iguarán, Émber, 148
Ikabarú, 225
ILO: Convention, 34, 78 106, 169; Convention on Indigenous and Tribal Populations, 48
Imataca Forest Reserve, 49
Indian, 'floating label', 159; -'*racionales*' distinction-makers, 7
indigeneity: anthropolgical criteria power, 36; 'anti-statist' assumption, 219; broad identifications of, 229; global capitalism dynamics, 229; imagery use, 99; label, 2; place names, 95; revalorized, 35, 37; Venezuelan criteria, 32

INDEX 285

indigenism: 'new'declaration of Barbados, 58; 'official, 59 'of liberation', 62, 177
indigenous activism/agency, 219; government programmes implementation, 167; non-Bolivarian candidates, 146; -non-indigenous alliances, 156; political and socioeconomic enfranchisement prioritized, 35, 104, 124, 126, 234, 239, 241; political candidates, 161; -state conflict, 165; tensions within, 163; *see also* collective actions
indigenous affairs pre-Chavez: anachronistic legislation, 46; government political history, 47
indigenous capitalisms, 230, 232–3, 235
indigenous collective action/mobilizations, 6, 72: 'co-option' criticism, 166; electoral, 125, 162; institutional capacity, 148; intra-political competition, 146; Latin America, 12; media initiatives, 122; multiethnic, 128; national-popular bloc relation, 85, 142, 241–2; non-electoral, 187; political agency, 236; state-sponsored, 172; state supporting, 16, 23, 218, 239, 241; sustained and proactive, 21; tactics, 158; *territorial issues, see below*; teleological preconceptions, 228, 235, 240; 21st century socialisms link, 217; -state relation, 173
Indigenous Committee for Mutual Assistance, Zulia, 56
indigenous communal councils and communes, 175–7; government emphasis, 110; state funding, 112, 150
indigenous communities: 'peasantization', 52; 'university villages', 118
'Indigenous crown', Capriles-Chavez competition for, 160
Indigenous Electoral Register creation of, 164

indigenous population/peoples: census percentages and fluctuations, 2, 28, 33–4, 107, 131; divergent interests/priorities of, 3, 7, 164, 172, 199, 208, 228, 235 educational institutions, 168–9; uneven geographic distribution, 129, 130, 151; urban, 35, 48, 115, 150
indigenous representation, party competition for, 137–40
'Indigenous Resistance Day', 93, 176; negative reactions, 97
indigenous rights 78, 104; legislation, 105; nationalist ambiguity towards, 42, 80; neoliberal framing, 230; NGO normative period, 14; place specific, 229; prioritizations, 126; socioeconomic realized, 113; 'standards ceiling', 106
indigenous territorial/land politics: antagonistic legislation, 50; determinants of, 37; demarcation and titling issues, 55, 76, 107–8, 175; gold, 222; minimal recognition of, 108, 110, 113; 1999 Constitution, 210; relative autonomy period, 51; rights campaign gains, 221
Indigenous University of Tauca, 142, 199
'indigenous value systems', Chenega claim, 231
'Indo-American socialism', 99, 180, 182
industrial working class, Latin America, 2
INE (National Statistics Institute), 38, 114, 127, 130;
information, right to, 121
Inter-American Indigenist Institute, 44
inter-tribal massacres, 67
Intercultural Bilingual Education Department, 118
international cooperation funding, 192–3
International Day of Indigenous Peoples, 101, 181
International Festival of Venezuelan Indigenous Culture, 122

International Institute of Statistics, 31
intra-indigenous political competition, 146
Iraq reconstruction, Chenega business with, 231
Irotatheri alleged massacre, 188–200
Istúriz, Aristóbulo, 77
IVIC (Venezuelan Institute for Scientific Research), 59

Jaua, Elías, 201–2
Jiménez, Pérez, 56
Jivi, La Rubiera massacre against, 67
jurisdictional power, religious orders, 39

Kariná community, 109
Kelly, J.A., 120
kidnaps, of military personnel, 226
Korta, José María, hunger strike, 199–202
Kuyujani organization, 152, 157

La Salida destabilization, 137
La Salle, Fundación, 59–62
Laclau, Ernesto, 89, 217
land: collective title to, 38, 112; communal title lack, 54; demarcation prioritizing, 109, 187, 196; demarcation, Perijá area, 195; grabs, 67, 83; responses to grabs, 65, 143, 168, 187; ownership regulations, 49; property individualization, 50; tenure regularizing goal, 45; titling issue, 82, 224; *see also* indigenous territories
Lara state, 131
Latin America: colonization history, 26; multicultural shift, 13–14; social support characteristics, 2; state role, 1
Latin-American Declaration of the Rights of Indigenous Peoples, 48
Law of Agricultural Reform, Fourth Republic, 51
Law of Demarcation and Guarantee of Indigenous Peoples' Habitats and Lands (LDGHTP), 38, 106, 108
Law of Indigenous Craftsmen and Craftswomen, 106
Law of Indigenous Jurisdiction, 198
Law of Indigenous Languages, 106, 183
Law of Missions 1915, 39, 47, 52, 193; repeal of, 41–2
Law of Reduction, Civilization and Indigenois *Resgurdos*, 50
Law of the Political-Territorial Division of Amazonas State, 49
Lehman, Kathryn, 121–2
León, Armando, 95
liberal multiculturalism, principles of, 105
Liga Socialista, 64
Linares, 100
literacy, indigenous population improvement, 116; states' different levels, 117
local councils, minimum indigenous representation, 131
LOPCI (Basic Law of Indigenous Peoples and Communities), 36, 42, 106, 129, 174, 184
LOPE (Basic Law of Electoral Processes), 38, 130; Article 144, 131; debate within, 164
Luepa military base, 114

Márquez, Gerardo, 81
Maduro, Nicolás, 12, 109, 160, 217; 2013 presidential campaign, 159
'magical state', Venezuela, 17, 134
Maldonado, Nicia, 100–1, 110, 145, 175–6, 178–80, 201, 224
Mapoyo Indians, 101
Maracaibo, Zulia state, 7
Maracay barracks, 91
María Lionza cult, 91
Marroquín, 62
Martínez-Alier, Joan, 223
MAS (Movement for Socialism), 64
Matos, Cecilia, 65
Media Rubio, Aristides, 94
Mendoza, Dayana, 6
MEP (People's Electoral Movement), 64

INDEX 287

mestizaje, ideology of, 80
Mexico, 67; indigenous mobilization, 15; state, 241
MIBAM (Ministry of Basic Industries and Mining), 222
'middle class', 11
military facilities, indigenous names, 91
mining, 109, 197; extensive small scale, 222; issue, 7; opposing indigenous positions, 53, 221–5
Ministry of Communes and Social Protection, 185
Ministry of Culture, 94
Ministry of Education, 43, 45, 100
Ministry of Health, Indigenous Health Department, 117, 120
Ministry of Higher Education, 117
Ministry of Home Affairs, 40; Direction of Cults, 44
Ministry of the Environment, 201
MINPI (Ministry if Indigenous Peoples), 37, 108–9, 112, 115, 123, 145, 169, 174–8, 180–2, 184, 198, 205; creation of 2007, 110, 173, 185; Perijá proposals, 199; priorities of, 111
Miranda state, 134
Misión Guaicaipuro, 123
Misión Robinson, 116
Misión Barrio Adentro, 119
Miss Amazonas, 6
missionaries: evangelical, 43; Salesian, 52
Montiel, Arcadio, 146
Montiel, Nemesio, 55, 57, 133
MOPIVE (Venezuelan Indigenous Peoples' Movement), 149
Morales, Evo, 181, 192, 214, 217, 219
Morón, Guillermo, 97
Moscoso, A., 95
Mosonyi, Esteban, 46, 68, 105, 133–4
Moviemnto por la Identidad Nacional, 61
MUD (Democratic Unity Roundtable), 136, 138, 146, 148; collapse of, 137
Muhr, Thomas, 19, 202
multi-organizationism, indigenous peoples, 142

MVR (Movement of the Fifth Republic), 74, 86, 145–6, 154/PSUV, 87

narratives, legitimizing, 88
National Assembly, 131, 175; elections 2005, 136, 178
National Commission for Indigenous Affairs, 41
National Commission for the Demarcation of Indigenous Habitat and Land, 108
National Commission of Demarcation, 108
National Council of Indigenous Education, Culture and, 107
National Endowment for Democracy, 193
National Experimental University, 117
National Health Public System, 121
national identity: defined, 88 flag redesigned, 94; the Indian as, 91
National Institute of Indigenous Languages, 183
national parks, creation of, 53–4
national sovereignty, 192; consolidation of, 209, 233–4; -indigenous rights relation, 78; principles, 194; recovery of, 43, 193 consolidation, 209, 233–4; principles of, 81, 194
National University Council, 117
nationalism: indigenous ingredients, 103; Latin American leftist, 42; right wing version, 84
natural resources, indigenous territories, 111
neo-extractivist governments, criticisms of, 215
neoliberalism, indigenous movements against, 232; 'nationalist' position, 83
new constitution, assembly dynamics, 238
New Geometry of Power, 165, 174, 208, 234
'New National Ideal', 90
New Tribes Mission: denunciation of, 61; expulsion of, 43

288 INDEX

New Zealand, 229
NGP, 176, 210
NotiMujer, CNN programme, 190
Nueva Esparta state, 131
Nuñez, Aloha, 178
nutrition, labels improvement, 115

OCAI (Central Bureau of Indigenous Affairs), 44-5, 57, 177; 'official' indigenism, 59
Ochoa Antich, Fernando, 84
Office for Indigenous Matters, 48
oil, 17, 233; emergence of, 51; industry lock-out 2002-3, 135; 1970s price boom, 46; Zulia state, 111
Olavarría, Jorge, 80
'Oligarchy', the, 10
Orinoco strip, oil, 111
ORPIA(Regional Organization of Indigenous Peoples of Amazonas), emergence of, 67
ORPIZ (Regional Organisation of the Indigenous Peoples of Zulia), 182
Otiza, Eliécer, 81

Panare people, 43; indigenous petroglyph, 94
Paraguay, 79
Paris Declaration of Aid Effectiveness, 194
PARLINVE Venezuelan Indigenous Parliament), 148-9
parroquias, 131
PCV (Venezuelan Communist Party), 57
PDVSA (oil company), CVM launching, 222
Pérez, Bartolomé, 148
Pérez, Carlos Andrés, 47, 65; first government of, 59
Pérez Jiménez, Marcos, 90; dictatorship, 197; regime collapse, 91
Pemón people, 43, 119, 225; Bolivar state, 109; Ikabarú sector, 224; indigenous communities, 7, 157; territory,
PEMON 08, 152, 154-6
People's Party, 56
Perijá area/region, Zulia state, 45, 198,
203, 223; expropriations payment promise, 202; MINPI proposals, 199; Yukpa land struggle, 196
'Permitted Indian', idea of, 230
Petras, James, 215
Piaroa community, 190; accusations against, 66; Hato San Pablo case, 68; Herman Zingg conflict, 62; lands, 66
Pizarro, Italo, 151-3
plurinationalism, 15
Pocaterra, Noelí, 75, 96, 182
PODEMOS (For Social Democracy), 164
'political associational space', 15
political -civil society ideological preconception, 170-1
Polo Patriótico, 71, 73, 79, 81-2, 85, 170
popular participation, facilitation of, 234
'popular power', 184
Porras, Florencio, 81
Portillo, Lusbi, 195
POS approach, 169
Postero, Nancy, 193
Poulantzas, Nikos, 18
Poyo, José, 85-7, 146-7, 182
PPT (Fatherland for All), 157, 164
Presidential Commission for the Protection, Development of Mining in the Guyana region, 224
Presidential Councils for Constitutional Reform and Communal Power, 99
Promotion and Application of Oral Written Usage of Indigenous Languages, 106
Proyecto Venezuela, 80
PSUV (United Socialist Party of Venezuela), 24, 74, 87, 97, 140, 146, 153, 156-7, 181-2, 186, 192, 194, 204; CONIVE relation, 170
Puerto Ayacucho, indigenous migration to, 220

Ramos, Alcida, 15
Rangel, José Vicente, 79
re-ethnication, 159
reactive indigenous action, 16
recall referendum 2004, 135

INDEX

referendum, 2007 defeat, 136
Regional Centres of Indigenist Action, 44
regional states, right to differentiated represent, 131
religious orders: indigenous colonization role, 40; official indigenous peoples power, 39
Relys, Leonela, 116
Republican independence, Latin America, declarations of, 26
resguardos lands; communal property regimes, 49; contradictory approaches, 50
resource extraction, effective rights to, 235
Robinsonian Technical Schools, 117
Rodríguez, Arturo, 152, 157
Rodríguez, Cherry, 157-8
Rodríguez, Jorge, 93-4
Rodríguez, Raúl, 180
Rodríguez, Simón, 89
Romero Izarra, Sabine, 198, 200-2, 204; assassination of, 122, 143, 197
Romero, Olegario, 201
Rosales, Manuel, 10
Russia, credit from, 210

Sanema people, 43, 221
Santaella, Yelitza, 182
SAOI, 121
Sarcos, Ivian, 6
Seventh Social Summit for Latin American and Caribbean Unity, 181
Second National Indian Congress, 41
self-determination, notions of, 113
self-identification, census, 29-30, 36
self-managed mining, 223
semi-subsistence economies, indigenous people, 3
separatism, land grab opposition accusation of, 83
Serbín, Andrés, 62
Simón Bolívar National Project, 184
Simón Bolívar satellite 2008, 114
Simoncito programme, primary education, 117
Social Christians, 59, party, 41

social democracy, policy orientation, 215
social identities, census determined, 29-30
social movements, characteristics, 181; concept, 168; fetishized, 214-16, 243; ideological preconceptions, 166; state-supporting, 166
social services, access to, 114
socialisms of the twenty-first century, 136, 172, 192, 214, 219, 243-4
socialism, -indigeneity mix, 99
socioeconomic development, Venezuela priority, 209
Soler, Mercedes, 190
sovereignty, see national sovereignty
Spain, independent media, 97
SRI (Integrated Rehabilitation Rooms), 119
State, the: Latin American, 1; history, 21; 'lobotomist, 218; supranational institutions 'socializing, 31; -society ideologized dichotomy, 240; Venezuelan deification of, 17;
State, the Bolivarian, 1, 13, 16, 18, 241; anti-neoliberal, 15; census design aim, 30; conflict incorporating, 20, 228; co-optive cliché, 240; debates about, 244; ideological condemnation of, 242; indigenous mobilization support, 172; indigenous organization invigorated, 20; political bases catalyst, 238; popular classes protection, 26-7; -social mobilizations dialogue, 228
substantive representation, 157
Sucre state, Chaima association, 132
Supreme Court, 75, 201
Supreme Tribunal of Justice, 48
sustainability, *just*, 211
symbols, concern, 98

TAWALA NGO, 148-9
Tierney, Patrick, *Darkness of El Dorado*, 46
TIPNIS project, Bolivia, 217; indigenous people for-and -against, 219

top-down power flows, simplistic depictions, 167
tradionality, objectivized notions, 114
'transcommunity networks', 15
Trienio Adeco period, 44

UCIW (Union of Indigenous Warao Communities), 182
UCV (Central University of Venezuela), 59
UIT, 201
UN (United Nations), 31; Food and Agriculture Organization, 115; Human Development Index, Venezuela rise, 115
Unidos por Venezuela, 140
Units of Indigenous Socialist Production, 112
Uriana Pocaterra, Atala, 86
Urimán, Pemon communities, 227
USA (United States of America) 229; 'civil society' donations, 193-4, 206; hostility to *chavismo*, 18; land, 53; international law violations, 231; USAID, 194
UVE (Union of Election Winners), 156

VAC, 68
Valles, Manuel de Jesús, 157
Van Cott, Donna Lee 64, 169
Varela, Iris, 192
Varí communities, 7
Velásquez, Patricia, 190
Veltmeyer, Henry, 215
Venevisión, 84
Venezuela, 212, 229; authoritarian accusations, 192; border territory, political autonomy, 221; census introduction 1873, 32; development model, 176; erratic indigenous affairs policy, 39; external interference in, 188, 206; government's indigenous support, 218; income poverty fall, 115; majority private media, hostile, 121; internal diversified production expansion weakness, 211; National Library, 94; National Plan of Development, 177; National Institute of Statistics, 34. 114; neocolonial legacies, 39; oil wealth, 244; oil-based economy, 211; political economy limits, 233;'populist tactics', 216; shares of state power, 238; sovereignty priority, 41, 243; structural differences, 9; uneven capitalist development, 220; USA hostility to, 18
Ventuari, land grab opposition, 83
Vicariate of Caroní, 40
Villalón, María E., 43

Warairarepano, 95
Warao people, 5; displaced, 6-7; land dispossession, 220
Wayaakua Indigenous Audiovisual Foundation, 122
Wayuu peoples, 119, 190; urban, 7
Wayuunaiki, bilingual, 122
women, Caracas *barrio*, 167

Yanomani people,, 190-1; Haximú massacre against, 67; killings of, 188
Yaruro people, 96
Yavari, Barné, 61
Ye'kuana people, 43, 61, 221; land grab opposition, 83; territory Upper Centuari, 66
Yo sí puedo literacy method, 116
Yukpa people, 143, 195; activists, 122; land claims, 194; movement, 196, 198, 203, 205-6; Serranía de Perijá, 24; violence against, 197

Zamora, Ezequiel, 89
Zingg, Hermann, 66; -Piaro community conflict, 62
ZIRUMA, 56
Zulia state, 55-6, 75, 151, 202; colonial legacies, 97; elections, 139; oil, 111